PRAISE FOR *REWIRED*

"An excellent guide to digital and AI transformation that provides an integrated approach to the key elements required for success, including talent-building, adopting new operating models, utilizing advanced technology, and embedding data. A must-read for any organization looking to stay competitive in the digital age."

Matt Anderson, Chief Digital Officer, The Carlyle Group

"Combining original research with real-world case studies, Lamarre, Smaje, and Zemmel demonstrate that digital and AI transformation has evolved light-years beyond systems and technology upgrades. They make the case that maximizing digital benefits today entails boldly reimagining your business, from strategy to delivery, to reflect the power of AI, data, and advanced analytics. This book details the talent management and organizational transformation ideas that should be top of mind for any leader seeking to move their company up the scale of digital maturity. With its clarity and comprehensiveness, *Rewired* will become the go-to playbook for people who want to harness digital innovation to drive competitive business outcomes."

Dr. Albert Bourla, Chairman and CEO, Pfizer

"Winning in the digital age requires a differentiating strategy, distinctive capabilities, and daring delivery. *Rewired* goes past the 'what' to delve into the 'how.' The book provides the details of what real change is about, and provides a compelling playbook for today's leaders who are ready to make the leap."

Bettina Dietsche, Chief People and Culture Officer, Allianz Group

"*Rewired* is a practical and thoughtful guide for *becoming* digital, where technology and data fuel the model for companies to operate as digital enterprises. Being digital is an everlasting journey that requires constant reimagination of the talent, organization, and underpinning technology and data to create competitive advantage. This book gives insight into the capabilities and frameworks needed to win."

Julie Dillman, Executive Vice President; Senior Executive, Operations and Technology; and Digital Transformation Officer, Chubb Group

"*Rewired* is the best reference guide on digital transformation I have seen, with a detailed view of how to get it done and get results. We are on a journey to reinvent ourselves as a leader in digital printing and digital packaging solutions. *Rewired* will be recommended reading for my team."

Ted Doheny, President and CEO, Sealed Air Corporation

"If your business has both digital opportunities and challenges and an aspiration to succeed, whether you're in the boardroom or the project room, and whatever your industry, *Rewired* is for you. It combines a clear blueprint about what matters with clear guidance about how to get it done, while providing detailed pragmatic frameworks and suggestions to assist you on your way. It is a must-read reference book, practical guide, and solution-provider. Keep it close at hand – I will!"

Rona Fairhead, Board at Oracle; Life Peer, UK House of Lords; Chair at RS Group plc; former Chair and CEO, Financial Times Group Ltd

"As the authors of *Rewired* argue, every executive will be working for the rest of their careers at using technology to outcompete. That seems especially true as AI becomes an ever-larger part of our lives and businesses, forcing us to rethink how to change, and making *Rewired* both timely and timeless. But this book helps to put AI and technology into perspective by breaking down the mechanics of change and itemizing all the things you need to do in order for technology to have an impact on your business – from building a digital talent bench to implementing modern software engineering practices to organizing the enterprise to deliver continuous digital innovations."

Roger W. Ferguson Jr., Board at Alphabet Inc., Corning, and IFF; former President and CEO of TIAA

"*Rewired* provides a thorough, yet easy-to-follow guide to developing and implementing a digital and AI transformation. While no transformation is ever easy, *Rewired* provides a clear roadmap to build your enterprise capabilities and concrete examples that will greatly increase your organization's odds of success."

Jeff Harmening, Chairman and CEO, General Mills

"One of the major challenges of a digital and AI transformation is the technology that underpins it – technology is complex, fast-changing, and it's essential for any company that wants to build great digital experiences. For many executives that reality can be quite intimidating. But facility with technology is now essential for any executive. *Rewired* is among the best books I've read, explaining what executives need to know at a level that is both understandable and sufficiently detailed to be meaningful. This is a great manual for those executives who want to really understand technology."

Peter Jacobs, CEO, ING Bank Netherlands

"Technology is changing so quickly that at times it seems it's impossible to keep up. But *Rewired* shows the way forward by not just clarifying the role of technology, but also showing how to apply the technology in order to achieve a competitive advantage."

Dr. Markus Krebber, CEO, RWE AG

"Reimagining business in the digital age is an imperative for today's enterprise leaders – and *Rewired* is a practical guide that takes them through the journey of building or changing business processes, capabilities, culture, and customer experiences to deliver sustainable value. In typical McKinsey fashion, this insightful book makes the challenge of tech-enabled transformations all that more approachable and actionable!"

Chua ("SK") Sock Koong, Board at Bharti Airtel, Prudential, Royal Phillips, Ayala Corporation; former CEO, Singtel

"Digital transformation is one of those phrases that many people use but not many understand. Lamarre, Smaje, and Zemmel have undertaken a unique service in filtering through the complexity and making it navigable. Digital transformation for a large company is complex, no matter how you cut it. But *Rewired* provides a clear map for how to build all the pieces and bring them together so that companies can not only change, but also capitalize on the potential offered by new technologies to build competitive advantages."

Chuck Magro, CEO, Corteva Agriscience

"The story of digital at adidas has been the story of how to do many things well, at the same time, across a global organization. The scale of that challenge is fantastic, and has required us to develop a sometimes-bewildering array of new capabilities while still staying true to what makes us special for our consumers. *Rewired* both captures that complexity and provides a clear set of actions and steps to manage it. This book is an absolute must-read for any executive with aspirations for leading a multinational company and turning the promises of digital into reality."

Martin Shankland, Executive Board Member for Global Operations, adidas

"To stay competitive and at the forefront of any industry, it's clear that businesses must continuously adapt and evolve with technology. *Rewired* tackles the key question of how: providing a blueprint for how to transform a business and preparing for the complexities that come with the journey."

Robin Vince, President and CEO, BNY Mellon

"*Rewired* provides a 'Unified Field Theory' based on all the elements that create specific actionable approaches to help companies move from disjointed digital projects to an end-to-end true digital enterprise. The book provides the C-suite team with the guidance needed to align purpose, people, processes, and technology, and transform the firm's operating model, cadence, and results. Only through the C-suite team owning the journey can you become a digital leader in your competitive space and create sustainable value for customers, shareholders, and other stakeholders."

Ron Williams, Board at Boeing, agilon health, Warby Parker; Chair and CEO, RW2 Enterprises; former Chair and CEO, Aetna

Rewired

Rewired

The McKinsey Guide to Outcompeting
in the Age of Digital and AI

Eric Lamarre, Kate Smaje,
and Rodney Zemmel

WILEY

Published by John Wiley & Sons, Inc., Hoboken, New Jersey.
Published simultaneously in Canada.

For general information on our other products and services or for technical support, please contact our Customer Care Department within the United States at (800) 762-2974, outside the United States at (317) 572-3993 or fax (317) 572-4002.

Wiley also publishes its books in a variety of electronic formats. Some content that appears in print may not be available in electronic formats. For more information about Wiley products, visit our web site at www.wiley.com.

Library of Congress Cataloging-in-Publication Data is Available:

ISBN: 9781394207114 (hardback)
ISBN: 9781394207138 (ePDF)
ISBN: 9781394207121 (epub)

Cover Design: Wiley
Cover and Author Images: © lvcandy/Getty Images; Courtesy of McKinsey/Craig Gordon; Courtesy of Dirk Kikstra

SKY10050787_071023

Contents

What we mean by digital and AI transformation

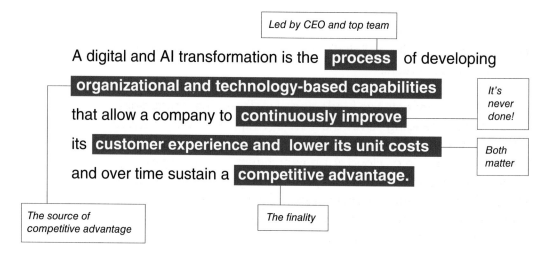

A digital and AI transformation is the **process** of developing **organizational and technology-based capabilities** that allow a company to **continuously improve** its **customer experience and lower its unit costs** and over time sustain a **competitive advantage.**

Led by CEO and top team

It's never done!

Both matter

The source of competitive advantage

The finality

Introduction

The enterprise capabilities that turn digital and AI into a source of ongoing competitive advantage

Business leaders will be digitally transforming their companies for the rest of their careers.

That statement reflects two fundamental realities: one is that digital is constantly changing. Over the past decade, digital has seeped into almost every aspect of our lives driven by the confluence of new technologies (e.g., cloud, AI), new architectural paradigms (e.g., micro-services, APIs), and new ways of building software (e.g., agile, DevSecOps), all inherited from the tech industry. And we haven't even scratched the surface of generative AI, edge computing, quantum computing, and other frontier technologies.[1]

As long as tech continues to evolve, your business will need to evolve.[2] For this reason, the word *transformation* itself is a little misleading because it implies a one-time program with an end. In fact, a digital transformation is a journey to continuously increase competitiveness.

The second fundamental reality is that digital and AI transformations are hard. In our most recent annual survey on the subject, 89% of companies have launched a flavor of digital transformation. But they only captured 31% of the expected revenue lift and realized just 25% of total expected cost savings.[3]

There are, unfortunately, no quick fixes. You can't simply implement a system or a technology and be done. We see from the digital leaders that there isn't one "magic" use case. Instead, it's about having hundreds of technology-driven solutions (proprietary and off-the-shelf[4]) working together that you continuously improve to create great customer and employee experiences, lower unit cost, and generate value. And creating, managing, and evolving these solutions requires companies to fundamentally rewire how they operate. That means getting thousands of people across different units of the organization working together and working differently. It means bringing on new talent and developing accelerated learning loops that harness their skills and help them grow. As important as technology is, digital and AI transformations are also very much about developing new organizational capabilities.

No company is a stranger to this struggle. Even the tech darlings we all know have had to invest, experiment, fail, and adapt to succeed.[5] Take Amazon's retail business. It has automated vendor onboarding, inventory replenishment, pricing, and order fulfillment. All these processes were automated with proprietary solutions developed by thousands of cross-functional teams composed of business, tech, and operational experts. But it didn't start that way – even Amazon wasn't the "Amazon" we now know early on. It rewired itself by investing in the technologies and enterprise capabilities - and continuously improving them over time - to become digital to its core."[6]

While Amazon's success is well known, there are also good examples of large, established companies that are winning the digital and AI transformation race, and creating greater digital distance between themselves and their rivals. Those successes are based on hard-won lessons that have coalesced into a recipe for what works. This book is that recipe. This book is their story.

Digital as a source of competitive advantage

Not so long ago, executives at established companies would often choose to delay changes to their core systems because "it would be cheaper and less risky to do it later when the system has been tested and proven by others." Executives would say, "We want to buy standard packages . . . it's too expensive and complicated to build custom ones." Technology was of course needed to run the company, but it rarely provided a competitive advantage because any company could buy the same technology from vendors. The advantage, if there was one, was to deploy these systems on time and on budget, and to make good use of the capabilities purchased.

This has all changed and been flipped on its head. Companies still purchase systems from vendors to run their enterprise, but the rise of digital technologies and the related new architectural paradigms and ways of developing software are making it possible to also develop and maintain proprietary applications. As the software industry matures and evolves, a *software supply chain* has emerged where you can develop applications by assembling them from existing software *building blocks* and develop new code only where necessary. These developments, and new ones on the horizon such as generative AI, are radically reducing the cost and time to develop proprietary applications, and making it possible for any company to compete on that basis now.[7]

So, where are those examples of established companies that have built a competitive advantage from digital and are being rewarded for it? Many factors impact a company's performance and, let's be honest, it takes time to transform a company deeply enough that the results will show on their financial performance. Nevertheless, the question remains fundamental. Established companies are making substantial organizational and financial commitments to digital. The low success rate raises questions if this is all worth the effort.

Our own analysis from surveys over the years has clearly indicated that top-performing companies achieve significant improvements when they implement a series of digital practices.[8] Our most recent survey of more than 1,300 senior business executives, for example, reveals that 70% of top performers use advanced analytics to develop proprietary insights; 50% use AI to improve and automate decision making.[9]

Building on this baseline, we set out to develop some hard, empirical data that ties digital transformation to financial outperformance. We turned to the banking industry, where we have a unique benchmarking data set for 80 global banks in developed markets. And banking is a sector that has been digitally transforming for 5–10 years, providing enough time to see the effects of transformation.

Our research covered the 2018–2022 timeframe and focused on a group of 20 digital leaders and 20 digital laggards, which helped bring into sharp relief three major insights:[10]

1. **Digital leaders outperformed.** Digital leaders had better return on tangible equity (ROTE) – a key financial metric in banking - and had improved it more as well. Likewise for P/E ratio. Over this time period, digital leaders outgrew laggards with better operating leverage. As a result, they grew total return to shareholders (TSR) 8.2% annually versus just 4.9% for laggards. Digital leaders were financially rewarded.

2. **Competitive advantage comes from end-to-end business model transformation.** We looked at four measures of business model transformation in banking and how these measures progressed over time for our digital leaders and laggards (Exhibit I.1). The first metric looked at customer adoption of a mobile banking app. While leaders stayed ahead of laggards, both made robust improvements. That may seem surprising at first, but it's not. As soon as a bank introduces a new mobile feature, others follow within 6–12 months. The mobile app is table stakes in banking; it does not provide competitive differentiation. Most banks have managed to build a digital team that can develop and improve its mobile app.

   Now, let's look at the other three metrics: digital sales and staffing levels in the branch network and in contact centers. These metrics reflect true operational outperformance, and this is where leaders show accelerating improvements over laggards. Improving these metrics is much more difficult because each one requires an end-to-end process transformation.

Core digital transformation metrics in banking

▨ Laggards ■ Leaders

Mobile app adoption

% of total customers active on mobile app over past 90 days

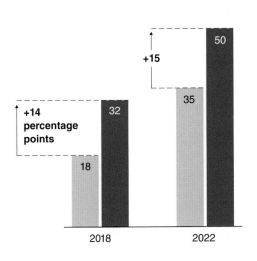

Digital sales

% of sales through digital channel

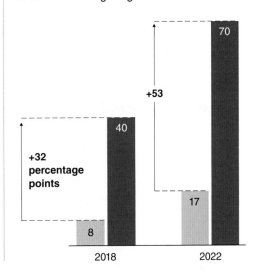

Branch network staffing

Percentage point change in average branch network FTEs per 100k customers

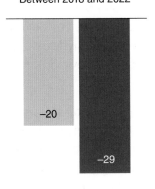

Contact center staffing

Percentage point change in average inbound contact center FTEs per 100k customers

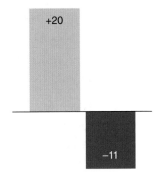

Source: Finalta Global Digital Benchmark. Global Contact center metrics only available after 2019

EXHIBIT I.1

At the front end of this process, leading banks integrate personalization analytics and digital marketing campaigns to bring relevant offers to (potential) customers. In the middle of the process, they create an omnichannel experience where branch and contact center professionals have the tools and data to support customers at any stage of the sales journey, even if that journey was started online. These leading banks are also able to provide customer approvals in real time thanks to automated credit risk decisioning. At the back end of the process, they drive customer self-servicing through well-designed digital workflows enabled by a modern data architecture. In short, the digital transformation goes beyond the front-end mobile app to also transform marketing, sales, servicing, and risk management.

Importantly, digital leaders are much faster at realigning sales and servicing capacity as customers shift their banking online. This seems simple but it's not. It requires a shift in incentives and performance management across the entire bank. This level of cross-functional alignment is core to what differentiates digital winners in any industry.

3. **Digital leaders build better enterprise capabilities.** We researched the underlying practices of leaders and laggards. Clear differences emerged. Leaders have gone further in building a quality digital talent bench, with a focus on creating an environment in which top-notch engineers thrive. They have adopted a new operating model that brings people from business, technology, and operations together to work in small, agile teams that continuously improve customer experience and lower unit cost through automation. They have built a modern and distributed technology and data architecture grounded in the cloud that allows the entire organization – not just IT – to develop digital and AI-based solutions. In short, they invested in building capabilities – talent, operating model, technology, and data – that in turn are used by their organization to develop great digital experiences and continuously improve them.

At the end of the day, the leadership teams at digital winners are bolder in reimagining their core business and more cohesive in how they come together as a team – breaking out of their traditional functional silos – to realize their vision. They invest more strategically in building differentiating capabilities – both organizational and technological – that become their source of competitive advantage. Over time, these capabilities create ever-improving customer experiences and drive lower unit cost. In this way, they become rewired to outcompete and financial rewards follow.

We have found this to be true in every industry, whether B2B or B2C, products, or services. Every sector has the opportunity to create significant value from a digital transformation. It's just a question of knowing how.

The "How"

Many will be familiar with the basics of a digital and AI transformation and its promises of value. Some have had robust early successes. But a digital and AI transformation with the scale and momentum to drive business-altering value is another ball game.

What's been missing for executives is a detailed perspective on *how* to build the enterprise capabilities to achieve impact at scale. This book answers that "how" question. It is a manual for leaders who are ready to roll up their sleeves and do the hard work needed to make their transformation successful. It examines the unique issues and opportunities created by technologies such as smartphones, the Internet of Things, artificial intelligence (including machine learning and deep learning), augmented and virtual reality, big data and real-time analytics, digital twins, APIs, cloud technologies, and others. Any digital and AI transformation relies on a mix of these technologies to develop digital solutions.

This guide is the same one our McKinsey teams around the world use when working with our clients on their digital and AI transformation. The result of constant development, refinement, and learning in the field over the past five years, *Rewired* translates McKinsey's lessons into a *how-to* guide that is proven to work.

Those lessons are organized into six sections each corresponding to an enterprise capability: it starts with creating top team alignment on the value and the plan; next, it addresses how to build the delivery capabilities to develop competitively differentiating digital solutions, and finally it covers change management aspects to drive adoption across end-to-end business processes and effectively scale across the enterprise (Exhibit I.2).

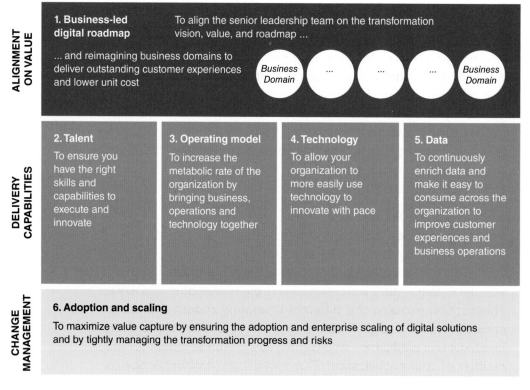

EXHIBIT I.2

The six sections each cover an essential enterprise capability. No digital and AI transformation can be successful without addressing all of them – that's a key finding from our own retrospective of McKinsey's client work in this space over the past decade. For the book, we also included a section that explores how three companies navigated their digital and AI transformation journeys. At a high level, these sections cover:

Section One: Creating the Transformation Roadmap This section explains how to focus and align the leadership team on a North Star vision and how to reimagine the business with technology. The resulting decisions are translated into a detailed roadmap that is both rooted in impact and clear about the new capabilities needed to deliver. When evaluating stalled digital and AI transformations, we find that many of the issues encountered can be traced back to missteps at this stage.

Section Two: Building Your Talent Bench You can't outsource your way to digital excellence. Companies need to have the capabilities to build and evolve their proprietary digital solutions, and that requires quality digital talent. Established companies often think they can't compete with digital natives for talent, but they can and do. This section details how to develop a talent roadmap that is as detailed as your digital one, including how to create an organization that can not only hire the best but also create an environment where they thrive.

Section Three: Adopting a New Operating Model Perhaps the most complex aspect of a digital and AI transformation is developing an operating model that fosters customer centricity and speed. That's because it touches the core of the organization, its management processes, and how scores of teams work. This section explains the different operating model choices to consider – from a digital factory to an organization built around products and platforms – and guides you in your selection for the realities of your organization. This section also highlights how to establish and scale make-or-break capabilities such as product management and user experience design.

Section Four: Technology for Speed and Distributed Innovation This section explores how to build a distributed technology environment that makes it easy for hundreds, if not thousands, of teams to provision the services they need to quickly build digital and AI solutions. We cover the necessary modern software engineering practices, including DevSecOps (development, security, and operations) and MLOps (machine learning operations), that have become central to achieving high-development velocity, code quality, and peak live operational performance.

Section Five: Embedding Data Everywhere This section reviews the critical decisions required to architect data thoughtfully for quality, easy consumption, and reuse. Only then can the power of AI be unleashed. We explore how to develop and deploy data products (the data that is packaged into easy-to-consume formats for other applications) in a way that provides the greatest benefit to the business. This section also tackles the often-tricky data governance and organizational issues that can undo even the most promising data products.

Section Six: The Keys to Unlock Adoption and Scaling One of the most dispiriting aspects of a digital and AI transformation is how even the best digital solutions just don't have the impact they're supposed to. Companies typically invest in the initial solution development but chronically underinvest in driving user adoption and scaling across the enterprise. This section explores those change management challenges, with a focus on how to address at a sufficiently granular level the technical, process, and human issues that keep great solutions from delivering their full value.

Section Seven: Transformation Journey Stories We finish the book with an in-depth look at three companies – Freeport-McMoRan, DBS, and the LEGO Group – that we consider leaders in digital and AI transformation. This section shows how the six elements covered in this book come together for these exemplar companies, from how they built up their capabilities to how they worked as a team to deliver on the value. These cases highlight the turns in their journey, challenges they overcame, and how they succeeded in creating distance over their competitors.

This guide provides an integrated perspective on how these elements work best with one other. The digital roadmap in Section One, for example, aligns with the value tracking method in Section

Six. The digital talent presented in Section Two aligns with the operating model design in Section Three. This integrated approach is fundamental to successful digital and AI transformations, and it was one of our primary motivations for writing this book as we find many companies struggle to establish overall transformation coherence.

What this book is . . . and isn't

Don't expect a coffee table book with quotable stats about digital and AI transformations. We feature instead practical artifacts – McKinsey frameworks, process flows, technology architecture diagrams, workplans, how-to checklists, and team staffing models, among others – that are the necessary tools to be successful in this work.

This book is for leaders and practitioners who are responsible for shaping and executing their company's digital and AI transformation. That includes the CEO and those in the C-suite who invariably are called to play a major role in such an undertaking, but also any executives responsible for leading tech-related change in their business unit or function.

We also wrote this book for executives frustrated by reading dozens of articles and books on the topic and still feeling confused and uncomfortable with technology. This book covers what executives need to know to be effective in deploying digital technologies in their business. We do not focus on a specific technology, but we do explore the broad array of technologies digital transformations need to achieve their goal.

Similarly, this book does not focus on specific digital solutions. Every industry and every process within these industries will use different digital solutions to better serve customers and lower unit cost. For example, in the consumer packaged goods industry, revenue management solutions are critical to commercial performance.

In mining, solutions that focus on maximizing process yields are key. Instead, this book examines how to figure out which digital solutions to build, and then how to go about building and deploying them.

We wrote *Rewired* to flow sequentially in the way companies typically encounter each topic in a digital and AI transformation. But we also wrote each section and chapter to be self-contained so that those who are further along the journey or responsible for a specific part of it can use this book as a reference guide, consulting chapters that are most relevant to the challenges they are facing.

As we all know, digital is a fast-moving field and the state-of-the-art is constantly evolving. The content in this book is based on the fourth generation of our own internal digital and AI transformation method at McKinsey. We update our method every 18 months or so, and our intent is to periodically update this book to give you a clear sense for how the field is evolving, from a practitioner's standpoint. We hope this book will become a useful and reliable guide for you on this exciting journey.

It's still Day 1 for digital and AI transformation

How companies navigate the digital world to achieve sustainable competitive advantage is the defining business challenge of our time. For digital and AI transformations to scale and deliver on its promises, the top team needs to be ready and willing to undertake the organizational "surgery" required to rewire their business so they can outcompete with technology.

A digital and AI transformation is ultimately an exercise in constant evolution and improvement – it's just the modern way that businesses will work. If you accept this premise, it will change your perspective for how you approach the job at hand. To borrow Jeff Bezos's expression, it's still Day 1 for digital and AI transformation.

Notes

1. Michael Chui, Roger Roberts, and Lareina Yee, "McKinsey technology trends outlook 2022," McKinsey.com, April 22, 2022, https://www.mckinsey.com/capabilities/mckinsey-digital/our-insights/the-top-trends-in-tech.

2. Simon Blackburn, Jeff Galvin, Laura LaBerge, and Evan Williams, "Strategy for a digital world," *McKinsey Quarterly*, October 8, 2021, https://www.mckinsey.com/capabilities/mckinsey-digital/our-insights/strategy-for-a-digital-world.

3. Laura LaBerge, Kate Smaje, and Rodney Zemmel, "Three new mandates for capturing a digital transformation's full value," McKinsey, June 15, 2022, https://www.mckinsey.com/capabilities/mckinsey-digital/our-insights/three-new-mandates-for-capturing-a-digital-transformations-full-value.

4. A proprietary solution is a solution built with off-the-shelf and custom-developed software as well as data sets to solve a business/user problem. If the proprietary solution makes a meaningful performance difference and it is difficult for competitors to replicate, then it provides a competitive advantage.

5. Steven Van Kuiken, "Tech companies innovate at the edge: Legacy companies can too," *Harvard Business Review*, October 20, 2022; https://hbr.org/2022/10/tech-companies-innovate-at-the-edge-legacy-companies-can-too.

6. Colin Bryar and Bill Carr, "Working Backwards: Insights, Stories, and Secrets from inside Amazon," St. Martin's Press, 2021.

7. Our internal research at McKinsey on the benefits of generative AI on 200 of our software developers suggests a greater than 25% productivity gains in developing code (This research is soon to be published).

8. Michael Chui, Bryce Hall, Helen Mayhew, Alex Singla, and Alex Sukharevsky, "The state of AI in 2022—and a half decade in review," McKinsey.com, December 6, 2022, https://www.mckinsey.com/capabilities/quantumblack/our-insights/the-state-of-ai-in-2022-and-a-half-decade-in-review.

9. Laura LaBerge, Kate Smaje, and Rodney Zemmel, "Three new mandates for capturing a digital transformation's full value," McKinsey.com, June 15, 2022, https://www.mckinsey.com/capabilities/mckinsey-digital/our-insights/three-new-mandates-for-capturing-a-digital-transformations-full-value.

10. Publication of this research in Harvard Business Review is pending.

Creating the Transformation Roadmap

A business-led roadmap is the blueprint for a successful digital and AI transformation

When evaluating stalled digital and AI transformations, we find that many of the issues can be traced back to insufficient planning and alignment.[1] Misunderstanding among leadership at the strategic planning stage will invariably lead to muddled execution in your digital and AI transformation.

We typically see five serious sins: leaders have a different conceptual understanding of digital so they talk past each other; leaders focus energies on pet projects that don't deliver much value; they focus too much on technology solutions, and miss the crucial people and capability needs; the transformation is scoped too broadly so invest-ments are spread too thin; and, lastly, the CEO delegates responsi-bility to another executive in the C-suite.[2]

If one of these issues is afflicting your company, call a timeout. No matter where a business is on its transformation journey, it's never too late to reset. By clarifying what you want to achieve and align-ing around a plan to do it, you can create tremendous excitement and conviction about the journey ahead. The following chapters will guide you on how to develop a roadmap and establish a strong foundation for your digital transformation:

Chapter 1: Get your top team inspired and aligned. Take the time to establish a common digital language, learn from other industries, develop a shared vision, and explicitly agree on a set of commitments that match your ambitions.

Chapter 2: Choose the right transformation "bite size." The root cause of most struggling transformations is an inappropri-ately scoped effort that is either too small to achieve meaningful impact or too big and complex to deliver.

Chapter 3: Have business leaders define what's possible. When business leaders step up to define ambitious yet realistic trans-formation goals of their business domains, they set in motion the flywheel of change.

Chapter 4: Figure out what resources you need to achieve what you want. Agile pods are small, multidisciplinary teams tasked with delivering the reimagined business. You need to figure out what kinds and how many you need.

Chapter 5: Build capabilities for now and the next decade. You are fundamentally upgrading the capabilities of your organization to outcompete in the age of digital and AI. Be clear on what those capabilities are and how to build them.

Chapter 6: The digital roadmap is a contract for your C-suite. It details specific plans to transform business domains with investments and benefits. And it articulates a plan to build enterprise capabilities with measurable maturity end-points.

Chapter 7: The ultimate corporate team sport. Every C-suite executive will need to do their part for the company to succeed on its digital transformation journey.

Notes

1. Dennis Carey, Ram Charan, Eric Lamarre, Kate Smaje, and Rodney Zemmel, "The CEO's playbook for a successful digital transformation," *Harvard Business Review*, December 20, 2021, https://hbr.org/2021/12/the-ceos-playbook-for-a-successful-digital-transformation; Celia Huber, Alex Sukharevsky, and Rodney Zemmel, "5 questions boards should be asking about digital transformation," *Harvard Business Review*, June 21, 2021, https://hbr.org/2021/06/5-questions-boards-should-be-asking-about-digital-transformation.
2. Jacques Bughin, Tanguy Catlin, Martin Hirt, and Paul Willmott, "Why digital strategies fail," McKinsey.com, January 25, 2018, https://www.mckinsey.com/capabilities/mckinsey-digital/our-insights/why-digital-strategies-fail.

Chapter 1

Get your top team inspired and aligned

You rush a miracle man, you get rotten miracles.

—Miracle Max from "The Princess Bride"

Three elements of successful digital transformations are foundational and universal: vision, alignment, and commitment. While these elements are important in any transformation, digital and AI transformations often don't receive the same rigor when it comes to setting targets and goals. That's a classic symptom of a business that is either treating digital as a side effort or of leadership that doesn't understand digital well enough to know what's possible.

Because digital and AI transformations have an impact on so many parts of the business, investing the time to get these foundations right pays significant dividends in terms of clarity and unified action.[1]

Vision

Vision is both a shared understanding of what the ultimate, high-level goal of a transformation is, and its value. Vision is more than aspiration, it's the underlying "why" and acts as the company's North Star in the transformation that provides a clear destination for all the activities and solutions outlined in the roadmap. The tactical goals and objectives for teams and the missions they work on should all point toward this common vision. Some companies choose a different term, but whatever term is used, it needs to be clear and relevant for the entire business's digital and AI transformation efforts.

What makes a good vision? Strong vision statements have some common ingredients: an aspiration, often anchored around the customer, as well as a time dimension and a quantification of significant value. The vision needs to inspire and be framed so that the company's employees can all understand it. The best vision statements go beyond simply being inspiring aspirations like "unmatched customer service" to provide more specifics, like "Deliver personalized, proactive outreach at multiple points during the customer journey." For one company, it was "Provide a frictionless customer and employee experience by leveraging AI across our core operational processes to deliver industry-leading customer satisfaction and a 15% lift in EBIT in three years."

From a good vision, you can then be clear about how you intend to reimagine the business and identify the capabilities needed to deliver on that vision (see Exhibit 1.1). One touchstone: anchor the transformation vision in the overall business strategy of the company.

Alignment

Alignment means more than agreement—it means everyone understands their respective role and what they need to do. This is important because digital and AI transformations always require tight cross-functional collaboration. For example, sales, marketing, pricing, customer service, and order fulfillment must transform together

Digital vision example

Example for a consumer packaged goods company

ASPIRATION

Business goals

Drive new sources of growth via direct-to-consumer personalization and become the best CPG company in serving our retail customers

Financial goals

Create $1 billion lift in verifiable annual earnings before interest and taxes (EBIT) by 20XX

REIMAGINING OUR BUSINESS

Insights-driven consumer journey

Enable personally relevant consumer interactions via tailored messages, offerings, and experiences

Innovation

Leverage data-mining to better understand unmet consumer needs and accelerate renovation of core categories

Category and customer growth

Develop insights and execute strategies to profitably grow categories and serve as thought partner to retailers

Supply-chain advantage

Support optimal level of complexity and service at the lowest delivered cost

NEW DIGITAL CAPABILITIES

Talent

Field a core bench of digital talent, and increase digital proficiency of the broader workforce

Agile operating model

Create empowered interdisciplinary teams, deployed to and led by the business to develop our proprietary digital solutions

Tech

Adopt modern, open, modular cloud-based architecture; build and customize for competitive differentiation

Data

Invest in developing proprietary data assets that will differentiate our customer and consumer experience

EXHIBIT 1.1

if the company is to successfully shift to online channels. These end-to-end process collaborations are the rule, not the exception, in digital transformations.

It's critically important to get alignment right. Research proves it: companies reporting successful transformation efforts are nearly four times more likely than unsuccessful ones to report "a shared sense of accountability for meeting the transformation's objectives."[2]

It's not unusual at this early stage for leaders to be misaligned when it comes to the digital and AI transformation. Executives on the leadership team often approach a digital and AI transformation with different priorities and perspectives that might conflict. In many cases, the top team lacks both a common understanding of digital and pattern recognition for the business possibilities offered by digital technologies. Even at the most fundamental level, leadership may not have a common understanding of questions such as: What is artificial intelligence? What does a data engineer do? Why does DevSecOps matter? There are dozens of questions like these around which leadership must build a common language, a shared understanding, and real conviction for the potential that digital might offer in their business , and what will it take to capture it.

For this reason, it's always a good idea at the start of a transformation to create an experiential leadership learning journey composed of go-and-see visits to other companies that are further along their digital journeys, executive training to learn about the basics of digital and AI, and art-of-the-possible workshops to build pattern recognition and conviction on how digital can transform different areas of the business.

You should plan on having each top executive invest a minimum of 20 hours of learning before they can be ready to productively engage in defining a digital roadmap with their colleagues. In our experience, this is the most important thing you will do in the early stages of your transformation.

Commitment

No transformation is possible without commitment. Commitment is more than budget allocation, which is necessary but not sufficient. Commitment is C-suite leaders making themselves individually and jointly accountable for delivering the vision and the related benefits based on resources invested.

Executive commitment, which should be firmly in place by the time the roadmap is completed, is reflected in four ways:

1. **A digital business case worth rolling out of bed for.** Business leaders must be ready to commit to clear business performance improvements in customer experience and/or return on investments. At this stage, ask yourself: Will our plan truly transform the business? Are the investments commensurate with the opportunity? On this last point, be careful of falling victim to "digital magic," that is, investing very little but expecting to create a huge amount of value. There is no such thing as "digital magic."

2. **Real investments behind building foundational enterprise capabilities.** While some investments should be tied to specific digital opportunities, others should be focused on building foundational capabilities in (a) digital talent, (b) operating model, (c) the technology stack, and (d) the data environment. In the early days of a digital transformation, you might expect a 50/50 investment split between creating specific solutions and building capabilities. Recent analysis shows, in fact, that top-decile economic performers are significantly ahead of their peers in many areas of foundational technology investment.[3] Be careful, however, of developing long timelines and creating an excessive drain on your P&L. Digital transformations take real investment, but that spend should be divided up into manageable timelines with a clearly articulated focus on payback periods. After an initial period of investment, you should be building value along the way, not at some far-off time.

3. **CEO-led transformation governance.** Successful transformations are sponsored by the CEO. Only the CEO can create the cross-functional alignment required to succeed and make bold decisions around the building out of enterprise digital capabilities. Create a transformation office (TO) and staff it with your most capable people (more on this in Chapter 30).

4. **Executive resolve and role modeling.** CEOs and other line executives have plenty of other responsibilities, of course, but they still need to devote meaningful amounts of time to the transformation. They should role-model being customer focused, collaborative, tech savvy, and agile – all qualities of great digital leaders.

They should be curious and continuously learning about the potential of technology. They should be down in the trenches observing the successes and challenges faced by their teams in implementing new digital solutions. The roadmap should explicitly define what is expected of senior leaders (see more in Chapter 7).

Notes

1. Kate Smaje, Rodney Zemmel, "Digital transformation on the CEO agenda," McKinsey.com, May 12, 2022, https://www.mckinsey.com/capabilities/mckinsey-digital/our-insights/digital-transformation-on-the-ceo-agenda.
2. "Losing from day one: Why even successful transformations fall short," McKinsey.com, December 7, 2021, https://www.mckinsey.com/capabilities/people-and-organizational-performance/our-insights/successful-transformations.
3. "The new digital edge: Rethinking strategy for the postpandemic era," McKinsey.com, May 12, 2022, https://www.mckinsey.com/capabilities/mckinsey-digital/our-insights/the-new-digital-edge-rethinking-strategy-for-the-postpandemic-era.

Chapter 2

Choose the right transformation "bite size"

Pick battles big enough to matter and small enough to win.

—Jonathan Kozol

Many companies set their digital and AI transformations up to struggle from the start by getting the scope of the change wrong. Some companies start too small, believing an incremental approach will lower risk. This is a mistake. Successful transformations need to change something meaningful in the business, where there is a noticeable amount of value at stake and the impact can be measured. You won't get far transforming a house by repainting the living room; you need to take on something much more substantial, like remodeling the kitchen.

Others, with the best of intentions, go too big too soon, and try to transform the whole company all at once. This is generally too disruptive, too expensive to do right, or too difficult to tackle as a first project, and usually fails. More commonly, companies spread bets and resources too thinly across an uncoordinated set of activities and initiatives. This results in a lot of activity but not much value.

The domain-based approach

The right approach is to identify a few important and self-contained domains in the business and rethink them completely. As many as 80% of successful interventions in a struggling digital transformation are based on re-anchoring the scope to drive a concerted effort against a well-defined domain.[1] Taking this approach starts with identifying what the domains are. A domain is a subset of your enterprise that encapsulates a cohesive set of related activities. There are a few ways to define domains (see Exhibit 2.1).

Companies can determine for themselves how best to draw a circle around a set of business activities to define a domain that makes the most sense. The key is to define a domain that's large enough to be valuable and noticeable to the company, but small enough to be transformed without being unduly impacted by dependencies with other parts of the business. How many total domains are there for a company? The right number is about 10–15 for a monoline business. For a conglomerate, the right unit of analysis will be the strategic business unit, so domains are defined at that level. For the purposes of a digital transformation, however, select two to five to focus on transforming first. It is possible to go bigger and do more domains at the beginning. However, doing so requires a significant near-term investment, more coordination, and more talent. It may also carry more risk and will almost certainly require significant external resourcing and may deprive the organization of some early learnings. So be thoughtful about which and how many domains to tackle.

Three ways to define a domain

Workflow/Process

High-value business processes like asset maintenance, customer care, or procure-to-pay

Journeys

Interaction-intensive processes like customer onboarding, providing customer advice, or buying a product online

Function

Traditional business functions, such as sales, finance, marketing, or supply chain

Most companies choose to organize their domains by workflows or journeys, as this tends to offer the greatest value to customers and/or employees.

Example of domains in a consumer packaged goods company

FRONT OF HOUSE	OPERATIONS	SUPPORT FUNCTIONS
Personalized marketing	Integrated supply chain planning	People
Store execution	Logistics	Finance
Digital engagement	Manufacturing	Legal
Innovation/R&D	Procurement	
Revenue management		

EXHIBIT 2.1

Prioritizing domains

Prioritizing which domains to go after first requires an assessment along two broad dimensions: value potential and feasibility (see Exhibit 2.2). Executives will recognize this simple way of prioritizing opportunities but they should pay attention to the criteria that drive the assessment.

Domains are prioritized based on value and feasibility

Example consumer packaged goods company

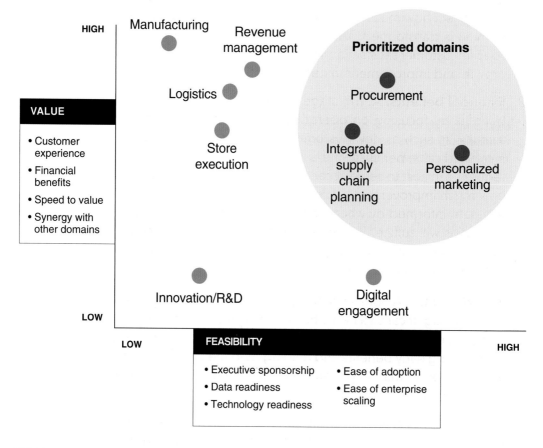

EXHIBIT 2.2

At this stage, a high-level estimate of the value potential based on a combination of outside-in analysis and discussions with senior leaders and industry experts will suffice. Most companies struggle with this kind of estimation because they lack experience understanding what might be possible with digital. To address this issue, consider using benchmarks from successful companies (even outside of your sector). Key value considerations include:

1. **Customer experience.** Improving the customer experience should be considered the "first among equals" when it comes to considerations. Most successful digital and AI transformations are centered around the customer and meeting their needs. It helps to benchmark the current experience versus competitors, and project how much the experience would improve once the domain is transformed. This should translate into measures of specific customer satisfaction improvement as well as of customer growth and improvement in net value per customer.

2. **Financial benefits.** At this stage you want to estimate financial benefits by focusing on operational key performance indicators (KPIs), such as new customer growth, reduction in churn, increased value per customer, improvement in process yield, or reduction in cost to serve. It can be difficult to precisely estimate how much improvement could be achieved at this stage, so an estimate informed by what others have achieved in analogous industries will suffice. Be careful not to downplay the potential at this stage. This is only for prioritization purposes and it is not yet the business case.

3. **Speed to value.** A domain-based transformation should typically generate significant value within six to 36 months, depending on the domain. This is often an important consideration in terms of providing early benefits and helping fund the transformation. We have found that, in general, AI-intensive opportunities pay off more quickly.

4. **Synergy.** If you are transforming more than one domain, synergy between them is a compelling point of leverage. Synergy can be evaluated in terms of three primary elements: (a) data reuse across solutions, (b) tech stack reuse across solutions, and (c) shared change-management efforts. For example, if you develop a new mortgage sales platform and a new credit-card sales platform at the same time, you would only need to retrain your thousands of branch sales representatives once.

Assessing feasibility is a combination of understanding technical and data readiness, the change-management effort required, and the domain leadership's capacity to commit. The most important considerations are:

1. **Strong executive sponsorship.** You need to be clear whether the executives in the given domain are fully on board. A unit may be ripe for digital transformation, but if there are competing priorities, such as implementing a new IT system or completing a major compliance remediation effort, then it might not be the right time to transform it.

2. **Data and technology readiness.** On the data side, the core questions to assess are the ease of moving the necessary data fields to the cloud and the quality of the underlying data. At this stage, a cursory analysis is needed, but more diligence will be required if this domain is selected. On the tech side, the core questions to assess are quality of the cloud architecture, the performance of the underlying core systems, and the ease of accessing data and applications with application programming interfaces (APIs). Your enterprise architects will be best positioned to make this assessment. Note that legacy technology – or the demands on large existing core systems, such as an ERP upgrade – is often used as an excuse for not making progress. These issues, of course, need to be understood, but are not a reason for inaction. Legacy mindsets are a bigger challenge than legacy technology.

3. **Ease of adoption.** By understanding the scope, intensity, and risks involved in the change effort, companies can identify potential obstacles to the adoption of a digital solution. For example, carrying out change in a unionized environment may involve negotiations that can require time to carry out effectively.

4. **Ease of scaling.** Assuming you successfully develop the digital solution, assess how easy it will be to scale it across the enterprise? How complex will the change management challenge be? How many different data environments will the solution operating in? These questions matter in getting the full value.

The output of this value-feasibility analysis should highlight two to five domains to prioritize. What's important at this point is that you are not looking for precision – it does not matter if the measurements are exactly right at this point. View this more as a way to structure the conversation with the management team. Refining estimates will happen in the next step as part of reimagining the domain.

In their words: Avoiding fragmentation and collaborating better

The enemy of any go-to-market digital transformation is fragmentation, especially in a company of Sanofi's size. . . . you need to ruthlessly prioritize, and recognize that six months down the road, new shiny objects could creep in to dilute your initial objectives, and slow down your ability to create big wins.

Today, we invest less in aggregate than we did three years ago, yet for the chosen priority projects, we devote more resources. Our iterative agile build cycles go faster and involve users in the development process, resulting in solutions that are much more relevant and impactful.

A second obstacle to success is us, the leadership, the management team. Everybody likes to have their sphere of business power, which in the past was linked to a specific, often siloed, P&L. The digital future is not like that. You need to be more open, able to empower, delegate, and collaborate. Nurturing digital capability is another factor. We had to train up a critical mass of people who could understand digital in order to attract and retain digital talent. Previously, we didn't move fast enough and rejected innovative ways of working introduced by the new talent, which led to frustration and rapid churn.

—Dr. Pius S. Hornstein, Global Head, Digital Global Business
Units, Sanofi

In some cases, management will have a clear view of where the value is and decide to go after that domain immediately, skipping the prioritization step (see an example of this in the Freeport-McMoRan case example in Chapter 33). This can be a good approach when management is clearly aligned and the value from the domain is meaningful. In practice, this can also be a useful way to build conviction in the organization by clearly demonstrating the value companies can capture or protect with digital and AI.

One large agricultural company decided to go this route by focusing initially on its commercial domain by supporting its agronomists in better serving its growers (customers) and in making it easier for these growers to do business with the company. The CEO and the top team were experiencing competitive pressure from new digital entrants and felt there was a number of customer pain points they could address quickly to improve cross-selling and retention.

While jumping quickly to address a trial domain can work well, leadership needs to guard against just launching another pilot that generates interest but doesn't materially transform the business. That's why it is so important to take the time to conduct a thorough domain reimagination effort, as described in the next chapter.

Note

1. Tim Fountaine, Brian McCarthy, and Tamim Saleh, "Getting AI to scale," *Harvard Business Review*, May–June 2021, https://hbr.org/2021/05/getting-ai-to-scale.

Chapter 3

Have business leaders define what's possible

Without leaps of imagination, or dreaming, we lose the excitement of possibilities. Dreaming, after all, is a form of planning.

—*Gloria Steinem*

In each domain targeted for transformation, the goal is to identify multiple interrelated solutions that, when implemented, will *meaningfully* impact performance for the better. Note the emphasis on "meaningfully." Too often, companies will shoot for marginal improvements over their current rates, but that tends to constrain thinking to operate within the traditional boundaries of the legacy business. Small thinking leads to small results, often not worth the effort of the transformation. Our rule of thumb is that a robust digital roadmap should deliver 20%+ EBITDA improvement.

We recommend following a simple five-step process to develop a robust business case for each domain (see Exhibit 3.1).

Five steps for the domain reimagination

Problem to solve

Articulate the business problem to be solved – user unmet need or process pain points. Be clear on the improvement lever to activate to solve the problem.

Solutions and use cases

Identify the digital solutions and underlying use-cases required to address the "problem to be solved."

Data and tech requirements

Assess the data landscape and technology stack against the target solution architecture. Understand the gaps and investments needed.

Impact and investments

Estimate the impact these solutions could achieve by specifying how each lever/KPI could improve. Roughly estimate the required investments.

Implementation plan

Articulate change management requirements to realize the full value and develop an implementation sequence. Specify leadership and accountabilities.

EXHIBIT 3.1

Step 1 is a clear articulation of the business problem to be solved. What are the customer/user unmet needs? What are the process pain points? There are typically two approaches to do this:

1. **Zero-based journey design** uses design thinking to define end-user personas and identify unmet needs along the experience journey through user interviews and workshops. This approach is preferred in service-intensive industries where differentiation on the basis of great customer experiences is prized. The resulting journey maps provide the starting point for reimagining the user experience. Working with designers helps ensure this approach is built around the customer or user unmet needs (read more on user experience design in Chapter 16).

2. **End-to-end process mapping** involves breaking down the core business into a set of processes, identifying waste, pain points, or missed opportunities in the way the value is delivered. This approach is often preferred in operations-intensive industries where process uptime and achieving low unit cost are fundamental to competitiveness.

Step 2 aligns the unmet needs of the user or process pain points against a specific value lever (see Exhibit 3.2). For each value lever, identify potential digital solutions (e.g., apps or data assets) that users or customers will use as part of the improved experience you intend to provide. For example, it could be a new mortgage sales platform for branch bankers or a setpoint optimizer for operators of copper concentrators. Each solution should activate at least one value lever. Organizing by levers helps formulate a clear "from . . . to . . ." improvement assumption and it provides a measurable key performance indicator (KPI). Companies struggling with digital transformations often identify solutions that are not explicitly tied to business value through measurable KPI improvements.

Each solution will be made up of use cases or data assets needed to deliver that solution. In the case of a mortgage sales platform solution, for example, a use case could be customer onboarding or automated credit checking. Typically, transforming a domain will require a few solutions and each solution will in turn contain a few use cases. Use cases are supported by digitized workflows, analytic models, and data.

Step 3 goes deeper into the technology and data-related aspects of the solutions to be developed. What is the target architecture for these solutions and the underlying data? Is the current technology stack able to accommodate it, and, if not, what will have to be changed? Likewise on data. This step does require expert guidance from solutions architects.

Step 4 assesses the investments and expected benefits. The biggest mistake made at this stage is false precision. In the world of digital and AI, the payback should be 5× or more on your investment. Being +/−30% right on investments and benefits is therefore sufficient. The investments in the tech and data architecture need to be properly allocated, as most of these investments will be reused by other solutions. Often companies manage those in a separate effort to build out their common tech and data enablers.

Step 5 develops an implementation sequence with expected resourcing and benefits over time, including change management efforts required to realize the full value. This step tends to be casu-

Cascading from business domain to value levers, solutions, and use cases

Business domain	DOMAIN			
Value levers	LEVER I	LEVER II		LEVER III
Solutions	SOLUTION 1 SOLUTION 2	SOLUTION 3		SOLUTION 4
Use cases/ models	Use case 1.1 Use case 2.1	Use case 3.1		Use case 4.1
	Use case 1.2 Use case 2.2	Use case 3.2		Use case 4.2
	Use case 1.3	Use case 3.3		Use case 4.3
		Use case 3.4		

Business domain	A customer/user journey or a core business process – sizeable enough such that the value from transforming it would be meaningful
Value levers	Core business outcomes that are driven by the transformation of the domain, such as new customers, churn, cost to serve, NPS, etc.
Solutions	Solutions provide value to a customer or a user, such as a weather app or a mortgage sales platform
Use cases	A solution is typically composed of use cases. In the case of a weather app, the use cases might be forecasts for temperature, humidity, and wind. For a mortgage sales platform, the use cases might be customer onboarding, customer credit check, and mortgage pricing calculator

EXHIBIT 3.2

Case example: A CPG company improves its personalization capabilities

Case study: Personalized marketing

Personalized marketing domain at a CPG company

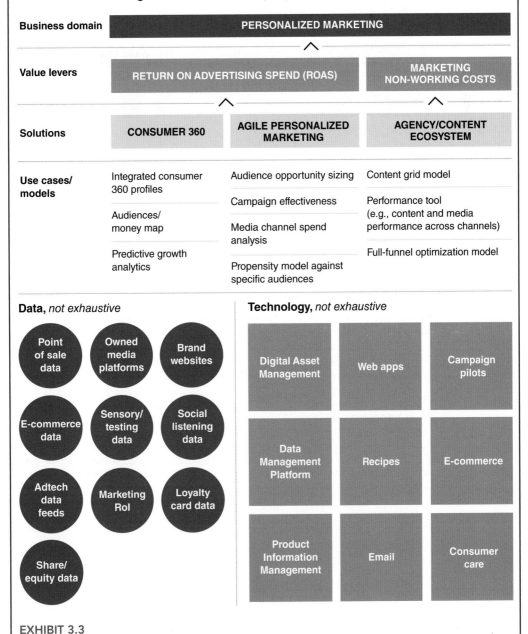

Business domain	PERSONALIZED MARKETING		

Value levers	RETURN ON ADVERTISING SPEND (ROAS)	MARKETING NON-WORKING COSTS

Solutions	CONSUMER 360	AGILE PERSONALIZED MARKETING	AGENCY/CONTENT ECOSYSTEM

Use cases/ models	Integrated consumer 360 profiles	Audience opportunity sizing	Content grid model
	Audiences/ money map	Campaign effectiveness	Performance tool (e.g., content and media performance across channels)
	Predictive growth analytics	Media channel spend analysis	Full-funnel optimization model
		Propensity model against specific audiences	

Data, *not exhaustive*

- Point of sale data
- Owned media platforms
- Brand websites
- E-commerce data
- Sensory/ testing data
- Social listening data
- Adtech data feeds
- Marketing RoI
- Loyalty card data
- Share/ equity data

Technology, *not exhaustive*

- Digital Asset Management
- Web apps
- Campaign pilots
- Data Management Platform
- Recipes
- E-commerce
- Product Information Management
- Email
- Consumer care

EXHIBIT 3.3

A consumer packaged goods company was looking to improve its personalized marketing capabilities to forge a much closer relationship with its customers, and increase returns on its advertising spend. To capture that value, the company developed solutions to deliver detailed customer insights and analytics to drive personalized customer marketing interactions.

They then identified the use cases, data, and technology needed to deliver those solutions. For example, they built out a marketing technology infrastructure to optimize and manage the messaging across multiple channels, including email, programmatic display advertising, retailer media, and paid social advertising. The domain transformation architecture is shown in Exhibit 3.3. As a result of this concerted effort, the messaging drove measurable increases in engagement across the targeted customer groups, often at multiples of existing business-as-usual engagement levels.

ally addressed but it is fundamental to achieving the impact. Read more about this in Section 6.

How to think about emerging technologies such as Generative AI

The fast-moving developments in technology create a unique challenge for digital and AI transformations: How do you build an organization powered by technology when the technology itself is changing so quickly? There is a fine balance between incorporating technologies that can generate significant value and dissipating resources and focus chasing every promising technology that emerges.

McKinsey publishes annually on the more important emerging tech trends based on their capacity to drive innovation and their likely time to market. As of this writing, the research identified 14 tech trends that have the potential to revolutionize how businesses operate and generate value.[1] While it remains difficult to predict how tech-nology trends will play out, you should be systematic in tracking their development and their implications for their business.

This book is not the place to go into detail about these trends – we encourage you to track McKinsey's annual review of technology trends to do that. But we do want to highlight generative artificial intelligence (GenAI), which we believe has the potential to be a significant disruptor on the level of cloud or mobile. GenAI designates algorithms (such as GPT-4) that can be used to create new content, including audio, code, images, text, simulations, and videos. The technology uses data it has ingested and experiences (interactions with users that help it "learn" new information and what's correct/incorrect) to generate entirely new content.

These are still early days and we can expect this field to change rapidly over the next months and years. In assessing how to best use GenAI models, there are three application types:

1. Content generation. Broad functional models that will become adept at automating, accelerating, and improving existing knowledge work (e.g., GPT-4, Google's Chinchilla, Meta's OPT). For example, marketers could leverage GenAI models to generate content to fuel targeted digital marketing at scale. Customer service could be fully automated or optimized via a "knowledge sidekick" monitoring conversation and prompting service reps. GenAI can rapidly develop and iterate on product prototypes and construction drawings.

2. New discoveries. Industry-specific models that can not only accelerate existing processes but develop new products, services, and innovations. In pharma, for example, application models that use common techniques (e.g., OpenBIOML, BIO GPT) can be deployed to deliver speed and efficiency to drug development or patient diagnostics. Or a GenAI model can be applied to a massive pharma molecule database that can identify likely cancer cures. The impact potential and readiness of generative AI will vary significantly by industry and business case.

3. Coding (e.g., Copilot, Alphacode, Pitchfork). These models promise to automate, accelerate, and democratize coding. Existing models are already able to competently write code, documentation, automatically generate or complete data tables, and test cybersecurity penetration – although significant and thorough testing is

necessary to validate outcomes. In our own recent research at McKinsey, we have a greater than 25 percent productivity improvement among our software developers when using Copilot.

In the context of a digital transformation, it's important to consider a few things when it comes to GenAI. First, any understanding of the value of GenAI models needs to be grounded on a clear understanding of your business goals. That might sound obvious, but as interest in GenAI surges, the temptation to develop use cases that don't end up creating much value for the business or become a distraction from the digital transformation efforts will be significant.

Secondly, like any technology, extracting at-scale value from GenAI requires strong competencies in all the capabilities covered in this book. That means developing a range of capabilities and skills in cloud, data engineering, and MLOps, and finding GenAI specialists and training people to use this new generation of capabilities.

Given this necessity, it will be important to revisit your digital and AI transformation roadmap and review your prioritized digital solutions to determine how GenAI models can improve outcomes (e.g., content personalization, chatbot assistants to increase website conversion). Resist the temptation of pilot proliferation. It's fine to let people experiment, but the real resources should only be applied to areas with a real tie to business value. Take the time to understand the needs and implications of GenAI for the capabilities you're developing as part of your digital and AI transformation, such as the following:

Operating model: Dedicated, responsible GenAI-focused agile "pods" are required to ensure responsible development of and use of GenAI solutions. This will likely mean closer collaborations with legal, privacy, and governance experts as well as with MLOps and testing experts to train and track models.

Technology architecture and delivery: System architecture will need to adapt to incorporate multimodal GenAI capabilities into end-to-end work flows. There will need to be an evolution at multiple levels in the tech stack - data layer, model layer, UX interface - to ensure adequate integration and responsiveness in your digital solutions.

Data architecture: The application of GenAI models to your current data will require you to rethink your networking and data pipeline management to account for not just the size of the data, but the massive change frequencies that we can expect as GenAI learns and evolves.

Adoption and business model changes: In almost any scenario, we can expect that GenAI will offer a partial activity substitution, not a complete one. We will still need developers. We will still need contact center employees. But their job will be reconfigured. That may be much more of a challenge than the technology itself, especially since there is a significant "explainability gap" with GenAI models. This means that users are likely to not trust them and, therefore, not use them well (or at all). Retraining employees so they know how to manage and work with GenAI models will require substantial efforts to capture the promised productivity gains.

Digital trust: GenAI represents significant trust concerns that companies need to identify. Given that national data privacy regulations vary by maturity and restrictiveness, there remains a need for policies relating to usage of proprietary or sensitive information in third-party services and accountability in situations of data breach. Similarly, companies will need to think through, and track, intellectual property developments (particularly around IP infringement) as well as biases that are likely to manifest through unrefined GenAI models.

It's also becoming clearer that, in a world where everyone will have access to "intelligent" content, the ability to competitively differentiate yourself will increasingly depend on proprietary data and execution capabilities.

Note

1. Michael Chui, Roger Roberts, and Lareina Yee, "McKinsey technology trends Outlook 2022," McKinsey.com, April 24, 2022, https://www.mckinsey.com/capabilities/mckinsey-digital/our-insights/the-top-trends-in-tech.

Chapter 4

Figure out what resources you need to achieve what you want

How could you have a soccer team if all were goalkeepers?
How would it be an orchestra if all were French horns?

—Desmond Tutu

The organizing unit in a digital and AI transformation is the agile pod (sometimes called a squad, scrum, agile team, or cross-functional team). A pod is a cross-disciplinary team of about 5–10 people that owns the design, development, and production of a particular digital product or service for an extended period of time. Delivering the digital roadmap is basically an exercise in figuring out how many, and what type of, agile pods you need to get the job done.

We won't go into detail here about how these agile pods work (you can find that in Chapter 13). However, it's important to cover the basic construct of agile pods with a focus on roles because you cannot complete the digital roadmap if you don't specify the resources needed.

Pod composition

Agile pods have a product owner (also sometimes called a product manager or pod owner), a scrum master,[1] a group of relevant digital technologists, and business subject matter experts (see Exhibit 4.1). Most pod members are dedicated 100% to the pod because that's the most effective way to achieve high-development velocity (although there are some exceptions for certain shared resources, such as solution architects and agile coaches).

Recent research has shown that having the team working together in a physical location is preferable but not necessarily a critical driver of agile pod performance, especially if time zone differences are reasonable.

Pod archetypes

There are two important considerations when deciding on the staffing composition of a pod. First, what type of solution do you want to develop? For example, an analytics-intensive solution requires deep data engineering and data science expertise. On the other hand, a customer-facing solution requires more skills around user experience design and software development. In general, most companies will define three to six different archetypes of pods (see Exhibit 4.2). While the exhibit presents three classic pod archetypes, others exist, such as a digital marketing pod, connected pod (i.e., IoT), or core system integration pod.

The second consideration is the life stage of the development effort. In the initial discovery phase, you need expertise to scope the work, design the solution, prioritize use cases, and frame the business case. In the proof-of-concept phase, you need more "builders" (including

Typical roles in an agile pod

Not exhaustive

BUSINESS

Provide business and functional expertise

 Product owner
Defines and prioritizes product roadmap and backlog

 Subject matter expert
Brings expertise and knowledge of business, functions, operations, legal, risk, and compliance

 Business/process analyst
Brings understanding of end-to-end business process, supports development of business case, OKR tracking, and change management effort

DESIGN

Create user experience for the solution

 Design lead
Leads customer-centric design, develops user engagement plan, and conducts user testing

 UI/UX designer
Creates user experiences that capture business value and meet customer needs

ENGINEERING

Conceptualize technical architecture, develop code, and run solution in production

 Software engineer[1]
Develops code, writes unit tests, and drives integrations

 Data engineer
Builds data pipelines to drive analytics solutions from different data sources

DATA SCIENCE/AI

Analyze data to identify key insights for the solution

 Data scientist
Analyzes and mines business data to identify patterns and builds predictive models

 Machine learning engineer
Implements ML models into production ensuring performance and stability of model

SUPPORT[2]

Deliver additional guidance to the team

 Scrum master
Oversees scrum process and helps the self-managing team achieve its goals

 Agile coach
Supports and coaches the scrum team on agile development practices

Note: List is not exhaustive.

1. Software engineers cover full-stack developers, solution architects, cloud engineers, and DevOps engineers.
2. These roles diminish as pods gain maturity.

EXHIBIT 4.1

Pod archetypes and typical staffing by solution life cycle

Examples — will vary by industry and company

DIGITAL INTENSIVE SOLUTIONS

Solution life stages

Discovery	Proof-of-concept/MVP	Production	Change management
1 Product owner	1 Product owner	1 Product owner	1 Product owner
1 Design lead	1 Scrum master	1 Scrum master	1–2 Change agents[3]
0.5 Software engineer[1,2]	1 Design lead	1 Design lead[1]	1 Business analyst[1]
1 Business/process analyst	1 UI/UX designer	1 UI/UX designer	
1 SME	2–3 Software engineers[1,2]	2–3 Software engineers[2]	
	1–2 SMEs	1–2 SMEs	

ANALYTICS INTENSIVE SOLUTIONS

Discovery	Proof-of-concept/MVP	Production	Change management
1 Product owner	1 Product owner	1 Product owner	1 Product owner
0.5 Data scientist	1 Scrum master[1]	1 Scrum master[1]	1–2 Change agents[3]
0.5 Data engineer	2 Data scientists	1 Change agent	1 Business analyst[1]
1 Business analyst	2 Data engineers	1 UI/UX designer[1]	
1 SME	1 Business analyst	1 Data engineer	
	1 SME	2 Machine learning engineers	
		1 Business analyst	

DATA INTENSIVE SOLUTIONS

Discovery	Proof-of-concept/MVP	Production	Change management
1 Data product owner	1 Data product owner	1 Data product owner	1 Product owner
1 Data architect	1 Scrum master	1 Scrum master	1–2 Change agents[3]
1 Data engineer	1 Data architect	1 Data architect	1 Business analyst[1]
1 Data SME	2–3 Data engineers	2–3 Data engineers	
1 Business analyst	1–2 Software engineers[2]	1-2 Software engineers[2]	
	1–2 Data SMEs		

1. Optional/as needed. 2. Software engineers cover full-stack developers, solution architects, cloud engineers, and DevOps engineers. 3. Pod members who are active promoters of change, working to embed new solutions and build organizational buy-in by embracing new processes, addressing questions and concerns, and resolving implementation challenges.

EXHIBIT 4.2

designers and software engineers) who can rapidly develop, test, and iterate to deliver a minimum viable product. In the production phase, you need engineering capabilities to ensure the solution is secure, performs effectively, and can scale.

While pod staffing evolves through the lifecycle of a solution, there is never a handover from one pod to another. In fact, maintaining continuity for key roles, such as the product owner, is key to ensuring a coherent development effort.

With these archetypes defined, it becomes easier to assess the resource needs of your digital and AI transformation. At a minimum, you should plan one pod per solution on your digital roadmap. If the solution is complex, you may have more pods focusing on different use cases. Assigning archetypes to solutions takes some experience and practice but it will soon become second nature.

Estimating overall talent needs

Once you have assigned pod archetypes to each of your digital solutions, it becomes straightforward to understand the overall talent needs of the transformation, or at least the needs for the first 18 months or so (see example talent needs in Exhibit 4.3). These essentially become the marching orders for your Talent Win Room team (see Chapter 9). These needs will evolve over time as solutions mature and new ones get added. You should revisit this process on a quarterly basis.

Note

1. Scrum master roles are often covered by product owners in more mature agile organizations.

Estimating overall talent needs

Archetypes for each use case per quarter

		Q1	Q2	Q3	Q4	Q5	Q6
DOMAIN: PERSONALIZED MARKETING							
Solution: **Build consumer 360 data asset**	Use case: Ingest internal data	Data Discovery	Data Discovery	Data PoC	Data PoC	Data Prod.	Data Prod.
	Ingest external data	Data Discovery	Data Discovery	Data PoC	Data PoC	Data Prod.	Data Prod.
	Build API and consumption interfaces	Data Discovery	—	Digital PoC	Digital PoC	Digital Prod.	Digital Prod.
Activate digital marketing campaign	Develop personalized offerings	Analytics Discovery	Analytics PoC	Analytics Prod.	Analytics Prod.	Analytics Prod.	Analytics Prod.
	Activate paid search	—	Digital Discovery	Digital PoC	Digital PoC	Digital Prod.	Digital Prod.
	Activate own e-commerce site	—	—	Digital Discovery	Digital PoC	Digital PoC	Digital Prod.
DOMAIN: SUPPLY CHAIN							
Build supply chain digital twin	Build inbound material data twin	Data Discovery	Data Discovery	Data PoC	Data PoC	Data Prod.	Data Prod.
	Build operations transformation data twin	Data Discovery	Data Discovery	Data PoC	Data PoC	Data Prod.	Data Prod.
	Build outbound finished products data twin	Data Discovery	Data Discovery	Data PoC	Data PoC	Data Prod.	Data Prod.
Develop digital control tower	Develop on-time delivery metrics	Digital Discovery	Digital PoC	Digital PoC	Digital Prod.	Digital Prod.	Digital Chg. mgmt.
	Develop predictions based on sc twin	—	—	Analytics Discovery	Analytics PoC	Analytics Prod.	Analytics Prod.
DOMAIN: PROCUREMENT							
Create spend transparency	Consolidate spend data	Data Discovery	Data Discovery	Data PoC	Data PoC	Data Prod.	Data Prod.
	Create data for product specification fields	—	Digital Discovery	Digital PoC	Digital PoC	Digital Prod.	Digital Prod.
	Upload in spend analytics tools	—	—	Digital Discovery	Digital PoC	Digital PoC	Digital Prod.
	Develop should-be analytic models	—	—	Analytics Discovery	Analytics PoC	Analytics Prod.	Analytics Prod.

		Q1	Q2	Q3	Q4	Q5	Q6
Estimated roles needed	Product owners	3	6	14	20	16	16
	Data architects & data engineers	23	22	37	20	38	38
	Design leads & UI/UX designers	2	6	18	20	26	24
	Software engineers	1	4	26	43	30	29
	Tech leads	11	10	10	8	10	10
	Data scientists & ML engineers	1	3	5	9	10	10
	Scrum masters & agile coaches	11	13	32	15	24	24
	SMEs	3	7	16	27	16	14
	Other	14	14	10	20	11	14
	Total	**69**	**85**	**168**	**182**	**181**	**179**

EXHIBIT 4.3

Chapter 5

Build capabilities for now and the next decade

You cannot escape the responsibility of tomorrow by evading it today.

—Abraham Lincoln

What you have defined on your digital and AI roadmap will necessarily be focused on the next two to three years. But you are also building the enterprise capabilities that will make it possible for your company to digitally innovate for the next 10 or more years.

This long-term view to building capabilities, in fact, is what differentiates the digital leaders from those who are looking for a quick fix by going after a sprinkling of use cases. Developing the necessary enterprise capabilities requires a plan and real investments that will serve the immediate needs of the priority domains but also the longer-term needs of the organization as it pursues more digital and AI innovations.

This starts with developing a shared viewpoint of the current state of digital capabilities to understand what is immediately possible and what will be needed to realize the long-term vision. Do you have the software engineering skills required? Can your operating model scale to hundreds of pods? Is your critical data easy to consume?

Once organizations have a shared fact base about where they are from a capability perspective, they are better able to make realistic plans about what is possible over what period of time.

Assessing foundational digital capabilities

There are four core capabilities required to deliver digital solutions: talent, operating model, technology, and data. Sections Two through Five in this book explore each of them in detail. But understanding where a company stands against good practices on these capabilities is a prerequisite to knowing what to do to improve them. You can do this by benchmarking your business against companies that are further down the journey, not just in your industry but, preferably, in industries that are ahead of yours in terms of digital transformation.

You may wonder why the digital capabilities of a bank may be a good benchmark for a resource company. It's because core digital capabilities are industry-agnostic to a large extent. Digital talent is largely the same. Agile practices are the same. Modern technology architecture and software engineering practices are the same (although reference architectures can vary by industry). In other words, domains and how they get reimagined tends to be specific to the industry but core capabilities are not.

Assessing digital capabilities

Capability ranking survey results by category, on scale of 1–5[1]

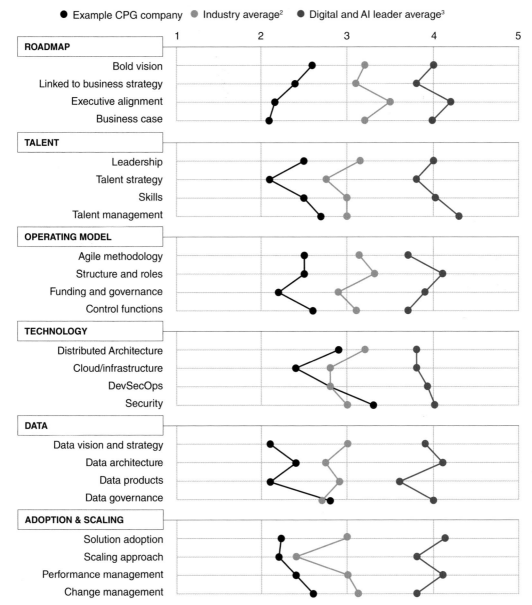

● Example CPG company   ● Industry average[2]   ● Digital and AI leader average[3]

1. 1 = lagging; 5 = best-in-class. 2. Average of top quintile of companies (from CPG industry) in the McKinsey Digital Quotient (DQ) database, across geographies. 3. Average of top quintile companies in the DQ database, across industries and geographies

EXHIBIT 5.1

The benchmarking effort is carried out by surveying employees using a standardized survey instrument. Exhibit 5.1 provides a good example of the output from a consumer packaged goods company.

Surveys have their own limitations so it's also a good idea to have independent experts conduct interviews with executives and managers across different business units and functions. This will bring additional color and perspective in interpreting the score. Finally, the executive team should take the time to visit exemplar companies to understand their digital journey and how they have gone about building their digital capabilities. This will help better calibrate the investments and efforts required.

Another useful assessment approach is a "lookback," a review of progress and roadblocks that the company has experienced in developing and delivering digital solutions. This is particularly helpful for companies that have started the journey but feel stalled. The lookback should start with establishing the portfolio of solutions that you will investigate. Through stakeholder interviews, you can then classify and categorize each solution by how far it has progressed along each stage of value along the maturity funnel (see Exhibit 5.2).

This exercise is particularly useful in identifying root causes when a digital transformation has stalled. Exhibit 5.2 is from a global food producer. Upon analyzing its digital spend of $130 million in 400 digital solutions, the company had a few important realizations. First, its $130 million of overall spend on digital was reasonable albeit on the low side in light of its overall $1 billion IT spend. Our rule of thumb is that digital transformation spend should be about 20% of IT spend or more, although this is very situation specific.

Second, the projects were subscale. With an average spend of $325,000 per project, this portfolio was far too skewed toward pilots and experimentations.

Look-back perspective on digital investments

Global food producer example

PROJECTION PROGRESSION		NUMBER OF SOLUTIONS	RUN-RATE POTENTIAL OF SOLUTIONS AT THIS STAGE % of total company EBITDA
IDEA	Idea validated to address business problem	160	<1%
PILOT/ TESTING	Concept tested and ready for business case	35	<1%
PROPOSAL	Business case approved and solution build starts	30	<1%
IMPLEMENTATION	Partial roll-out	35	<1%
PRODUCTION	Full roll-out and scaling	20	<1%
STOPPED	No longer active	120	<1%

EXHIBIT 5.2

Third, the overall impact potential of this portfolio is negligible – overall EBITDA would improve by less than 1% even if 100% of the projects were successful (as mentioned in the previous chapter, another one of our rules of thumb is for a robust digital roadmap to deliver 20%+ EBITDA improvement). Finally, too many projects were stopped and too few were making it to production – again, a sign that the company was doing too much bottom-up piloting.

In aggregate, these are the symptoms of a company where the senior business leaders have not invested enough time to reimagine how they might outcompete with proprietary digital and AI-based solutions.

These findings were eye opening for the top team. They immediately realized they needed a more top-down approach to better manage their spend. The first step was to stop most ongoing projects and consolidate the spend on their commercial and operations domains. They then mandated the senior leaders in these areas to build truly transformative digital roadmaps, and to concentrate their investments in both developing fewer but higher-impact solutions and building the talent and technology capabilities to continue improving them. They also earmarked sufficient investments to make the necessary changes to work processes and train users. Within 18 months, they delivered $150 million-plus incremental margin per year.

Scoping your capability-building needs

With your baseline capability assessment and domain reimagination plans in place, it becomes relatively straightforward to build the capability-building plan and related investment needs. Essentially, this is an exercise in scoping out the work that you need to do and the resources you need to have to build the necessary capabilities, which you can then feed into the overarching digital roadmap (see more on the roadmap in Chapter 6).

Exhibit 5.3 shows the specific elements in the capability-building plan of a consumer-packaged goods company for the first 18–24 months of its transformation.

Partnering to accelerate capability building

When developing your capability-building plans, you will likely need to rely on third parties to supplement or complement your current capabilities as you build them out. In doing so, be careful not to out-source the core digital capabilities that will be central to developing competitive differentiation. You may initially partner to build these capabilities in the short term, but the mid- to long-term view is to keep in-house those capabilities that are fundamental to creating value.

Key elements of a capability-building plan

Typical elements for first 18–24 months

TALENT	OPERATING MODEL	TECHNOLOGY	DATA	CHANGE MANAGEMENT
Talent needs: number and type of technologists needed, for year 1, at minimum (Ch. 4)	Approach to train teams in agile working methodologies (Ch. 13)	Future-state tech stack architecture to support priority domains (Ch. 17)	Plan for accessing and conditioning key data elements for priority domains (Ch. 24)	Setup of transformation office (Ch. 30)
Talent sourcing: setup of Talent Win Room (Ch. 9) and sourcing plan (Ch. 10)	Future state operating model and transition plan (Ch. 14)	Approach to address cloud migration needs for priority domains (Ch. 18)	Building of priority data products (Ch. 25)	System to track value created by digital solutions (Ch. 30)
Training programs for executives, domain leaders, and pod members (Ch. 12)		Approach to implementing DevSecOps and support developers (Ch. 18)	Future-state data architecture (Ch. 26)	Broad-based organizational training on digital (Ch. 32)

← Resourcing and investment required per quarter →

EXHIBIT 5.3

We've seen four types of partnerships that can work when properly scoped and structured:

1. **Umbrella:** Like hiring a general contractor for building a house, you might partner with a firm that helps plan and organize the transformation, perhaps supplies some talent, and helps you vet and organize other suppliers of talent, technology, and data. It is best to work with a single umbrella partner to avoid misalignments and coordination complexity.

2. **Talent:** Using partners to source talent can significantly increase speed and flexibility. The right partner can deploy a team of skilled experts to your business in a matter of days, and then leave when no longer needed. They can also provide upskilling services and training. Such partnerships may be necessary at first

but should be designed to diminish over time as you build up your own capabilities.

3. **Technology:** Partners can help house, process, and protect applications and data. Cloud service providers (CSPs) provide an ever-increasing array of services and capabilities, particularly around data and analytics (read more in Chapter 18). Other software providers may also be relevant depending on the solutions you build (e.g., marketing tech stack technologies for digital marketing). You may also need specific tech partnerships around more specialized capabilities like geolocation or penetration testing.

4. **Data:** Third parties can provide important supplemental data. Public data sources, data brokers, and data marketplaces all offer a range of data and data-related services. Companies need to carefully think through data access protocols, intellectual property, and cybersecurity risks.

Effective use of partnerships is ultimately based on how well a company knows what its capability gaps are and how well it can structure the partnerships to fill those gaps in the near term while building them out for the longer term.

Chapter 6

The digital roadmap is a contract for your C-suite

A goal without a plan is just a wish.

—*Antoine de Saint-Exupéry*

The final output of the business-led roadmapping process is the implementation roadmap and the related financial plan.

Exhibit 6.1 shows an actual example of a digital roadmap for a CPG company. Note the specific domains (personalized marketing, supply chain, and procurement) and how the capability-building efforts happen in parallel. This roadmap is limited to the first three domains. In years two and three of this transformation, these domains add additional solutions to continue their transformation and new domains get launched.

It's not helpful to plan further out than two to three years. Invariably things will change and you will learn a lot in the first year. Be clear on the prize you are going after and flexible about the journey to get there.

There are five markers of a good digital and AI transformation roadmap:

1. Domains and the underlying digital solutions are sequenced in a way that will produce meaningful value in the short and medium terms.

2. Domain transformations are explicitly tied to improvements in operational KPIs, which in turn tie to value creation. Business leaders are committed to the domain roadmap and the expected benefits have been baked into their business objectives and incentive plan.

3. The overall plan explicitly accounts for the buildout of enterprise capabilities – talent, operating model, technology, and data – and includes the investments required and the time needed to achieve maturity.

4. The overall financial plan is clear and reflects a realistic but aggressive time and investment horizon. It is essential to have financial metrics just as rigorous as if it were a typical cost or revenue transformation, and that progress can be measured in months, not years.

5. Change management for the entire transformation and for specific solutions is incorporated. The Transformation Office has developed a change management program and a clear governance model, and it has articulated measurable quarterly milestones (more on this in Chapter 30).

The digital roadmap is leadership's moment to "stack hands" in agreement. The roadmap essentially becomes a contract that leadership signs on to deliver.

Strategic roadmap for the entire transformation

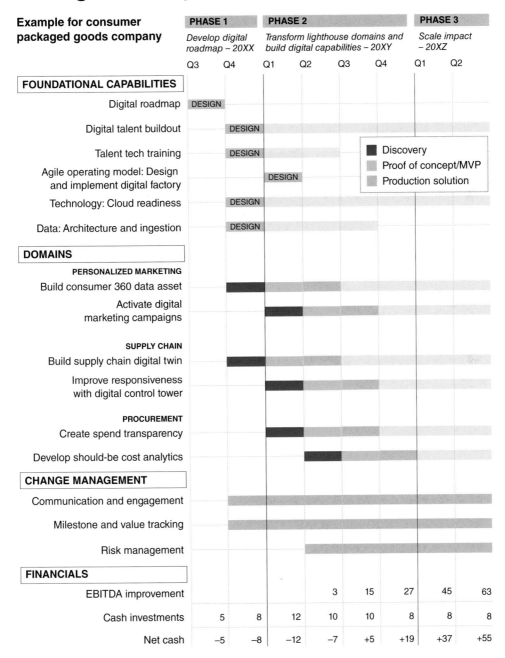

Example for consumer packaged goods company

	PHASE 1	PHASE 2	PHASE 3
	Develop digital roadmap – 20XX	Transform lighthouse domains and build digital capabilities – 20XY	Scale impact – 20XZ

Q3 Q4 Q1 Q2 Q3 Q4 Q1 Q2

FOUNDATIONAL CAPABILITIES

Digital roadmap — DESIGN

Digital talent buildout — DESIGN

Talent tech training — DESIGN

Agile operating model: Design and implement digital factory — DESIGN

Technology: Cloud readiness — DESIGN

Data: Architecture and ingestion — DESIGN

Legend:
- Discovery
- Proof of concept/MVP
- Production solution

DOMAINS

PERSONALIZED MARKETING
Build consumer 360 data asset

Activate digital marketing campaigns

SUPPLY CHAIN
Build supply chain digital twin

Improve responsiveness with digital control tower

PROCUREMENT
Create spend transparency

Develop should-be cost analytics

CHANGE MANAGEMENT

Communication and engagement

Milestone and value tracking

Risk management

FINANCIALS

	Q3	Q4	Q1	Q2	Q3	Q4	Q1	Q2
EBITDA improvement				3	15	27	45	63
Cash investments	5	8	12	10	10	8	8	8
Net cash	−5	−8	−12	−7	+5	+19	+37	+55

EXHIBIT 6.1

Chapter 7

The ultimate corporate team sport

No one can whistle a symphony. It takes a whole orchestra to play it.

—Halford Luccock

Leadership is crucial in any transformation but the intense, cross-functional nature of a digital and AI transformation requires a much greater level of collaboration across the C-suite. Everyone has an important part to play and without it, the transformation success will be at risk.

The CEO

Because digital and AI transformations require heavy cross-functional collaboration and the building of shared enterprise capabilities, the CEO (or division leader, in the case of conglomerates) plays an essential role. They are responsible for creating top-of-the-house alignment and architecting the new enterprise capabilities to avoid organizational misunderstandings.

The CEO is particularly important in convening and rallying leadership around the need for transformation, and regularly communicating the vision, alignment, and commitment to reinforce it. There are also far-reaching knock-on effects of a digital and AI transformation on end-to-end processes such as having to reduce servicing capacity in bank branches when customers increasingly use their banking app to complete certain tasks. Since these knock-on effects can touch so many different parts of the organization, it's up to the CEO to continually recalibrate and realign across the entire business system to capture the full gains.

The CEO also has an important role in holding people accountable for the transformation results with a constant focus on key progress metrics and a tight alignment of management incentives. As a rule of thumb, the CEO will invest two to four days per month in ensuring the success of the transformation, and somewhat more at the start.

The chief transformation officer

While the CEO is involved and accountable for the digital transformation, a dedicated leader is responsible for day-to-day activities and driving the transformation. This transformation officer typically reports directly to the chief executive and will be the face of digital for the organization, even if that person is acting in a temporary capacity – this role typically lasts two to three years (in some cases, a chief digital officer will have this role, or be a co-leader). By that time, the transformation should have shifted from being a special initiative to having been integrated into the day-to-day management routine.

This leader should be able to create and promote a compelling vision, have an end-to-end understanding of how the company works, and have a strong intuition for where digital and AI might transform it. They are a respected executive with the capacity to influence the C-suite and implement strong program management discipline. For this reason, the transformation leader is generally an internal hire.

The typical responsibilities of a transformation officer at the start of the transformation will include:

1. Designing and leading a digital leadership learning journey for executives

2. Working with the leadership team in developing their digital roadmap

3. Working with HR and IT to ensure proper talent, technology, and data assessments are completed around the priority domains

4. Developing, in collaboration with business, finance, IT, and HR, a view of the investments and resources required, and expected benefits

5. Creating strong engagement around the digital transformation at the executive committee and one or two levels down in the organization, and over time across the entire organization

During the execution phase, the transformation leader's responsibilities evolve to include managing the progress of the transformation, overseeing training and change management programs, and addressing specific issues as they arise (read more about this in Chapter 30).

The CTO, CIO, and CDO

These three tech-related roles may or may not exist in your organization. Some companies have all three. Others may combine two or all of them into a single role. This varies and it often depends on the skill set of the individuals.

- The CIO (chief information officer) typically focuses on improving the inner workings of the company with technology. They oversee the company's core systems and technology infrastructure. The CIO provides critical architectural guidance and plays a leadership role in defining/evolving the target state cloud architecture.

- The CTO (chief technology officer) typically works on improving customer offerings with technology. They oversee applications that touch the customer directly like a banking ATM or the software applications in a car. The CTO's role in the transformation can take many flavors, depending on the exact responsibilities they have at your company. If the role is heavily product oriented, the CTO will naturally focus on developing or evolving the product's digital roadmap.

- The CDO (chief digital officer) in some cases acts as a co-leader of the transformation, and typically creates new digital experiences for customers or internal users. The CDO will play a central role in supporting each priority domain in defining the architecture of the digital solutions envisioned, scoping the resource requirements for delivery, and overseeing digital solution delivery. During implementation, they oversee the delivery of these solutions and build the related capabilities.

You'll note some overlap between the CDO role and the CIO and CTO. The major difference, however, is that the CDO brings a new skill set that CIOs or CTOs may not have. They are well versed in modern software development and in advanced AI and data methods. They live and breathe agile, and can recognize good agile practices. They can scope the delivery of a complex digital solution, defining the number of pods required, the talent mix needed, the duration, and the right OKRs. They also understand how a modern technology stack is put together.

The truth is that these three roles are increasingly blending as CIOs and CTOs become increasingly savvy with modern digital technologies and ways of working. To launch a digital and AI transformation, you will need all three roles to contribute. Section Four of this book explains the different technology-related aspects that the CDO/CIO/CTO will need to oversee.

The chief data officer

If your company has a chief data officer, they will lead the development of the data architecture, the definition of data products, and the implementation of an effective data governance (covered in Section Five).

The CHRO

The CHRO (chief human resources officer) plays a crucial role early in the transformation to secure the digital talent needed and to put in place the talent management practices that will help develop and retain digital talent (covered in Section Two).

The CFO

The CFO (chief financial officer) oversees the development of the transformation business case as described earlier in this section, and the tracking of the value realization (which you can read more about in Section Six of this book). In addition, they will be central to rethinking the planning and funding approaches of the company to make them more agile (covered in Section Three).

The chief risk officer

The chief risk officer is responsible for architecting how the first line of defense and second line of defense play their roles in the context of having multiple agile development teams. They will also need to understand how to respond to new risks, such as data privacy and cybersecurity, that a digital and AI transformation may generate (topics covered in Sections Three and Six, respectively).

Leaders of business lines and business functions

Leaders of business lines and functions (e.g., operations, marketing, sales, procurement, supply chain, R&D) that sit at the C-suite level oversee important business domains that are likely to be high-value areas on the digital roadmap. Chief marketing officers, for example, have a critical role in reinventing how to attract customers who may be interested in the company's products or services, personalize offers to them, and measure in near-real-time customer satisfaction at different stages of their online experience. Business line and business function leaders need to play active sponsor roles in the reimagination of their domain, as well as be curious about understanding the art of the possible. They need to be bold in shaping a transformation vision, and agile in embracing new ways of working.

Getting Ready
Section One

The following is a set of questions to help you home in on the right actions to take:

Is your top team able to articulate the business's vision and how technology will contribute to achieving it?

What are the top business domains you are focusing on – are they the ones with the best chance to generate attention-grabbing value and are they really feasible?

Can your top team articulate the expected benefits and investments required to transform your priority domains? Are you clear on how you will create sustainable competitive advantage?

Are your resources aligned to the two to five well-defined and cohesive domains that can generate real impact?

Are you clear on the new enterprise digital capabilities needed and will you make the necessary investments to build them?

How well can your top team articulate their roles and responsibilities – as well as those of their teams – in delivering on the digital roadmap?

Building Your Talent Bench

Creating an environment where digital talent thrives

No company can outsource its way to digital excellence. Being digital means having your own bench of digital talent – product owners, experience designers, data engineers, data scientists, software developers, etc. – working side by side with your business colleagues.[1]

For this reason, digital and AI transformations are first and foremost people and talent transformations.[2] And you can't start soon enough because you need to mobilize technologists to start delivering against the digital roadmap, and securing the right talent has the longest lead time compared to any of the other priorities.

Executives from legacy businesses should not think they need to cede top digital talent to Silicon Valley companies. Established companies with inspiring agendas and real commitment to people have been successful in creating a bench of digital technologists. Many have proven this.

The best digital talent programs go way beyond hiring to creating and delivering on exciting employee value propositions, developing more agile and digital HR processes, and committing to creating an environment where the best talent gets better. This section will show you how.

Chapter 8: Core versus noncore capabilities – strategic talent planning. Develop a clear view of the talent you have, the talent you need, and a plan to close the gap. This might seem easy, but it's not.

Chapter 9: The talent team that can build your digital team. Create a team that understands how to find, hire, and retain digital talent.

Chapter 10: Hiring digital talent when they're actually interviewing you. You don't have to be a tech company to win top talent. Develop a compelling employee value proposition and a hiring and onboarding experience that is grounded in what candidates and employees want and need.

Chapter 11: Recognize distinctive technologists. This is easier said than done. It requires being able to tell people with great tech skills apart from the others, and building dual career paths for digital talent without completely changing your company's talent management framework.

Chapter 12: Fostering craftsmanship excellence. Because technology is evolving so rapidly, digital talent places a premium on on-the-job learning and development - so should you.

Notes

1. Sven Blumberg, Ranja Reda Kouba, Suman Thareja, and Anna Wiesinger, 'Tech talent techtonics: Ten new realities for finding, keeping, and developing talent', McKinsey.com, April 14, 2022. https://www.mckinsey.com/capabilities/mckinsey-digital/our-insights/tech-talent-tectonics-ten-new-realities-for-finding-keeping-and-developing-talent
2. "In disruptive times the power comes from people: An interview with Eric Schmidt," *McKinsey Quarterly*, March 5, 2020, https://www.mckinsey.com/capabilities/mckinsey-digital/our-insights/in-disruptive-times-the-power-comes-from-people-an-interview-with-eric-schmidt.

Chapter 8

Core versus noncore capabilities – strategic talent planning

We have to go for what we think we're fully capable of, not limit ourselves by what we've been in the past."

—*Vivek Paul*

Do you have a talent roadmap that is as detailed as your technology roadmap? That question can catch many executives off guard. And if the answer isn't yes, it's critical to put in place a thoughtful and realistic plan.[1]

Workforce planning is the process of translating the digital road-map and vision – a plan of prioritized solutions and the teams (or pods) needed to create them – into actual talent requirements. This includes inventorying the talent you already have and matching it against the talent you need to deliver on your digital roadmap (discussed in Chapter Six). From this analysis, you can develop an action plan to fill the gap. You might think this is overly simplistic but in fact this is riddled with complexities.

What talent do you need in-house?

Every company faces the same strategic question when it comes to digital and AI transformations: "Do we need to own this talent?" Executives will argue that technology is not their core business – offering mortgages or extracting resources is. They may also argue that they have heavily outsourced IT capabilities in the past, so why should it be different for digital and AI?

The reality, however, is that if a company wants to competitively differentiate itself through digital solutions, it needs to have the talent that will provide this differentiation in-house. Our analysis of companies that are digital leaders – whether they be in the tech field or in more established industries – clearly shows that they always own a core bench of digital talent. We have yet to see a company that outsourced its way to digital excellence.

The reason it's so important to have your own bench is that it allows the technologists to work closely with their business and operations counterparts to develop and continuously improve digital solutions. That proximity enables fast development cycles. Furthermore, the technologists gain precious understanding of the business context. A data scientist will be many times more productive in developing a revenue management solution for a consumer packaged goods company if they understand consumer pricing dynamics, brand positioning, and the data environment of the company. Context matters to developing great digital solutions.

Having said that, not everything digital is a competitive differentiator. Many capabilities, such as services that cloud providers offer, or highly specialized skills, such as penetration testing that ensures an application is cyber secure or geolocation services to track a user, may all be critical to a digital solution, but may not be the source of competitive differentiation for your business. If that's the case, these capabilities should be sourced.

It may also be that you need to accommodate scaling your digital team up and down over time to accommodate changes in the business environment. That could also be a reason to contract for flexible capacity – but understand that there is no free lunch. These team members may provide flexibility but they will not be as productive as your in-house resources because they lack context and are not as invested. As a rule of thumb, the goal should be to have 70–80% of your digital talent be in-house and leverage external support for the rest.

It takes time to build a high-quality digital bench. Companies at the start of a digital and AI transformation will often heavily rely on external parties and, in parallel, kick-start their digital talent acquisition machine and their upskilling journey for employees. Over time, they will substitute their contractors with their own people. Depending on how bold the ambition is, often after one to two years, they can typically reach the 70–80% in-house target state.

A consumer packaged goods company, for example, kicked off its digital transformation with five pods staffed largely from its lead consulting partner because it did not have that talent in-house. At the same time, it recruited top tech talent at a rate of about 10–15 people per month. In less than a year, it was able to largely replace the members of its consulting partner with its own people.

Understanding the digital talent you have

Knowing what digital talent you have is a much harder task than at first it might seem. That's because you need to identify the skills and proficiency of the existing talent – merely inventorying job titles doesn't get you there (see Exhibit 8.1).

Digital talent skills taxonomy

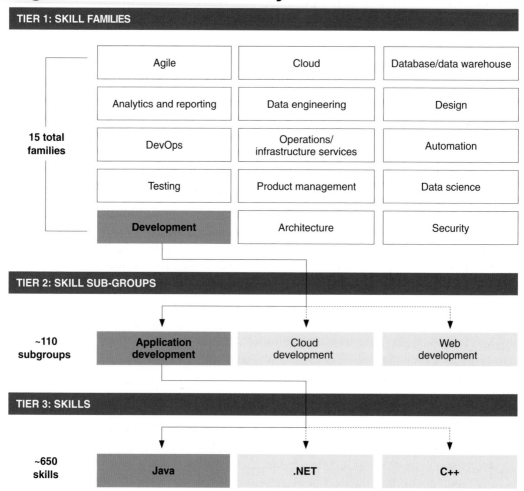

EXHIBIT 8.1

This precise level of skill mapping rarely exists in most organizations. That is, knowing someone is a "Java Web Developer," for instance, is much more useful than just knowing someone is a developer. Similarly, a cloud engineer is quite different from a data engineer, and while you'll likely need both, you'll need to understand clearly what they do so you can make the best use of their skills. Just as important, the technical skills landscape changes quickly as the need for machine learning engineers and generative AI engineers shows, so you will need to stay on top of how it evolves.

Most organizations can fairly easily establish the headcount in roles across job families through mapping HR data to a simplified taxonomy. The more important step is to understand the skills and proficiency of that talent because that lets you know who can actually do the work.

Typically organizations have no reliable way of pinpointing differences in skill proficiency across their people, especially technologists. Running a query on the HR system barely gives you a starting point. Four approaches are useful for assessing the skills of existing digital talent:

1. **Manager assessment.** Starting with a quick top-down manager's assessment is helpful if you need to select, say, 30–50 people from a pool of a few hundreds. This will help classify your existing talent along a skills taxonomy and get a sense of the level of expertise by using observable behaviors. For instance, an engineer who is assigned simple tasks and needs constant oversight is classified as a novice. At the other end of the scale, an engineer who is seen as a leader in their field is classified as an expert. Note that you will need to control for judgment based on each manager's own skills.

2. **Individual self-assessment.** A skill survey is useful to get an in-depth assessment across the entire IT/digital workforce. This approach is needed when hundreds, if not thousands, of people need to be inventoried and assessed. The survey will help employees self-assess against a detailed taxonomy of technical and functional skills. Third-party tools are available to do this and it is relatively easy to deploy across a large employee population. The technique suffers from inherent biases in self-assessments. Note that women traditionally will rank themselves lower than men, so the assessment will need to be adjusted.

3. **Online testing.** Third parties, such as Hackerank, Codility, CodeSignal, and TestGorilla, offer specific online coding tests that are useful in assessing the specific baseline skill level of

highly technical people. These tests are by far the most precise in assessing technical coding skills but they can be disruptive for an organization and generate anxieties or conflict, so it's important to thoughtfully manage this process.

4. **Technical interview.** This uses a combination of formal technical testing and personal interviews to assess skills. These kinds of assessments are fairly labor intensive, and usually done only for key roles. To be effective, these interviews must be conducted by senior technologists who have achieved skill mastery in the specific discipline. Too often, companies confuse a senior executive in IT as someone with technical mastery. That is often not the case.

Case example: How one company figured out the talent it really had

A specialized financial services company designed a new digital sales support tool for its large field sales organization. Its digital unit was charged with developing the new digital experience and, while the initial pilot was successful, the application failed to scale suffering from data replication and latency problems. The root cause was an underskilled digital team.

Using Hackerank to test the 100-person digital team, the business learned that only 20% of the technologists had a passing grade of 50% (see Exhibit 8.2). No wonder the company's application was riddled with architectural and engineering issues. It is interesting to note that a third of the resources came from third-party contractors who did not perform any better, a problem we often see.

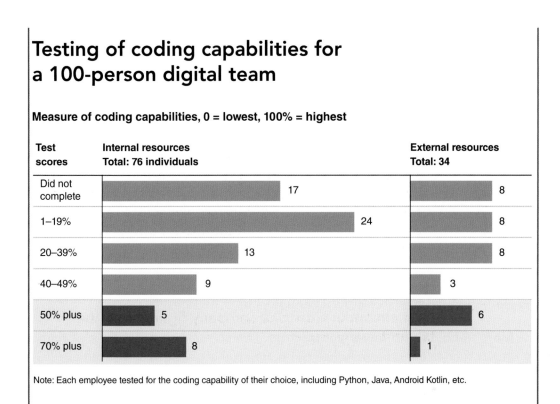

Testing of coding capabilities for a 100-person digital team

Measure of coding capabilities, 0 = lowest, 100% = highest

Test scores	Internal resources Total: 76 individuals	External resources Total: 34
Did not complete	17	8
1–19%	24	8
20–39%	13	8
40–49%	9	3
50% plus	5	6
70% plus	8	1

Note: Each employee tested for the coding capability of their choice, including Python, Java, Android Kotlin, etc.

EXHIBIT 8.2

Determining the talent gap

Once the current state of skills assessment is complete, you can match it against future talent needs as established by the digital roadmap. In making this determination, it's important to consider two key factors that companies often overlook: one is that hiring for "job description" rather than actual skills, which is a big risk. The value of a great developer is commonly accepted to be 5–10 times greater than that of an average developer. And two, you should not forget to look for important intrinsics for the digital age, such as flexibility, the ability to communicate and collaborate, and, perhaps most important of all, learning aptitude.

Case example: A global insurance company fills its talent gap

Let's take a look at a talent gap analysis for a global insurance company (see Exhibit 8.3). This exercise covered all its internal tech talent. Employees assessed their own skill level on a skill of 1 (novice) to 5 (expert) for key roles identified in the digital plan. The company mapped their current state against their future needs to identify the gap. The output provided a clear view of where their talent priorities were (in this specific exhibit, competency levels 1 and 2 are grouped under novice, while 3 to 5 are grouped under competent).

The company's approach to filling its talent gap highlights important insights that apply to many companies driving a digital and AI transformation:

1. **More in-house and fewer contractors.** This company is aggressively bringing its tech talent back in house by changing the mix from 39% internal/61% external to 70% internal/30% external. That's massive. It is not only a wise strategic move but it also yields savings (assuming no changes in geographic footprint).

2. **More doers and fewer checkers.** This company is hiring a massive number of integration engineers (also known as full-stack engineers) and data specialists, while reducing headcount in skill categories historically associated with waterfall development like program management and managerial roles. In essence, they want more people who can deliver code and fewer people who manage and oversee, thus providing a 15% lift in effective development capacity while reducing headcount by 15%. This is only possible because agile development approaches enable a flatter and more empowered organization.

3. **More competent practitioners and fewer novices.** The competency levels of the business's existing employees are well below what is needed. A talent "pyramid" in the digital age should be more the shape of a diamond, with more competent-level practitioners in the middle and fewer novices at the bottom. Even if this talent is more costly, the productivity level of competent-level engineers is substantially higher than the differential in pay and will lead to productivity gains[2].

Example of digital and technology talent gap analysis

Global insurance company Ⓝ Novice Ⓒ Competent ▪ Resources to release ■ Resources to add

Category	Chapter	Current state		Future needs		Difference	
		Ⓝ	Ⓒ	Ⓝ	Ⓒ	Ⓝ	Ⓒ
Software	Front-end engineering						
	Integration engineering	502	410	514	2,056	−12	−1,646
	Full-stack engineering						
	QA engineering	44	36	27	108	+17	−72
Architecture	Architecture	33	80	26	103	+7	−23
Infrastructure	SRE	47	78	27	108	+20	−30
	DevOps	12	19	27	108	−15	−89
	Cloud engineering	6	10	11	43	−5	−33
	Infrastructure engineers	113	184	66	263	+47	−79
Data and analytics	Data and analytics	74	91	54	216	+20	−125
Security	Security	84	102	34	136	+50	−34
Design	Experience design	4	7	9	34	−5	−27
Product management	Product owner	96	179	69	275	+27	−96
Agile	Agile practitioner	15	55	11	44	+4	+11
Other	Program manager	58	217	3	14	+55	+203
	Leadership (e.g., VP+)	0	198	0	64	0	+134
	Nonpod roles (e.g., Admin)	0	362	0	274	0	+88
Internal FTEs		1,088	2,028	878	3,846	+210	−1,818
Total internal		3,116		4,724		−1,608	
Total external		4,826		2,024		+2,802	
Internal; external		39%; 61%		70%; 30%			

Note: Based on tech talent skills survey with 1 (novice) through 5 (expert) scale, where novice means participants who rated 1 to 2 while competent means participants who rated 3 to 5.

EXHIBIT 8.3

You now have all the inputs necessary to translate the digital roadmap into a hiring plan (see Exhibit 8.4). This essentially becomes the marching orders for the talent team in charge of building your digital bench (see more about this team in the next chapter). In determining how to execute the plan and fill the talent gap, you will need to inevitably strike the right balance in sourcing people across hiring, contracting, or upskilling existing employees (see more on this in Chapters 10 and 11). You will need to take into account the timing of the digital solutions build, how important core versus non-core talent is to the business, and costs. Inevitably, priorities shift as the digital transformation progresses, so it's important to regularly align the hiring plan with the roadmap.

Estimating overall talent need and building a hiring plan

Global agriculture company

TALENT NEED				HIRING PLAN (Cumulative)					
				Q1			Q2		
Role	Demand	Supply	Gap	Hire	Contract	Reskill	Hire	Contract	Reskill
Product owner	20	2	18	5	5	0	8	0	10
Scrum master	10	3	7	5	2	0	7	0	0
Change agent	5	Many	–	0	0	0	0	0	0
Design lead	3	0	3	1	0	0	2	0	0
UI/UX designer	17	0	17	3	7	0	6	7	0
Data scientist	6	1	5	2	0	0	3	0	2
Data engineer	18	5	13	5	7	0	10	3	0
Software engineer	43	12	31	8	13	0	12	15	2
Machine learning engineer	3	0	3	0	0	0	1	0	0
Tech lead	8	2	6	2	2	0	5	1	0
Data architect	2	0	2	0	1	0	1	0	0
Agile coach	5	0	5	2	2	0	4	1	0
Business analyst	15	Many	–	0	0	0	0	0	0
SME	27	Many	–	0	0	0	0	0	0
Total	**182**	**NA**	**110**	**31**	**39**	**0**	**59**	**27**	**14**
					70			100	

EXHIBIT 8.4

Notes

1. Dominic Barton, Dennis Carey, and Ram Charan, "An agenda for the talent-first CEO," *McKinsey Quarterly*, March 6, 2018, https://www.mckinsey.com/capabilities/people-and-organizational-performance/our-insights/an-agenda-for-the-talent-first-ceo.
2. Peter Jacobs, Klemens Hjartar, Eric Lamarre, and Lars Vinter, "It's time to reset the IT talent model," MIT Sloan Management Review, March 5, 2020, https://sloanreview.mit.edu/article/its-time-to-reset-the-it-talent-model/.

Chapter 9

The talent team that can build your digital team

People who need people are the luckiest people in the world!

—Barbra Streisand

Many HR organizations find themselves with relatively slow recruiting and onboarding processes, rigid compensation frameworks, and outdated learning and development programs for digital talent. That's a problem if you want to build a digital talent bench and retain your high performers.

Transforming your entire HR organization and underlying HR processes to make them digital ready, however, could take a few years. We have found instead that setting up a special team focused on adapting your current HR processes with a focus on digital talent is the most pragmatic – and successful – way forward. When done well, this approach has helped organizations move quickly while addressing fundamental HR challenges specific to digital talent. We call this special unit the Talent Win Room (TWR) (the "room" could be physical or virtual, but the key point is that it's a dedicated team). The primary mission of a TWR is to build and continuously improve all facets of both the candidate and employee experience.

The TWR requires a C-level executive sponsor, typically the CHRO and/or CDO, and a full-time senior HR executive serving as the team leader. The TWR is an interdisciplinary team that mirrors the working habits and behaviors of an agile pod. It is made up of tech recruiters and HR specialists with relevant expertise in: talent planning; recruiting and onboarding talent; talent management; talent development; and diversity, equity, and inclusion. The team is augmented with part-time functional specialists as needed (e.g., legal, finance, communications, marketing). Exhibit 9.1 shows the typical composition of a TWR and sample metrics that it drives.

The TWR should work in the same way agile pods do by focusing on the "customer" – in this case the candidate or employee – and working quickly and iteratively to redesign and execute new HR processes specific to them (Chapter 13 covers agile ways of working). From a candidate standpoint, an agile HR team is the first sign of an organization walking the walk by demonstrating speed, relevance, and agility.

Case example: How a large agricultural business set up a TWR

A large agriculture company decided to bring key digital capabilities and roles in-house. They stood up a TWR and trained the team to have a candidate-centric mindset along with adopting agile ways of working. The TWR modernized talent sourcing by using contract-to-hire and active digital channels (e.g., TopCoder, GitHub, Stack Overflow), elevated the interview experience to include coding exercises, and implemented a candidate tracking system to manage the end-to-end journey. Within six months, they had successfully built an 80-person digital bench.

Typical roles in a talent win room (TWR)

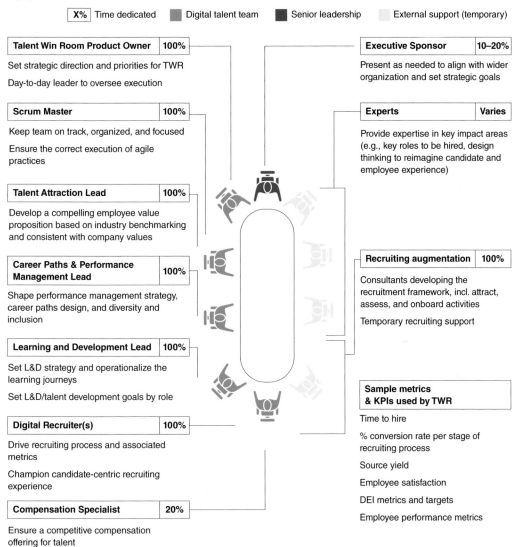

X% Time dedicated ▨ Digital talent team ▮ Senior leadership ▨ External support (temporary)

Talent Win Room Product Owner | 100%

Set strategic direction and priorities for TWR

Day-to-day leader to oversee execution

Scrum Master | 100%

Keep team on track, organized, and focused

Ensure the correct execution of agile practices

Talent Attraction Lead | 100%

Develop a compelling employee value proposition based on industry benchmarking and consistent with company values

Career Paths & Performance Management Lead | 100%

Shape performance management strategy, career paths design, and diversity and inclusion

Learning and Development Lead | 100%

Set L&D strategy and operationalize the learning journeys

Set L&D/talent development goals by role

Digital Recruiter(s) | 100%

Drive recruiting process and associated metrics

Champion candidate-centric recruiting experience

Compensation Specialist | 20%

Ensure a competitive compensation offering for talent

Executive Sponsor | 10–20%

Present as needed to align with wider organization and set strategic goals

Experts | Varies

Provide expertise in key impact areas (e.g., key roles to be hired, design thinking to reimagine candidate and employee experience)

Recruiting augmentation | 100%

Consultants developing the recruitment framework, incl. attract, assess, and onboard activities

Temporary recruiting support

Sample metrics & KPIs used by TWR

Time to hire

% conversion rate per stage of recruiting process

Source yield

Employee satisfaction

DEI metrics and targets

Employee performance metrics

EXHIBIT 9.1

A TWR isn't something you spin up and down. A typical Fortune 500 company, for example, will need 200–2,000 digital technologists, which can take one to three years to build. Once at that level, you will continue to hire to make up for natural turnover (typically 5–10% per year). In addition, other HR activities will intensify (e.g., career path design, performance management, and career progression and compensation strategies). The TWR capability should become permanent, although the focus will evolve over time, most often becoming a core building block to shape and integrate best practices into a renewed HR function addressing additional talent pools. As this team becomes permanent and slowly grows its mandate, we often see organizations stand up multiple TWRs to tackle other organizational talent priorities in similar ways.

Chapter 10

Hiring digital talent when they're actually interviewing you

I never minded coming in and reading. They should know if I'm the right person, and I should know if I want to do a movie.

—Jodie Foster

To find and keep good people – both internal and external – you will need to get inside the heads of your digital talent to know what they want. That's because top talent has a high bar in terms of what they're looking for from an employer – in effect, they're also interviewing you. You win the hiring game by offering what digital talent values, and creating a hiring and onboarding experience that puts them at the center.[1]

A relevant, compelling, and authentic employee value proposition

In a world where top talent evaluates you as much as you do them, companies need to develop a compelling employee value proposition (EVP) that addresses what motivates top talent and is tailored to them.[2]

In their words: Elevating tech talent

There's a finite number of super-smart engineers who know what to build. These people go to the companies that take them the most seriously. They go to companies where they think leadership really understands what they do and understands how to build a first-class technology development culture. They go to places where they think they'll be appropriately rewarded but also where they'll be taken seriously, listened to, and respected. And they want to be in a place where people like themselves form a critical mass.

The problem that big, classic Fortune 500 companies have is the same problem they had 20 years ago. I thought the problem would shrink over time, but I'm not sure it has. That problem is that the true technologists inside so many big companies are not the primary people at the company. They're not treated as first-class citizens.

Just look at the org chart. For so long, companies put their technology people in the IT department. The IT department was so famously segregated and isolated that there are entire TV shows, like the great British comedy The IT Crowd, built around the idea of the nerds in the back room. Then, about 20 years ago, big companies got the message that maybe all their technologists should not be in the IT department. So they created what's typically known as the digital division, typically led by a vice president of digital. The good news is that the programmers run the digital division and are taken seriously there. But it's still a division. It's still a unit. That's a problem.

I'll give you an example: at Tesla, the engineers working on self-driving cars are the most important people at Tesla. Elon talks about them all the time, he talks to them all the time, and they're basically the leaders in the company. The people working on that stuff at traditional auto

OEMs are not. Maybe they should be, but they're not. They're still in this kind of "back room" thing. The people who have led the business for 40 years are the same kind of people who are now in charge.

That's the pattern. Tesla is run by the technologist who envisioned the entire thing and knows every aspect of how a self-driving electric car works. The big car companies are run by people who have more classical business training, who are not inherently technologists.

—Marc Andreessen, cofounder and general partner at venture
capital firm Andreessen Horowitz

One of the most important factors in attracting digital talent is to provide a work environment with development opportunities where they will be able to hone their craft by working on a modern technology stack with capable colleagues (see Exhibit 10.1). In essence, they want to be reassured that three years from now, their skill set will remain as valuable, if not more, as it is today. That's not the only factor that matters but it's consistently the most important one.

Most organizations have an EVP, but it will likely need to be updated and translated into a narrative that highlights a larger purpose, the importance of technology in meeting the company's mission, and its diversity and inclusion commitments in general. A good EVP provides both tangible and intangible aspects that demonstrate what a company stands for and what makes it unique (see Exhibit 10.2).

While elements of an EVP can be aspirational, it must be authentic. Recruits and employees can smell a disconnect between the stated EVP and the reality on the ground. When that happens, they leave and tell others. That can be devastating because tech people looking for a job read company reviews from third-party sites (e.g., Glassdoor, Blind) as their most common way to learn about companies. These outlets provide crucial insight into how your EVP is actually being experienced by at least some of your employees. Companies should monitor their reputation on these platforms with the same care and rigor they apply to monitoring industry or financial analysts.

The most important job factors for software talent

Percentage of software talent that chose a factor in the top three reasons why they took a job, plan to stay in a job, plan to leave a job, or left

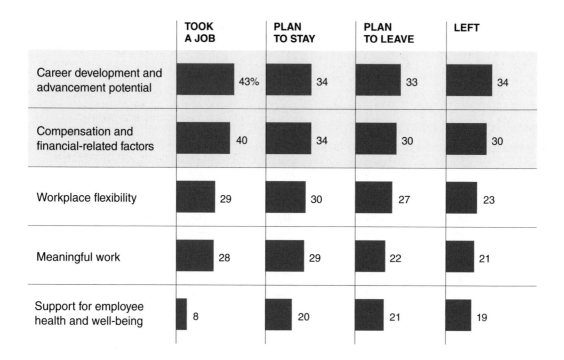

	TOOK A JOB	PLAN TO STAY	PLAN TO LEAVE	LEFT
Career development and advancement potential	43%	34	33	34
Compensation and financial-related factors	40	34	30	30
Workplace flexibility	29	30	27	23
Meaningful work	28	29	22	21
Support for employee health and well-being	8	20	21	19

Source: McKinsey Software Talent Great Attrition, Great Attraction Survey, 2022 (N = 1,532)

EXHIBIT 10.1

A recruiting experience built around the candidate

We have found that organizations are most successful in hiring when they shift their mindset from optimizing a step-by-step recruiting process to creating delightful candidate experiences.

Example EVPs – overall and digital

JOHNSON & JOHNSON PHARMACEUTICALS

OVERALL EVP: Working with Johnson & Johnson isn't just any job. Every day, we're creating life-changing treatments for infectious diseases, improving global health equity, and developing medtech innovations, pharmaceuticals, and consumer health products that enhance quality of life for people worldwide. From 3D printing and robotics that are transforming surgical procedures to drones delivering vaccines to remote regions, our work is bigger than all of us.

DIGITAL EVP: Imagine empowering AI with the accumulated medical knowledge of humankind, building natural language processing applications to make surgery safer or using machine learning to transform how rare diseases are diagnosed. Data science not only makes breakthroughs like these possible but accelerates our impact – it's how teams at Janssen R&D are shortening clinical trials, for example. And as the world's largest and most broadly based healthcare company, we're leveraging our expansive data sets to address the biggest health challenges of our time, from HIV to bladder cancer, lupus and COVID-19.

FREEPORT-MCMORAN

OVERALL EVP: Our skilled and versatile team finds, extracts, processes and provides the raw materials that connect the world. Copper. Molybdenum. Gold. The elements we supply play a crucial role in delivering the technology that drives the future.

We believe our greatest strength is our people. We respect and value the different ideas, beliefs, experiences, talents, skills, perspectives, backgrounds and cultures of our workforce. We strive for, promote and foster a workplace where everyone feels a sense of belonging, is treated with respect and their opinions are valued.

DIGITAL EVP: At Freeport we understand that our data does not reach its full potential until it is analyzed, and insights effectively communicated to the enterprise. You will work in close collaboration with mining operations, subject matter experts, data scientists, and software engineers to develop advanced, highly automated data products. You will be a champion of DataOps, DevOps, and agile practices; leading project teams and mentoring team members to realize their full potential.

Source: Johnson & Johnson and Freeport-McMoran company career websites

EXHIBIT 10.2

Exhibit 10.3 shows a typical recruiting process for companies and the many issues that bedevil it. Notice, for instance, how long the process can take. It's hard to compete for digital talent if the prescreen-to-offer timeline is longer than four weeks. When it takes too long, candidates feel they are dealing with a slow-moving company, not

Current state recruiting journey   **Financial services company**

PHASE	SOURCE / SEARCH (3-4 weeks)	SCREENING (1 week)

Step ①: **Create requisition**
Step ②: **Requisition approved by finance/HR**
Step ③: **Talent acquisition team assigns requisition to recruiter**
Step ④: **Post the position**
Step ⑤: **Digital application**

①: **Assess application**
②: **Schedule screening call**
③: **Conduct screening call**

Steps	①	②	③	④	⑤	①	②	③
Touch points	Recruiting system			LinkedIn, etc.	Application portal	Email	Email, phone call	Video conf.

Candidate experience
Actions, thoughts, feeling at key moments

Took forever to fill out the application

Motivated
Starts to look for new position or open to new opportunities

Excited/ curious/ uncertain
Reads job posting

OK
Applies for position

Anxious
Waits to hear back

Frustrated
Scheduling delayed

OK
Screening call

Upset
Looks elsewhere

Upset
Withdraws application

Recruiter experience

Searching for unicorns

Anxious
Doesn't know what's next in queue, doesn't have a pool of candidates

Over- whelmed
New requisition without warning

Stressed
Starts sourcing

Hopeful
Waiting for applications

Stressed
Screens basic info

Stressed
Waits for scheduling

Upset
Delays: Candidate lost

Hopeful
Conducts screening call

Hiring manager experience

Can't get my role prioritized

Stressed
Writes JD; Process is slow and tedious

Frustrated
Waits during requisition approval process

Stressed
Meets with recruiter to discuss what job requires

Hopeful
Posts to his own LinkedIn to increase exposure to his own network

Stack of candidate resumes to review

Frustrated
Gets the slate from recruiter

Frustrated
Sometimes, no visibility for what's going on

EXHIBIT 10.3

INTERVIEW (~2–4 weeks)

1 : Schedule interviews
2 : Conduct 1st round of interviews
3 : Conduct 2nd round of interviews
4 : Decision after interviews

OFFER (~1–2 weeks)

1 : Send verbal offer
2 : Negotiate verbal offer
3 : Final offer approval
4 : Formal offer
5 : Negotiate / sign

1	2	3	4	1	2	3	4	5	
E-mail	Video conference		Internal meetings	Phone call	Emails, phone call	Total Rewards	Email	Email, PDF	BEFORE ONBOARDING

Row 1

Schedule changes galore

Hopeful — Interviews with HM

Hopeful — Interviews with HM

Frustrated — Scheduling takes a long time

Upset — Finds position is not a good match

Overlapping interview questions

Frustrated — Waits to hear back

Excited — Receives offer

Upset — Rejected

Waiting and waiting

Stressed — Negotiates terms

Anxious — Waits for offer

Happy — Receives formal offer

Excited — Signs final offer

Stressed — In a period of silence

Row 2

OK — Waits for scheduling

Hopeful — Interview goes well

Lost candidates due to reschedule

Upset — Loses candidate

Frustrated — Hears that more candidates needed

Stressed — Tries to keep candidate "warm"

Excited — Verbal offer is given

Tired — Negotiates terms

Negotiation failure

Relieved — Written offer put into system

Anxious — Offer letter sent

Excited — Receives signed offer

Frustrated — ... if the candidate drops out

Row 3

Stressed — Preps for interviews, pulls panel together

Excited — Uses own interview structure

No standard interview guide and assessment

Excited — Found candidate

Frustrated — Passed on

How did candidate get this far?

Stressed — Decides on offer with panel, no other guidelines

Hopeful — Tells recruiter to extend offer

Stressed — Works with recruiter to negotiate terms

Relieved — Receives notification offer is approved

Excited — Receives signed offer from HR

Frustrated — ... if the candidate drops out

to mention the fact that in the meantime they have competing offers that take them out of the running for you. Remember, what candidates experience in the recruiting process sets the bar for what it will be like to work in your organization.

We have seen organizations succeed at finding and retaining their talent when they reimagine their talent approach. The best ones focus on creating a candidate-centric experience with an emphasis on how to make the moments that matter truly memorable (see Exhibit 10.4). It's important to have an experience that is thoughtfully designed and meets candidate and industry expectations. In Exhibit 10.4, notice the special experience moments, which convey to the candidate that this is a place where they will be valued.

Having a delightful recruiting experience is great, but it's not much use if you can't find the right candidates in the first place. While shifts in the economy have an effect, of course, on talent availability, finding top talent to meet your business's specific needs will always be a challenge.

First and foremost, this means you need tech recruiters, who are experienced and can speak the language of the candidates. Second, these recruiters need to be surgical about where to find candidates and engage with a variety of platforms and services that cater to tech talent. Enterprising recruiters, for example, shift their focus from traditional channels like general job boards to source-code repositories where engineers proudly post their work. They target communities such as GitHub and Reddit, places where technology talent congregates for non-job-search reasons.

Some companies host online competitions that allow organizations and prospective candidates to showcase their technical skills in partnership with digital platforms, such as currently-favored Topcoder and HireIQ. Digital-talent platforms such as Good&Co and Hacker-Rank are also helping companies more effectively assess a potential employee's match with the skill requirements and culture of the company. Pursuing these avenues requires digital recruiters who are well versed in tech recruiting.

Future state recruiting journey

Financial services company

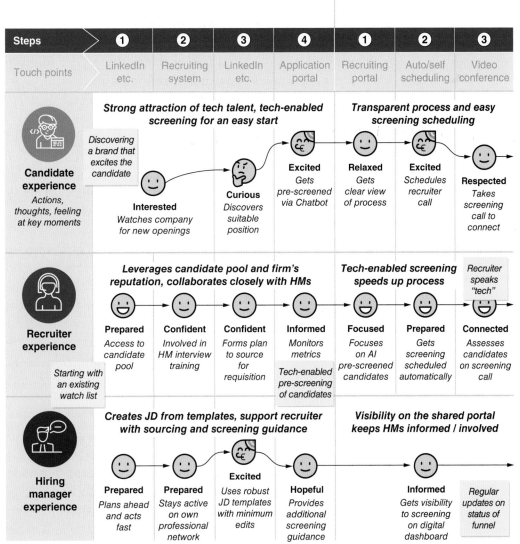

PHASE	SOURCE / SEARCH (1–2 weeks)	SCREENING (2 days)

SOURCE / SEARCH (1–2 weeks)
- Step ①: Brand building and planning
- Step ②: Job description creation
- Step ③: Job posting
- Step ④: Digital application

SCREENING (2 days)
- ①: Assess application
- ②: Schedule screening call
- ③: Conduct screening call

Steps	①	②	③	④	①	②	③
Touch points	LinkedIn etc.	Recruiting system	LinkedIn etc.	Application portal	Recruiting portal	Auto/self scheduling	Video conference

Candidate experience
Actions, thoughts, feeling at key moments

Strong attraction of tech talent, tech-enabled screening for an easy start

Transparent process and easy screening scheduling

- Discovering a brand that excites the candidate
- **Interested** — *Watches company for new openings*
- **Curious** — *Discovers suitable position*
- **Excited** — *Gets pre-screened via Chatbot*
- **Relaxed** — *Gets clear view of process*
- **Excited** — *Schedules recruiter call*
- **Respected** — *Takes screening call to connect*

Recruiter experience

Leverages candidate pool and firm's reputation, collaborates closely with HMs

Tech-enabled screening speeds up process

Recruiter speaks "tech"

- **Prepared** — *Access to candidate pool*
- *Starting with an existing watch list*
- **Confident** — *Involved in HM interview training*
- **Confident** — *Forms plan to source for requisition*
- **Informed** — *Monitors metrics* / *Tech-enabled pre-screening of candidates*
- **Focused** — *Focuses on AI pre-screened candidates*
- **Prepared** — *Gets screening scheduled automatically*
- **Connected** — *Assesses candidates on screening call*

Hiring manager experience

Creates JD from templates, support recruiter with sourcing and screening guidance

Visibility on the shared portal keeps HMs informed / involved

- **Prepared** — *Plans ahead and acts fast*
- **Prepared** — *Stays active on own professional network*
- **Excited** — *Uses robust JD templates with minimum edits*
- **Hopeful** — *Provides additional screening guidance*
- **Informed** — *Gets visibility to screening on digital dashboard*
- *Regular updates on status of funnel*

EXHIBIT 10.4

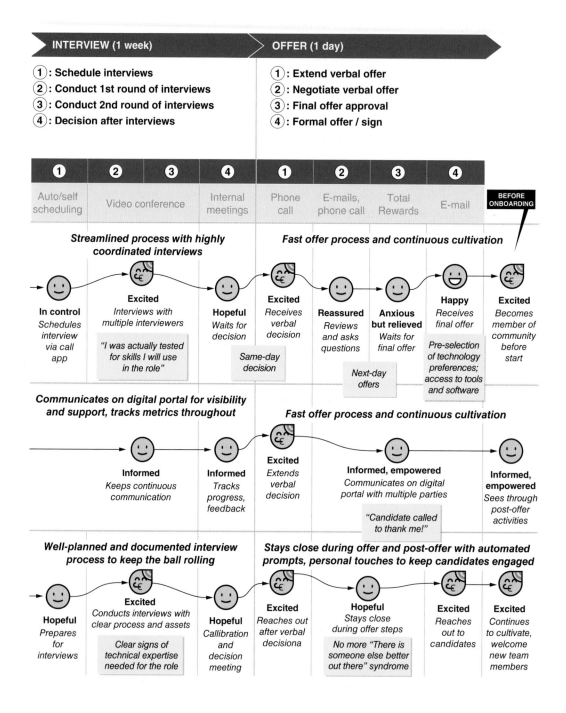

The interview process deserves special consideration. In too many cases, job descriptions are vague, interviews are poorly sequenced, interviewers are not calibrated to know what to look for, and the process takes too long – as many as 60 to 90 days. The most common pitfall is the struggle to test a coder's true expertise. Coding exercises are an important part of the process and need serious planning to do them well. Similarly, interviewers need to show up prepared, be engaged, and treat interviewing as a privilege, and not just another meeting on the calendar.

As part of the hiring process, some organizations prioritize anchor hires and senior leaders in a particular technical discipline. These individuals can help attract other exceptional talent through their personal networks and industry reputation. One leading North American industrial company looking to embark on a digital transformation prioritized bringing in a chief digital officer (CDO) who had credibility among technologists and in turn was able to attract three leading product owners and designers from similar organizations. The company then directed its recruitment efforts to people from large technology companies and well-regarded design agencies. Using this approach, the organization built its product and design team from zero to 30 people in about six months.

Finding anchor hires can take time, however, so it's important to proceed with mainstream hiring in parallel.

Finding talent internally

Many companies, in our experience, need to source a majority of their talent from outside to get the new capabilities they need. Internal transfers, however, carry several advantages: they are almost always easier, cheaper, and faster to find than any other method; and they come with an internal network and institutional knowledge.

When evaluating internal candidates, beware of two common pitfalls: recycling performance problems, and rebadging underqualified people without proper upskilling (see more on upskilling below). Establish qualification criteria and a screening process to make sure employees meet the bar. Know what good looks like and be willing to wait for the right person.

The best practice is to interview internal transfers in a similar way you would interview new hires, with a clear role description and expectations, including providing a bar for the craft proficiency for any role.

In digital and AI transformations, one of the roles that almost always needs to be filled internally is that of a product owner (or product manager), because their effectiveness depends partly on understanding the business and the organization. Good product owners are fundamental to the success of a digital transformation – more than any other role. It is particularly important to test their product management capabilities and experience and plan a serious upskilling program for those who fall short (for more on product management, see Chapter 15).

New employee onboarding journey

The time between when a candidate accepts the offer and when they join Day 1 is where the transition between the recruiter and hiring managers tends to fall apart. Too often, the new hires spend their first few weeks waiting for access to the right systems or code repositories, and to be assigned work with their new team. That's because onboarding new hires is a process that is owned by many parts of the organization.

Most companies will provide new hires with an overview of their role, responsibilities, and the expectations of them. Present them with an onboarding plan with clear goals and explain the performance management process during orientation. Where companies can go further is to provide an overview of the company's digital plans and where the new employee will be contributing. Context matters. We often say that business people need to learn about technology, but the reverse is also true. Technologists are most productive when they understand the business context, so be sure to include this in the onboarding plan.

The best companies assign an onboarding point of contact to help the new hire navigate the company. Ideally, this person is a colleague who will work with the new hire on their first assignment. Digital talent wants and expects to contribute immediately, so be prepared to deploy them directly into a real project Week 1.

Similarly, pay attention to the technology tools provided to new employees. Designers may expect to work on a Mac and use certain tools that allow them the greatest productivity, such as Sketch, InVision, or Balsamiq. Many organizations allow future employees to select their device preferences while completing employment paperwork. Developers should have access to code repositories immediately so they can get to work quickly. Data scientists will expect access to Python. The developer 'workbench' should be automated and clear enough that new developers are able to commit code by the end of Week 1 on the job.

Diversity, equity, and inclusion

Our research shows that companies that are leading in diversity, equity, and inclusion (DEI) are 36% more likely to outperform peers in EBIT margins, 27% more likely to create longer-term value, and 25% more likely to experience above-average profitability. By diversity, it's important to have a broad view that includes gender, ethnicity, experience, and neurodiversity.[3]

Leading universities have diversified their computer science, data science, and other STEM classes quickly, expanding the pipeline of talent available to employers. In addition to helping companies strengthen their staffing, this development also offers employers a path to meeting broader diversity goals, which in turn can make them more attractive to top talent, who increasingly view DEI as a core selection factor.

We have seen success when companies make sure that DEI factors are core elements of the EVP by communicating, for example, DEI support mechanisms that the company has in place. DEI should also be reflected in the candidate interview experience by developing inclusive job descriptions, conducting DEI training to help interviewers avoid subconscious bias, and having a diverse set of people doing the actual interviews. Consider adding DEI ambitions to your digital transformation dashboard. Finally, DEI should be part of the evaluation processes and succession planning.

Notes

1. Sven Blumberg, Ranja Reda Kouba, Suman Thareja, and Anna Wiesinger, "Tech talent tectonics: Ten new realities for finding, keeping, and developing talent," McKinsey.com, April 14, 2022, https://www.mckinsey.com/capabilities/mckinsey-digital/our-insights/tech-talent-tectonics-ten-new-realities-for-finding-keeping-and-developing-talent.
2. Vincent Bérubé Cyril Dujardin, Greg Kudar, Eric Lamarre, Laop Mori, Gérard Richter, Tamim Saleh, Alex Singla, Suman Thareja, and Rodney Zemmel, "Digital transformations: The five talent factors that matter most," McKinsey.com, January 5, 2023, https://www.mckinsey.com/capabilities/mckinsey-digital/our-insights/digital-transformations-the-five-talent-factors-that-matter-most.
3. Kathryn Kuhn, Eric Lamarre, Chris Perkins, and Suman Thareja, "Mining for tech-talent gold: Seven ways to find and keep diverse talent," McKinsey.com, September 27, 2022, https://www.mckinsey.com/capabilities/mckinsey-digital/our-insights/mining-for-tech-talent-gold-seven-ways-to-find-and-keep-diverse-talent.

Chapter 11

Recognize distinctive technologists

If you think it's expensive to hire a professional to do the job, wait until you hire an amateur.

—Red Adair

It's not realistic to expect an established company to completely change its approach to talent management to accommodate digital talent. Most companies, however, find that they can work within their current talent management framework to address the specifics of digital talent. Two areas that matter the most are compensation and performance management.

Adjust compensation to pay for skills

Compensation for technical skills is often dramatically misaligned with someone's value because rewards in traditional companies are often tied to tenure or number of employees supervised rather than engineering prowess. This leads to dissatisfaction, and it gives high performers a compelling reason to leave.

Modern companies celebrate technical career paths where individuals can have outsized impact on a company's performance based on their craft. This has given rise to dual career paths where technologists can grow either in a traditional managerial track or in an expert or engineering track (more on this in Chapter 12).

As you consider how to adjust your compensation framework for digital talent, keep in mind the following:

1. **Compensation is benchmarked to Big Tech.** Big Tech sets the bar and most other companies figure out where to peg their compensation, depending on their local market and the quality of talent they are competing for. This is even more true in a hybrid/remote world where talent can work from anywhere and can always be poached or more easily switch jobs. The Big Tech compensation bar will vary, of course, depending on the economic ebbs and flows of the tech industry, but that will nonetheless likely remain the standard. In general, most companies will settle for compensation levels that are between parity and 30% below Big Tech depending on markets and talent quality.

   In general, the compensation structure is skewed toward more substantial bonuses, thus providing a mechanism for premium total compensation for truly exceptional tech talent. Bonuses can be as much as 100% of the base salary for the top performers.

2. **Pay for skill at a granular level.** MLOps engineers make more than data engineers on average because that skill is scarce and in high demand. Inside each skill family, there needs to be a granular segmentation of levels driven by credentials. For example, Big Tech will have up to 10 levels of data engineers, each with different compensation ranges. To determine these skill markers, benchmarks can be helpful to understand the market for the talent you are looking for and provide data to ensure you are competitive for the skills you require.

   You will then need to do the work to figure out what the best markers are for the skills you want. That means establishing clear technology competency markers (TCMs) and leadership capability markers (LCMs) for different job families (see below for more details). That's not easy at first and it takes time to get it right. Exhibit 11.1 shows the TCM for a data scientist and for a senior principal data scientist at McKinsey.

3. **Nonmonetary aspects matter.** Take job titles, for example. Digital talent wants to be externally recognized by their peers. At the top of the technical "food chain," you have the distinguished engineer, someone who has solved some of the company's toughest technical challenges and has broad followership internally and externally. That title means something. The same is true of nearly all other titles related to digital talent – market recognition is important. Another important nonmonetary aspect is who will be their boss – the senior person who will essentially be helping them develop their craft. They will want to know if that person is indeed capable of being their mentor. Without strong technical talent in house, you may have trouble recruiting even if the compensation is competitive.

   Other nonmonetary rewards – including special assignments, the quality of the development environment, opportunities to present externally or attend special events, high recognition in the workplace, time for pro bono work, ergonomic home setup, access to mindfulness tools, etc. – can also have a persuasive effect. While you may not want to match the benefits and perks of Big Tech companies, you should be thoughtful about the

Career progression for a data scientist

Professional service firm example

Junior DS	Data scientist	Senior DS	Lead DS	Principal DS	Senior principal DS	Partner
Appren-ticing	*Requires technical guidance*	*Mostly self-sufficient*	*Leads technical workstreams*	*Leads large, complex tech-nical delivery*	*Provides technical delivery leadership & firm-wide expertise*	*Leads DS in Firm*

DATA EXPLORATION	Performs basic data quality assessment Performs basic exploratory analysis		Identifies data insufficiency, data quality or data bias issues and shapes solutions to address Continues to shape new technologies to surface data insights
DEFINITION OF THE ANALYTICS APPROACH	Has a growing understanding of the benefits and drawbacks of different methodologies, languages and assets		Understands long-term objectives for digital transformation; how current work fits into an overall technical roadmap Collaborates with business domain leads to craft an ambitious vision for next 1–3 years, and leads the technical thinking in scoping and developing technical roadmaps Helps identify technical skill gaps Combines latest advances in literature to overcome challenges that off-the-shelf DS/ML libraries cannot accommodate
FEATURE ENGINEERING	Can confidently construct/code features defined by herself/himself or others, working collaboratively with data engineering colleagues		Validates both business domain and functional features across predictive models but also key features guiding optimization constraints
APPLICATION OF ANALYTICS TECHNIQUES/ METHODOLOGIES	Performs analytics tasks with minimal guidance Has good knowledge of a number of leading methodologies and can apply appropriately, with limited guidance Can learn new methodologies quickly and apply with guidance Starts gaining familiarity with internal assets (e.g., Kedro)		Identifies opportunities for, and pioneers the use of new and innovative methodologies Holds the bar for technical validity of approaches, and defends that bar even under time/resource pressure Engages in R&D and external collaborations in order to identify trends and opportunities
OUTPUT AND VISUALIZATION	Generates plots/outputs that display relevant data optimally to guide problem solving, with guidance on choice/design of output		Shapes DS-related communications to senior leadership, translating complex technical outputs into compelling, clear, and contextualized messages Builds trust with senior business and technology leaders through breadth of knowledge and strategic thinking
ENGINEERING STANDARDS	Writes good, accurate production code with limited guidance Has growing familiarity with libraries and assets Follows software development and MLOps best practice with guidance		Proactively identifies opportunities to develop new technology assets and plays lead role in their development Aware of and ensures adoption of any latest significant advances in DS/ML technology and tooling Is responsible expert across multiple pods for coding best practices

EXHIBIT 11.1

few that are meaningful and signal your commitment to your digital talent.

4. **Manage the spillover to IT.** Some folks in your traditional IT organization will say, "I am a data scientist. Why can't I be paid the same as the data scientists just hired to work on digital solutions?" Of course, they should be paid the same, but only if they meet the technology and leadership capability markers. Be sure to clearly communicate those markers and, for those in your IT unit who meet them, make sure they are deployed on high-value efforts. If you don't manage this well, compensation comparisons will become untenable and cause people to leave.

In our experience, we have found that many established companies have sufficient flexibility in their compensation model to be able to recruit and retain digital talent. The trick is to use clear skill markers, external benchmarks, and thoughtful nonmonetary incentives.

Use tech competency markers in performance management

Managing performance in an agile and digital workplace is dynamic. While successful digital companies often retain annual written reviews, many have more frequent, informal ones. Best practices indicate managers should have frequent development discussions with their employees. In this approach, employees set their own objectives together with peers and their manager. There are frequent informal check-ins focused on professional development, and, where needed, course corrections.

Who does the evaluations and where the feedback comes from matters. Digital talent expects to be reviewed by someone who has mastery in their craft (or is at least better than they are). Many organizations have adapted some version of a "chapters" model, where people of like roles and skills are loosely organized as a community. The leaders of these groups take on many people responsibilities, including recruiting, performance management, staffing, skill development, and more.

The role of the manager is crucial and is often overlooked during digital and AI transformations. Managers should be frequently trained, especially on goal setting and one-on-one conversations with direct reports to discuss performance goals for the year ahead. For more formal performance reviews, consider incorporating feedback from multiple sources ("360° feedback"). Managers will seek feedback from the employee's advocates and colleagues, assess their performance with a review committee, and then share the feedback with the employee.

Good performance management requires a competency model that includes technical skills and knowledge areas expected within various job families (including skills markers, as discussed in the previous section). This baseline is important so the performance management process can remain fair and transparent. Tech talent wants to know the markers for success at every level. For example, what are the skill expectations for a junior data scientist to become a senior data scientist? This competency leveling becomes the center of your performance management process regardless of how frequently you formally run the process.

The best competency models define technical and nontechnical skills and knowledge areas necessary for success in a job in terms of measurable and observable characteristics and behaviors. The nontechnical ones are often tied to company values. They also map competencies and proficiency levels to specific roles and bands to define role requirements and enable career planning, promotion, and hiring decisions.

There continues to be a lot of experimentation in this area. For example, some organizations are shifting to formal reviews annually and informal ones throughout the year, decoupling reviews from promotions, keeping compensation raises on annual cycles, or digitizing just-in-time feedback. Successful employers stay current with such matters and are willing to test them and learn what works.

Chapter 12

Fostering craftsmanship excellence

Average players want to be left alone. Good players want to be coached. Great players want to be told the truth.

—Doc Rivers

Digital talent has a keen understanding that their value is closely tied to their skills. For this reason, they are particularly attuned to how well they can build their skills in their job. You may think: Isn't this true for all jobs? Yes, but it is particularly true for digital talent because the world of technology is evolving so much faster. Companies that can't deliver on this skill-building expectation shouldn't expect to keep their best people for long. There are two aspects of talent development where companies can support this aspiration:

flexible career paths that accommodate the development of great technologists, and learning journeys tailored to their needs.

Flexible career paths

While some digital colleagues want to progress into general management roles, more than two-thirds of developers don't want to become managers. These individuals instead prefer to keep their craft sharp and pursue ever more sophisticated digital challenges.

For this reason, digital organizations often have both manager and expert career paths (see Exhibit 12.1). A dual track also relieves common promotion pressures, including having technical paths that are less explicitly competitive than managerial ones, and fixing some compensation challenges by allowing those at the top of the expertise track to have pay levels comparable to those of senior executives, as discussed in the previous chapter.

Developing a dual-track career path requires developing comprehensive job architectures organized by job families, such as data science or data engineering. The expert track benefits from the development of a strong competency model with its clear expectations for advancement at each level. Note that while having more levels in the job architecture provides people with faster advancement and a sense of progression, it is also more complex to manage.

Tailored learning journeys

Broadly speaking, there are two elements in creating learning and development (L&D) journeys for digital talent: one is developing the specific training for your digital talent, which we discuss below. The other is creating an institutional capability to support broad-based enterprise trainings, which we cover in Chapter 32 as part of managing change across the enterprise.

Example of dual career tracks

Archetype	Description
Expert leadership	For those individuals who prioritize developing best-in-class thinking on a topic, refining their craft, and shaping customer expectations
People leadership	For those individuals who prioritize leading large teams, connecting work across departments, and managing customer expectations
Executive leadership	For those individuals who want to lead both People Managers and Experts to shape the structure, priorities, and work of the whole organization

DATA SCIENTIST EXAMPLE

IC – *Individual contributor*   **PL** – *People leadership*
EL – *Expert leadership*   **EX** – *Executive*

IC 1	Junior Data Scientist
IC 2	Assoc. Data Scientist
IC 3	Data Scientist
IC 4	Senior Data Scientist
IC 5	Lead Data Scientist

Assoc. Principal, Data Science	**EL 6**	**PL 6**	Data Science Manager
Principal, Data Science	**EL 7**	**PL 7**	Data Science Sr. Manager
Senior Principal, Data Science	**EL 8**	**PL 8**	Director, Data Science
Chief Data Science	**EL 9**	**PL 9**	VP, Data Science

EX 10

Chief Data and Analytics Officer (CDAO)

EXHIBIT 12.1

The core tenet of the modern training approach is that it's continuous, tailored, and targeted. This is a far cry from the more traditional training programs that too often feel like a "chore" rather than a chance to advance skills.

It's easy to get lost in this topic. Many HR organizations start with high ambitions only to find out after a few months that the task of developing these learning journeys and training programs for a plethora of digital roles and skill levels is overwhelming. Real pragmatism is needed here. We typically guide our clients to focus on the following three types of L&D programs for their digital talent, and to use external providers for the rest.

Build a digital "on-ramp bootcamp"

Thousands of people will join pods to develop a solution on your digital roadmap. People joining these pods come from different specialties and have differing levels of understanding about the company's digital vision, its agile ways of working, its user experience design framework, the company's technology stack, and the list goes on. For this reason, developing a "digital on-ramp" is the first training you should develop.

This training tends to be fairly customized and thus is best developed internally. The digital transformation office often assembles this program and leans on the company's L&D team to help shape and manage the training. Typically this learning is delivered as a bootcamp-style training (intensive, all-day, for a week) to kick off the launch of pods (see an example of a typical bootcamp schedule in Exhibit 12.2).

Establish learning journeys for digital talent

We cannot stress enough that skills are a top currency for digital talent, and being able to build skills is an important motivator for them. For this reason, it's crucial to invest in developing long-term learning journeys that support technology employees in developing the breadth and depth of their craft, as well as the behavioral skills that the organization also values.

Example of pod launch bootcamp

▢ Team working sessions   ▉ Reflections

	DAY 1	DAY 2	DAY 3	DAY 4	DAY 5
9 a.m.	Kick-off (Welcome from leadership, why are we here, broader transformation story)	Define team working agreements/ norms	Define MVP (Align on definition of an MVP, story mapping, draft product MVP)	Understand devops and how to use it (CICD pipeline and developer platform)	Share-out/demo with leadership (Team demonstration, gather feedback from leadership)
10 a.m.					
11 a.m.	Agile overview and simulation (Align on definition of Agile, mindsets and behaviors, Agile practices for teams. Simulation)	Stakeholder mapping (Stakeholder communication framework, develop stakeholder map)	Create backlog (Align on definition of backlogs, practice user story writing)	Define sprint cadence	Bootcamp retrospective
12 p.m.					
1 p.m.	Setting mission/vision (Align on the mission, crafting a vision statement)	Create product roadmap (Align on definition of a product roadmap, draft product roadmap)	Definition of ready/definition of done	Refine user stories for 2–3 sprints (Estimate stories, refine acceptance criteria, plan 2–3 sprints)	Sprint 1 planning (Review user stories for sprint 1, revise estimation, clarify acceptance criteria)
2 p.m.					
3 p.m.	Align on OKRs (Align on definition of OKRs, OKR writing practice, draft team OKRs)	Understand our technology and data architecture environment (What is relevant for the target digital solution)	Estimation (What are story points? Estimation techniques and planning poker, practice user story estimation)	Prepare for share-out/demo (Artifacts created during the week, demo format)	(Optional) Teamwork time (Team continues to refine artifacts, implements stakeholder engagement model, schedule sprint events, setup team collaboration tools)
4 p.m.					
5 p.m.	Retrospective	Retrospective	Retrospective	Retrospective	Note: Teams may modify this schedule based on team availability, time zones, and in-person/virtual/hybrid operating model
6 p.m.	(Optional) Teamwork time (Refine artifacts created during the day)	(Optional) Teamwork time (Refine artifacts created during the day)	(Optional) Teamwork time (setup team collaboration tools)	(Optional) Teamwork time (Dry run for demo, setup demo logistics)	

EXHIBIT 12.2

When designing learning journeys, it is important to differentiate between skill families. Resist the temptation to view all technical roles as interchangeable ("they are all engineers") and provide them with the same menu of learning options. Learning journeys for a front-end developer, product owner, or UX designer are all distinctly different. Clearly, this work can only be done by your most senior technologists. The learning journeys should also be organized by proficiency level and be aligned with career tracks and compensation.

Exhibit 12.3 shows what the learning journey for a cloud engineer could be. Note that these learning journeys last multiple years to deepen one's craft – you cannot expect to build real expertise, especially in highly technical areas, in a matter of months. These journeys should feature the full array of skills needed to build deep expertise in the corresponding field.

Since the kinds of skills developed in these programs are typically not specific to your company, it is best to outsource training delivery to organizations like Coursera, Udacity, Cloud Academy, and Udemy, which have a wide variety of rich programs. Many companies provide their digital employees with a yearly training stipend and leave it to them to find the best offering for their specific needs.

In short, focus your efforts on defining the skills expectations for each skill family and proficiency level, and let your employees figure out what offering in the market is best for them.

Reskilling with bootcamps

Reskilling is the process of retraining someone for a different role. This can be a significant undertaking and can take six to 12 months or more to complete (during which time employees won't be able to do their day-to-day duties). That being said, coding bootcamps are one of the most effective ways to build technical skills (e.g., JavaScript, CSS, C#, Ruby, Python) for various roles (e.g., front-end developer, back-end developer).

Sample learning journey for a cloud engineer

Role specific   Platform specific   Ways of working

Increased level of competency

NOVICE		COMPETENT		EXPERT

LEARN

What is Cloud?	Containers for production	Serverless computing	Cloud risk	Efficient Cloud development
Virtualization and deployment models	Applying Cloud to business scenarios	Cloud security specialization	Cloud cost management	Hybrid Cloud Modernizing Applications with Anthos
Intro to DevOps and Containers	Cloud development	Cloud SRE	Elastic CSP Cloud Infrastructure	
CSP Cloud fundamentals	Essential CSP Cloud infrastructure scaling and automation	Logging, monitoring, and observability in CSP Cloud	Reliable CSP Cloud Infrastructure	
Essential CSP Infrastructure Foundation	Getting started with Kubernetes engine	Getting started in Terraform for CSP Cloud	Engaging stakeholders	
Essential CSP Infrastructure Core services	Working with cross-functional teams	Scrum 101		
Problem solving	Embracing Agile fundamentals	MVP mindset		

APPLY

Define business problem statement for implementing Cloud	Create and manage Cloud resources	Set up and configure Cloud environment in CSP Cloud	Deploy and Manage Cloud Environments with CSP Cloud	Cloud Architecture: Design, Implement, and Manage
	Perform foundational infrastructure tasks	Automating Infrastructure on CSP Cloud with Terraform	Optimize Costs for CSP Kubernetes Engine	

EXHIBIT 12.3

The most effective approach is to partner with a specialized firm that offers these bootcamps, such as Turing School, Hack Reactor, CODE, and LeWagon. The best candidates for these kinds of bootcamps are typically those with empathy, grit, and a strong growth mindset; a strong aptitude for logical problem solving; and a passion for programming. Some of McKinsey's best software engineers have come from these programs. Nevertheless, it is difficult and expensive to reskill large numbers of people. Reskilling programs are typically used for talented individuals whom the company wants to invest in. It can be particularly effective for companies with quantitative- or engineering-based workforces.

Getting Ready
Section Two

The following is a set of questions to help you home in on the right actions to take:

Pull out your talent roadmap – is it as detailed and comprehensive as your technology roadmap?

Which are the skills that are core to your competitive differentiation and are you clear on what changes you need to make to find this talent?

Have your HR practices evolved to find, hire, and retain the best digital talent (e.g., prescreen to offer in four weeks, a compelling EVP, etc.)?

Is your company recognized as being a place where top talent wants to work?

Does your top talent believe they can grow and build a promising career in your company (check out your top talent churn numbers - do you know your 'key person' risk)?

Do you have a career track that values great technologists to the same degree that you have one that values excellent managers?

What are you doing to help your tech talent learn the business, and to continue fostering excellence in their craft?

Adopting a New Operating Model

Rearchitecting your organization and governance to be fast and flexible

The concept of agility has become so overused as to almost be cliché, but it remains at the heart of what it takes for companies to operate at the drumbeat of digital.[1] Building and scaling digital and AI solutions requires companies to be much faster and more flexible in the way they develop technology, and having an agile operating model is the way to get there. Developing that operating model, however, is perhaps the most complex aspect of a digital and AI transformation because it touches the core of the organization and how people work together.

Agile teams – or pods, the term we favor – are the most effective way to develop software-based solutions – that's no longer up for debate. But, while any company can get a handful of pods to work well, standing up and scaling hundreds, if not thousands, of them is another story.

This section covers the most critical working practices of well-functioning pods and, more importantly, what it takes to organize and manage a large number of them.

Chapter 13: From doing agile to being agile. Understanding what it takes beyond basic process changes to make agile pods work for peak effectiveness and impact.

Chapter 14: Operating models that support hundreds of agile pods. The three leading operating model options that have emerged to go from a handful of agile teams to supporting hundreds of them across all levels of the enterprise: digital factory, product and platform, and enterprise-wide agility.

Chapter 15: Professionalize product management. Product owners are the effective CEOs of agile pods. They are the linchpin for any operating model, and need prioritized focus and investment.

Chapter 16: Customer experience design: The magic ingredient. Those companies that are truly focused on the customer invest in understanding user motivations and translating that into an experience that both meets the need and delights.

Note

1. Daniel Brosseau, Sherina Ebrahim, Christopher Handscomb, and Shail Thaker, "The journey to an agile organization," McKinsey.com, May 10, 2019, https://www.mckinsey.com/capabilities/people-and-organizational-performance/our-insights/the-journey-to-an-agile-organization; "The drumbeat of digital: How winning teams play," *McKinsey Quarterly*, July 21, 2019, https://www.mckinsey.com/capabilities/mckinsey-digital/our-insights/the-drumbeat-of-digital-how-winning-teams-play.

Chapter 13

From doing agile to being agile

In most cases being a good boss means hiring talented people and then getting out of their way.

—Tina Fey

Our goal here is not to repeat the extensive literature that exists on agile. But it's important to understand the core concepts under-pinning agile ways of working and focus on what companies need to get right to be successful. Understanding how to effectively run agile teams and capture value from the new way of working is critical before scaling the model, which we discuss in Chapter 14.

Many companies have experimented with agile within or beyond the IT organization. When correctly implemented, even a small number of agile teams can quickly add value (see Exhibit 13.1). But companies run into problems when they focus too much on agile as a set of processes and not enough on agile as a new way to prioritize and focus resources on what matters. In these situations, management

Agile is a superior development approach

Benchmark of experienced agile teams performance versus teams using all other development methods

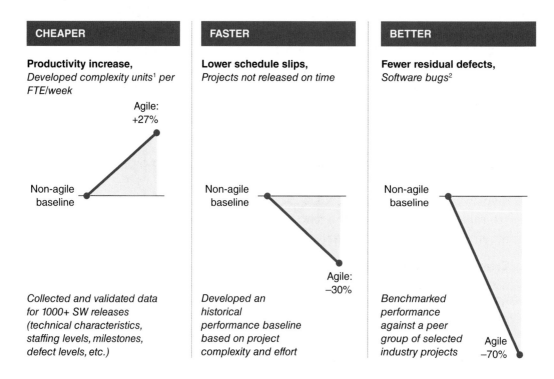

CHEAPER	FASTER	BETTER

Productivity increase,
Developed complexity units[1] per FTE/week

Agile: +27%

Non-agile baseline

Collected and validated data for 1000+ SW releases (technical characteristics, staffing levels, milestones, defect levels, etc.)

Lower schedule slips,
Projects not released on time

Non-agile baseline

Agile: −30%

Developed an historical performance baseline based on project complexity and effort

Fewer residual defects,
Software bugs[2]

Non-agile baseline

Agile −70%

Benchmarked performance against a peer group of selected industry projects

1. Units that possess a high amount of structure or information, often across multiple temporal and spatial scales
2. A problem causing a program to crash or produce invalid output

Source: Numetrics industry software database – 1,321 projects and analytics through patented normalizing algorithm (2021)

EXHIBIT 13.1

implements the rituals of agile, but then becomes disenchanted when the results don't follow, and blames agile. Simply implementing agile rituals without making corresponding changes to how to set objectives, configure teams, and enforce accountability for results will lead to poor outcomes.

Let's start with agile methodologies. There are a number of variations: scrum (named after the original name for the team), kanban,

SAFe (Scaled Agile Framework), and others. Each comes with its own language, cadences, and activities, sometimes leading to heated debate over which is better.

We don't think any of the labeling matters. Some of the best digitally-native companies don't even call the way they work "agile." Most organizations will get value from using the scrum framework and we've used it throughout this book, although we recognize that other approaches can be effective as well. What does matter, though, is developing four sets of defining characteristics that differentiate agile pods from legacy software development teams. They are:

1. **Mission-based with measurable outcomes.** Leadership gives each pod a clear mission grounded in the overall digital road-map. Each mission should focus on outcomes (or key results) that are measurable and that the pod can achieve in a reasonable timeframe (in months or quarters, not years).

2. **Cross-disciplinary with dedicated resources.** Pods are staffed with a mix of business, technical, and functional experts, each of whom brings a valuable capability or skill to the solution development effort. The pod should have, as much as possible, all the resources it needs to deliver on its mission, and these resources should be dedicated.

3. **Autonomous and accountable for achieving impact.** For this agile approach to succeed, pods need ownership over the work they do. This ownership covers not just developing the solution but also realizing the value from that solution. Pods are empowered to make solution development choices to achieve the mission. The product owner – the de facto pod lead – constantly prioritizes product development features in the backlog.

4. **Fast moving and focused on user needs.** The fundamental working approach of an agile pod is to test, learn, and continuously improve a solution based on a clear idea of what the end user needs. Pods work to produce something new and test it with end users every two weeks to collect direct feedback and adapt quickly. Pod members receive immediate feedback and execute on it.

In their words: Freeing up your product squads

One of the key shifts was focusing on the kind of value we were trying to drive. Changing the model to focus on the employee experience, as opposed to focusing on whether projects were delivered on time and on budget, was a fundamental change.

The second thing was really making the primary operating model revolve around the squad [i.e., pod], and making sure squads get whatever they need to set them up for success. That frees them to be self-directed, so that they can take charge of their direction and their decisions.

When you create that squad, you need a business product-owner role, you need a technical product-owner role, and you need scrum masters. It's the typical squad model from a technology standpoint. But making that shift from a project-oriented model, where some people are on board for only 20% of their time, is a fundamental and necessary shift.

It's not rocket science. It's just putting it all together in a model that makes sense for the work that needs to get done and remaining really focused and dedicated to that work, which is why you need a persistent team that exists beyond the initial delivery of the product you're trying to create.

We certainly benefited from that model, and I didn't have people calling me at all hours of the day and night asking, "What should I do about this project? How should I make this decision?" They were empowered to make those decisions for their products on their own, while reporting back to make sure we were aware of what was going on.

One way we try to evangelize this movement toward product-oriented technology is pointing out that you wouldn't launch a medical device or pharmaceutical product in the marketplace and then just walk away from it. You want to continually invest and support the development of that product in the marketplace. Why don't we do the same thing for technology? I think using that analogy sometimes helps people to understand and unlock some of that value.

—Tom Weck, CIO of corporate technology at Johnson & Johnson

Three ceremonies that matter most to drive agile performance

There is a misconception about agile that it is freewheeling and lacks sufficient management input and oversight. That happens in poor implementations of agile. In fact, when done right, agile is an effective way to manage performance because of its focus on results and the frequent checks on progress.

To achieve this, three ceremonies (a term that describes meetings with defined frequencies, durations, and goals) matter most (see Exhibit 13.2). Get these right and you succeed with your agile implementation.

Setting the mission and OKRs

This is the most important ceremony because this is when management provides direction and sets expectations (see #1 on exhibit 13.2). A mission is the work that a pod does for a year or longer. Management and each pod owner break down a mission into objectives and key results (OKRs) and set specific quarterly targets for the pod. Generally credited as the brainchild of the late Intel CEO Andy Grove, OKRs have proven to be effective in focusing teams on impact rather than activity. In practice, this is harder than it sounds and is often a major failure point in agile deployments[1]. The pod will translate its objectives into a product or solution roadmap that details how it will deliver its expected results.

Each OKR is tied to business outcomes, which everyone on the team shares. Objectives should be bold and specific. Keep the number of objectives manageable – fewer is better (generally one to three). Objectives should only be altered after careful consideration.

In their words: OKRs - Aligning on what matters

OKRs are a way of aligning on what matters most right now and then iterating on that, because it's not constant. Start-ups by their birthright are constantly calibrating a huge ambition with very little resource.

Agile cadence and performance management ceremonies

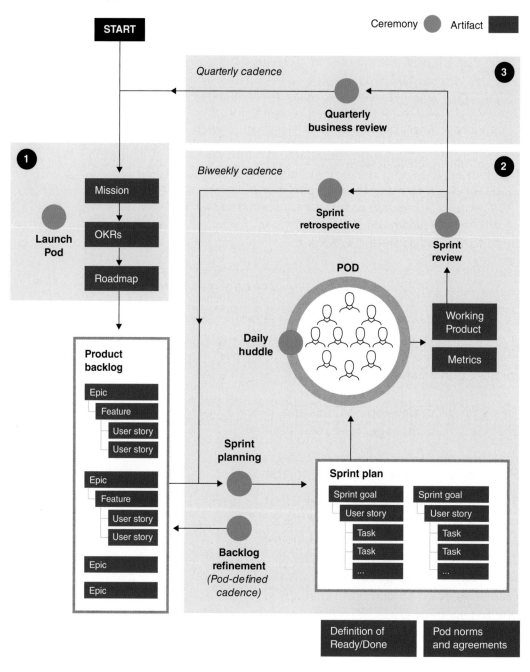

EXHIBIT 13.2

Their capacity relative to their ambition is wildly mismatched, which is both the exciting and the horrifying part of being in a start-up. They don't have unlimited time, money, and resources. So, if we had to make trade-offs of what mattered most, what would we trade in, what would we trade out? OKRs are a technique for larger companies to operate with the same notion of constraint, and that constraint helps drive choices.

The other thing that's powerful and very different to what preceded them is that OKRs put an emphasis on what awesome looks like, as opposed to what would be safe and have the most predictable result. It flips it to saying, "Okay, in the next 90 days, what is the best possible outcomes we could achieve?"

It's not about trying to look good in your KPIs. It's about trying to be amazing. I love that combination of bringing the ambition fully forward, and then given constrained capacity, what are we going to do first? What do we think moves the needles, and which needles matter most?"

—Deidre Paknad, co-founder and CEO of WorkBoard

Key results should be aggressive, to the point where they are occasionally missed, which is okay. In fact, key results are probably set too low if pods are always hitting them. Key results should be easily tracked, quantifiable, and tied to business value (see Exhibit 13.3).

This is the art of developing OKRs and, in our experience, this takes practice before management does this well.

Progressing and testing through sprints

The sprint is typically a two-week effort to develop features of a digital solution (see #2 in exhibit 13.2). Multiple sprints comprise a development phase (typically three months). The product owner (or manager) prioritizes the team's work for a sprint by developing a well-organized to-do list (also known as a backlog) of all the deliverables needed to complete the current sprint and the following one to two sprints.

Example of OKRs

Software solution that supports enterprise HR services

Objectives	Key results		Timing
1 Delight our current clients and deliver positive moments that matter every time	1.1	Develop a cohesive, consistent user experience across all three personas with 100% of user journeys implemented	Q2
	1.2	Drive error-free customer reports release rate to 95% from ~80%	Q1
	1.3	Increase average NPS to ~40 from ~13 for product V	Q2
2 Reduce direct costs associated with the product	2.1	Introduce and drive adoption of self-serve features to reduce call volumes by 10%	Q3
	2.2	Automate reports for queries that receive more than 100 service requests per quarter	Q3
	2.3	Reduce hosting costs by 20%	Q4
3 Improve customer retention by stabilizing the product	3.1	Match product uptime to SLA (99.995%) for the entire year	Q4
	3.2	Reduce number of critical incidents to 63 (from 83), and hot fixes by 50% (from 4 to 2)	Q3
	3.3	Achieve defect intake rate lower than defect resolution rate	Q2

EXHIBIT 13.3

The ability of a product owner to review and adjust priorities, escalate issues when needed, plan sprints, and think through dependencies is fundamental to the functioning of a pod. Most companies find themselves short of capable product owners (for more on product management, please read Chapter 15).

A two-week sprint concludes with a sprint review, and this is the opportunity for the pod to showcase their progress artifacts and keep itself honest that it is on track to deliver. It is also an opportunity for management – typically the domain leader – to celebrate the team and provide guidance.

The pod does *not* prepare formal, polished presentations for sprint reviews. That would be too onerous. Instead, it shares the work that's been completed. This is always a challenging cultural change for established companies.

The specific ceremonies of a sprint are described in Exhibit 13.4.

Governing through quarterly business reviews (QBRs)

The QBR, or quarterly business review, is when management takes stock of progress and value delivered, and redirects the team if needed. The QBR is a formal ceremony between the pod owners and the domain leader. It looks back at the progress of the past three months, adjusts OKRs for the next three months, and ensures OKRs are well coordinated across pods. Once this is done at the domain level, a second ceremony a level up brings together all domain leaders with the business unit leader. This is the opportunity to review domain-level OKRs and overall domain funding.

It takes time to design the specifics of how QBRs get embedded in the planning cycle of a company – how should QBRs link with strategic planning and budgeting? How should they be coordinated with quarterly and monthly executive committee meetings? Do they replace investment committee reviews?

QBRs are sometimes criticized for adding more meetings to the management agenda. This is not the case when implemented well. In fact, QBRs can reduce the number of management meetings by as much as 75%, as seen in the example of a US bank shown in Exhibit 13.5.

Agile ceremonies

CEREMONY	DESCRIPTION	EXPECTED RESULTS	FREQUENCY
Backlog refinement	Elements in the backlog are prioritized and fine-tuned to ensure they are ready for the upcoming sprint and the 1–2 following sprints	The backlog contains a number of user stories that have been prioritized, are well documented, and are comprehensive enough to potentially form the next sprint backlog	Every sprint (2 weeks)
Sprint planning	Used to ensure team agrees on the proposed amount of work, which is composed of several elements in the sprint backlog	Prioritized epics and stories[1] are allocated to sprints Assumptions, risks, and dependencies have been identified	Every sprint
Daily huddle	Serves to assess sprint progress and identify possible barriers	Every team member has 1+ tasks assigned for the day Status of user stories/tasks has been updated Blockers, if any, have been raised	Daily
Sprint review	Opportunity for teams to present new functionalities developed in the newly finished sprint	Feedback is provided to update or add future user stories	Every sprint
Sprint retrospective	Used to assess sprint productivity and identify improvement opportunities as well as strengths for the team	Team strengths have been identified Solutions to areas for team improvements have been identified and assigned	Every sprint
Quarterly business review	Performed at project start and every quarter to align OKR and product roadmap	Prioritized epics and stories are allocated to sprints Assumptions, risks, and dependencies have been identified OKRs for next quarter are set	Every quarter

1. Epics: large chunks of work that deliver full functionality (includes multiple stories and spans multiple sprints)
User stories: a feature from perspective of end-user

EXHIBIT 13.4

Streamlining of management forums from QBR implementation

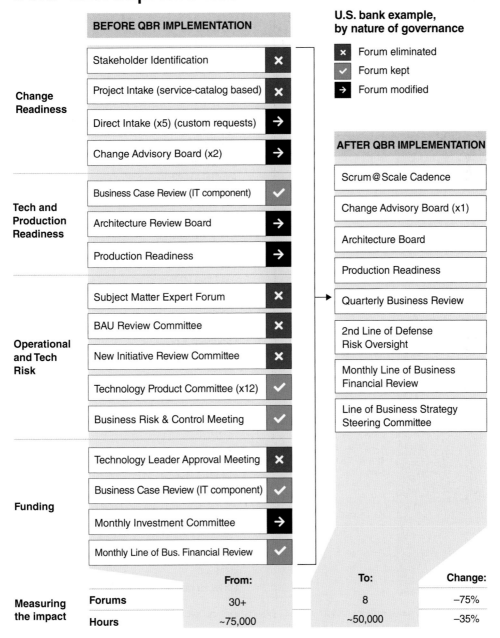

U.S. bank example, by nature of governance

✕	Forum eliminated
✓	Forum kept
→	Forum modified

BEFORE QBR IMPLEMENTATION

Change Readiness
- Stakeholder Identification ✕
- Project Intake (service-catalog based) ✕
- Direct Intake (x5) (custom requests) →
- Change Advisory Board (x2) →

Tech and Production Readiness
- Business Case Review (IT component) ✓
- Architecture Review Board →
- Production Readiness →

Operational and Tech Risk
- Subject Matter Expert Forum ✕
- BAU Review Committee ✕
- New Initiative Review Committee ✕
- Technology Product Committee (x12) ✓
- Business Risk & Control Meeting ✓

Funding
- Technology Leader Approval Meeting ✕
- Business Case Review (IT component) ✓
- Monthly Investment Committee →
- Monthly Line of Bus. Financial Review ✓

AFTER QBR IMPLEMENTATION
- Scrum@Scale Cadence
- Change Advisory Board (x1)
- Architecture Board
- Production Readiness
- Quarterly Business Review
- 2nd Line of Defense Risk Oversight
- Monthly Line of Business Financial Review
- Line of Business Strategy Steering Committee

Measuring the impact

	From:	To:	Change:
Forums	30+	8	−75%
Hours	~75,000	~50,000	−35%

EXHIBIT 13.5

Note

1. John Doerr, "Measure What Matters," Penguin Random House, 2018; Matt Fitzpatrick and Kurt Strovink, "How do you measure success in digital? Five metrics for CEOs", McKinsey.com, January 29, 2021, https://www.mckinsey.com/capabilities/mckinsey-digital/our-insights/how-do-you-measure-success-in-digital-five-metrics-for-ceos.

Chapter 14

Operating models that support hundreds of agile pods

The people doing the work are the moving force . . . My job is to create a space for them, to clear out the rest of the organization and keep it at bay.

—Steve Jobs

One of the biggest stumbling blocks in digital and AI transformations is the jump from running a handful of pods to running hundreds of them. While it's relatively easy to manage a handful of agile pods by exception and with extra effort, that is not sustainable when you expand to hundreds or thousands of pods.

To support that number of teams, companies need a more formal operating model. This chapter focuses on three fundamental models:

(1) digital factory, (2) product and platform, and (3) enterprise-wide agile. All three will vary based on a company's context and digital maturity, but they use the same building blocks.

Organizational building blocks

Three organizational building blocks make up any digital operating model (see Exhibit 14.1):

1. **Product or experience pods** develop and provide technology-enabled offerings or services used by customers and employees. Their immediate and primary purpose is to enable users to perform activities that create value. For example, a retailer's search engine contributes business value by making it easy for customers to find items on a website or mobile app.

   The word "product" was inherited from the software industry. Different companies use different terms that are more useful for their context. Financial services companies call them customer experiences; industrial product companies call them customer solutions. Regardless of the term used, "products" engage the customer or user directly through digital technologies.

   A group of product or experience pods working on the same end-to-end journey (e.g., customer onboarding) or process (e.g., yield optimizer) is called a domain (as described in Chapter 2). A domain is typically composed of 10–20 pods and led by a domain owner.

2. **Platform pods** are the back-end technology and data capabilities that support products. A retail search engine, for example, might rely on an inventory management platform that includes databases and interfaces to integrate with suppliers. Platform capabilities enable more effective scaling by providing functionalities that many product pods need to deliver their service.

Building blocks of agile operating models

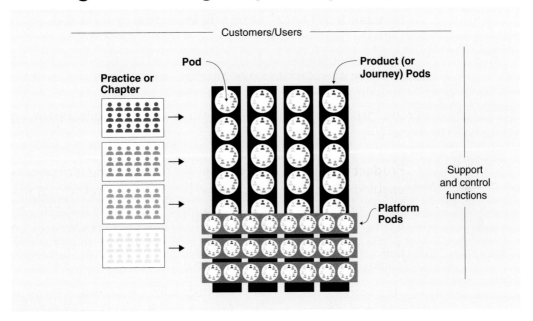

WHAT WE MEAN	EXAMPLES
Pod: Self-sufficient, cross-functional team with end-to-end accountability to deliver a product, experience, or service. *Alternate taxonomy: squad, cell, agile team*	(see below)
Product (or Journey) Pods: E2E delivery of a service or solution to a customer or user. *A collection of product pods is called a Product Group, Domain, Portfolio, Tribe, or Town*	Yield optimizer Pricing recommendation Customer on-boarding Website product search
Platform Pods: Grouping of similar technology assets, people, and funding to provide a (reusable) service to product/journey pods. *A collection of platform pods is called a Platform, Tribe, or Town*	Customer 360 data product Machine learning suite Core system Infra provisioning
Practice or Chapter: Organizational construct responsible for professional development of employees (separate from day-to-day direction done by the pod). *Alternate taxonomy: guild, communities of practice*	Data engineers Software engineers Product owners/managers

EXHIBIT 14.1

Platforms also typically contain 15 pods or more, and are led by a platform manager. Typical platforms include (a) data platforms such as Customer 360, (b) enterprise systems such as an ERP or a CRM, (c) platform-as-a-service (PaaS) applications such as user authentication or machine learning algorithms, and (d) infrastructure platforms (IaaS) that provide services such as cloud compute and storage.

3. A **chapter** is a group of people with the same role (e.g., product owners, data scientists, data engineers). Chapters are responsible for building expertise and maintaining common approaches to tasks. Chapter leads manage career paths, recruit individual employees, and provide performance evaluations. The role of the chapter lead is to staff people to pods based on its needs. The chapter also owns the exchange of best practices and the development of methods and standards. For example, the design chapter would define a standard design methodology.

   Chapters try to compensate for the fact that pods are cross-functional. Pods are great for bringing all the necessary expertise for the job, but they are inherently weak in providing development in one's craftsmanship. If you are the only data engineer on a pod, you don't have the opportunity to learn from other more experienced data engineers. The chapters help compensate for this shortfall.

   There are two versions of chapters: heavy and light. The heavy version is described above. The light version – often called a guild – is more of an informal network. It limits itself to providing best practice exchanges, and development and performance standards. The recruiting, staffing, and evaluation is left to domain or platform leads. Which model is best, light or heavy, is a subject of debate.

Operating model design options

In our experience, there are three main options for designing an agile operating model: (1) a digital factory model, (2) a product and platform model, and (3) an enterprise-wide agile model (see

Exhibit 14.2). Each model incorporates elements of the product, platform, and chapter building blocks described above.

Three operating model design options

	OPTION 1 **Digital factory**	**OPTION 2** **Product & platform**	**OPTION 3** **Enterprise-wide agile**
Description	A separate digital unit that builds digital solutions for business units using modern agile ways of working and multidisciplinary pods	Model brings together Business, Tech and operations in pods focused on improving customer/user experiences (so-called product pods) and pods dedicated to building services for reuse (so-called platform pods)	Extends benefits of agility beyond digital/tech, as many core operations and functions can benefit from agile collaboration
Typical configuration	10–50 pods Touches less than 2% of organization	50–1,000+ pods Touches 20–40% of organization	1,000+ pods Touches 80% of organization
Main advantage	Simplest model to implement	Integrates Business, Technology and Ops more closely and addresses evolution of platforms	Creates enterprise-wide agile culture
Prerequisites	Alignment of BUs in the funding and operating model of the factory	IT modernization required (e.g., talent, architecture, cloud, DevSecOps)	Organizational readiness for a full agile flip

EXHIBIT 14.2

The three models differ largely in the level of integration between business and technology resources and in how broadly the model is deployed in the organization. All three models are good models. Your choice will depend on how you intend to use technology as a competitive differentiator.

Many companies start with a digital factory because it is easier to implement. It's a great model when technology is a "strategic enhancer" to support the core business. Resource companies often fall in this category.

A product and platform model is especially relevant if technology is a main source of competitive differentiation, as in banking and retail. Some leading banks and retailers have transitioned or are currently transitioning from a digital factory to a product and platform model.

Those who opt for the enterprise-wide model want to extend the benefit of agile across the entire business, not just in the technology-intensive areas. We have seen banks, telcos, and retailers make this transition. This requires a serious multi-year commitment by the CEO.

Since each of these models is constructed from the same building blocks, you could progress from one model to the next and many companies do.

Note that many organizations often use a center of excellence (CoE) to bring digital expertise to their business units. Experience has shown, however, that this model is not a viable scaling option because it does not support cross-disciplinary teams and duplicates development efforts since there is no platform construct.

Digital factory model

The digital factory model is often the right place to start because it is self-contained and relatively rapid to implement (typically 12 to 18 months before it's fully operational, although it can get started in a matter of weeks).[1] At large enterprises, digital factories are embedded within divisions, whereas at smaller companies, a single factory serves multiple business units. Both the mining company BHP and Scotiabank implemented digital factory models when they started their digital transformations. Each had four to five digital factories serving their different divisions, with a coordination overlay to maximize code reuse and standardization.[2]

The digital factory is typically a physical place where people work together and is separate from the main business. The productivity and creativity benefits of co-location are real: coordination costs go down, decisions are made faster, and rework decreases. Remote working teams can also operate effectively, although it requires more purposeful and structured communication. Try to limit time zone differences across pod team members to three hours or less if you use a remote or hybrid model.

Exhibit 14.3 shows how one leading global hospitality company organized its digital factory, which houses over 400 employees.

A digital factory is typically a formal organizational unit that reports to the chief digital officer. It is organized in product pods and platform pods, houses all the relevant expertise (except for product owners), and it organizes them in chapters responsible for talent management and deployment.

Business units act as sponsors in the factory by funding and leading the work executed by product pods. They determine which opportunities get prioritized, set the OKRs, and provide funding. The business unit also provides the product owners and subject matter experts. In essence, the business units secure factory capacity for their digital needs. In return, the factory provides them with digital expertise to staff their product pods and platform-related services (e.g., cloud compute and storage, developer tools, core systems interfaces, or APIs).

The digital factory is responsible for running the platform pods. These are funded centrally or on a cost-sharing basis with the business units. As a rough rule of thumb, two thirds of the factory resources are typically deployed to product pods and one third to platform pods.

Annual budgeting is team-centric, not project-centric, meaning that it is based on the number of pods. This is often referred to as persistent funding as opposed to traditional project-based funding (see Exhibit 14.4). This funding model is also recommended for both product and platform as well as enterprise-wide agility operating models (see below).

Digital factory operating model

Hospitality example   XX   Estimated FTEs (internal and external)

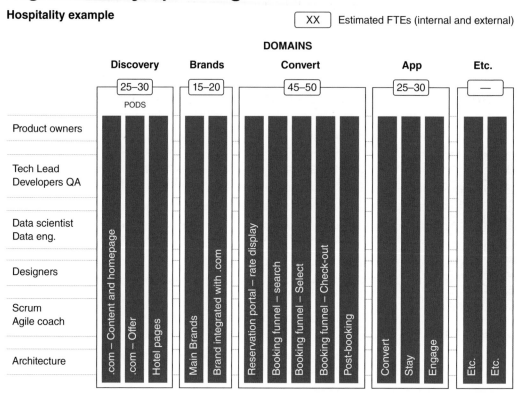

1. CMS = Content management system; 2. DAM = Digital asset management; 3. OTA = Online travel agency; 4.
API = Application programming interface; 5. CDP = Customer data platform

EXHIBIT 14.3

In our opinion, the digital factory model will remain relevant for companies where technology is important but perhaps not the most important driver of competitive differentiation. It provides a great way for business units to quickly secure world-class digital capabilities.

From project funding to persistent funding

	PROJECT FUNDING	PERSISTENT FUNDING
BUDGETING	Budgeting done by project on a yearly basis	Annual budget target is set at enterprise level and by domain (not by project)
FUNDING	Up to 50% of funding is getting absorbed into unplanned or lower-priority work	Additional funding released upon hitting milestones/stage gates
REVIEW	Projects are reviewed and prioritized yearly or biannually	Quarterly review and prioritization done during QBR

EXHIBIT 14.4

Product and platform model

The product and platform (P&P) model is being adopted by most software companies, leading global retailers such as Amazon, and leading global banks such as JPMorgan Chase.[3] Each has adopted a version of this model because it brings business, operations, and technology closer together to accelerate customer experience innovation and create a more scalable model through platform-based services.

The P&P model is a more evolved version of the digital factory and its deployment is at a much greater scale. While the digital factory model might manage 10 to 50 pods, the P&P model will typically have a few hundred and sometimes over a thousand pods for large companies.[4] That's because the model touches all technology resources and a substantial part of business and operations resources. Exhibit 14.5 shows the placemat design of a 1,000+pod P&P model for a leading international bank.

Product and platform model

Example for an international bank

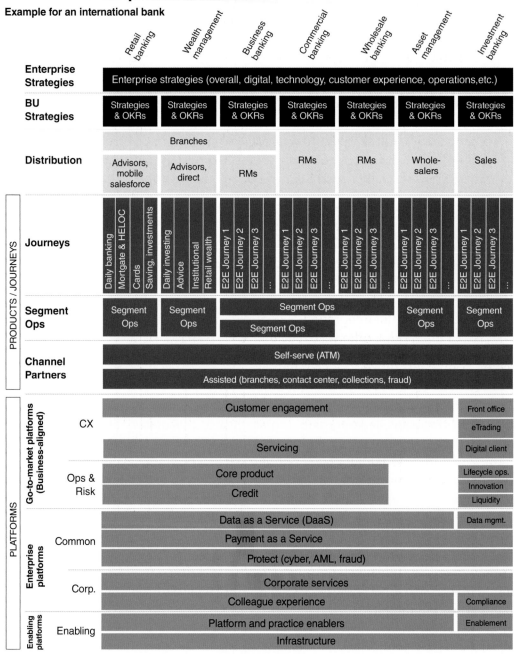

EXHIBIT 14.5

A P&P model differs from a digital factory in three ways:

1. The entire IT function is reorganized with application development and maintenance professionals usually joining product pods and infrastructure and core systems professionals becoming part of platform pods.

2. Technology undergoes a major modernization to enable the full potential of digital. This will mean moving to a more modular architecture, exploiting the new capabilities provided by cloud technologies, and adopting modern software development practices (for more on this, read Section Four, on technology).

3. As companies increase the number of agile pods, control functions such as risk management, cybersecurity, and compliance become a gating factor because they are brought in late to the agile development process, forcing pods to redo work. Or, even worse, pods try to circumvent these functions in the quest for greater speed but at the cost of uncontrolled risks. In a P&P model, thoughtful integration of control functions is an integral part of the model; otherwise it cannot scale (see sidebar).

When companies move to a P&P model, they are making a major strategic decision to realign large parts of the organization to better exploit technology in its core business. The flip into the new model typically takes one to two years, depending on the size of the company, and another one to two years to achieve full operational maturity. It's a major commitment that only the CEO – in tight alignment with the C-suite – can make.

The primary challenge in implementing a P&P model is to flip to the new model while continuing to run the business. Achieving this requires a clear blueprint for the target model and a well-oiled process to mobilize and launch pods with the right OKRs, proper staffing, funding, and agile governance. It is literally a case of flying the plane while building it.

We believe the P&P model will become the dominant model in industries where technology is the primary performance differentiator.

How to embed control functions into product and platform teams

While ideally every agile pod has dedicated control function resources, this is not feasible in practice. The first place to start is to make pods accountable for their risks as a first line of defense. This avoids the "not-my-job" issue that can drive sloppy work by the pods.

Agile teams can implement a comprehensive risk assessment process. This assessment covers all risks (including third parties, compliance, legal, regulatory, etc.) and is often supported, at least initially, by risk management professionals to ensure it is properly done (see Exhibit 14.6). The assessment automatically triggers involvement of specialized control functions (the second line of defense) depending on the risk level and type.

How risk management is embedded in agile operating model

US bank example

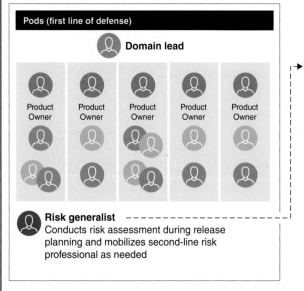

EXHIBIT 14.6

Risk discussions need to be part of regular agile ceremonies to ensure risks are addressed in a timely fashion. In these ceremonies, teams ensure clear roles for both the pod (first line of defense) and the control function (second line) in managing a specific risk (see Exhibit 14.7).

How risk assessment is embedded in the development process

MONITORING

Every quarter (if needed)

1 Risk identification
Risk assessment based on comprehensive risk taxonomy to identify risks at a granular, epic level

Initial assessment
Automatic triggers for involving specialized control functions

2 Risk professionals assignment
Risk professionals are assigned to co-design/consult risk-mitigating actions

During sprint

3 Refined risk assessment
Risk assessment can be retaken to update risk identification and rating as more clarity is obtained on the epic

Dashboard
Monitoring of risk levels and mitigation throughout the life cycle

4 Risk mitigation workflow
Risk mitigation stories identified and automatically generated into backlog of the pod

5 Mitigation executed
Stories assigned to pod members, business or risk professionals to execute mitigation

Post-sprint

7 Reporting and compliance
Risk mitigation actions documented for compliance, and sprint retrospective discussion

Compliance reports
Automatically generated and configurable reports

EXHIBIT 14.7

Best-in-class companies not only digitize the risk identification process but also automate risk controls ("security as code"). Addressing material risk areas in a timely fashion is an important part in achieving speed. This is extensively discussed in Chapter 22.

Enterprise-wide agility model

The benefits of small, diverse, customer-focused, and empowered teams are not confined to the development of digital solutions. Nearly any business function (sales, R&D, marketing, or product development, for example) or support function (HR or finance) can adopt, and benefit from, the same mindsets and ways of working to achieve greater productivity and employee satisfaction.

When deploying agile beyond digital/IT teams, however, new agile team constructs beyond cross-disciplinary pods are needed to suit the specific work being performed (see Exhibit 14.8). For example, self-managed teams are often used in contact centers to ensure end-to-end ownership of customer and cost outcomes, in a way that encourages continuous improvement. A "flow-to-work" pool of functional experts is used when a function (such as finance, HR, legal, etc.) wants to deploy its resources flexibly to the most pressing needs, often into the business (it's called "flow-to-work" because the resources "flow" to where the "work" is). Finally, "network teams" are often used in distribution and sales/store networks to bring daily-level coordination and alignment with less hierarchy and more hands-on leadership.

Companies that flip to a full enterprise-wide agile model such as ING, Spark NZ, or Walmart (Mexico) focus on reimagining the entire organization as a network of high-performing teams, each going after a clear, end-to-end business-oriented outcome, and possessing all of the skills needed to deliver.[5]

Exhibit 14.9 shows the placemat view of an enterprise-wide agile model for a midsize telecom operator. It deployed network element teams in channel distribution to flatten the organization and drive faster exchanges of best practice. In contact centers, it deployed self-managed teams to drive higher accountability for customer care, with spectacular results. In the area of corporate functions it used a flow-to-work model to enable faster redeployment of resources on critical projects. Finally, the core business was organized in cross-functional squads (or pods) as we have described them previously in the P&P model.

Four archetypes of agile units

CROSS-FUNCTIONAL UNITS

Example: Product teams (pods)
Used in digital factory, and P&P

Product owner steering

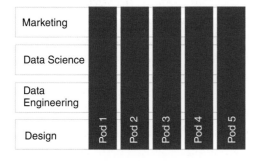

SELF-MANAGED TEAMS

Example: Contact center
Each team is accountable for the end-to-end
experience of a subset of customers

KPI-based steering

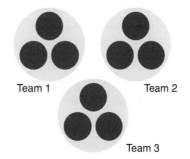

FLOW-TO-WORK

Example: Functional experts
Deployed to teams with the most pressing needs

Special project teams   *Pool experts*

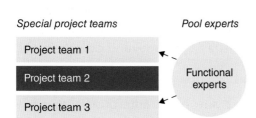

NETWORK ELEMENTS

Example: Distribution
(stores, sales teams)

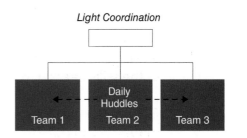

EXHIBIT 14.8

This model delivered a more than 20% reduction in overall headcount while improving customer satisfaction and overall revenue
per customer. As importantly, it achieved this result while increasing
employee satisfaction, which reached a +78 NPS three years into the
transformation (up from +22).

Enterprise-wide agile operating model

Midsize telecom operator

Agile organizational building blocks

■ Cross-functional pods   ■ Self-managed teams   ■ Flow-to-work pools   ▢ Network elements

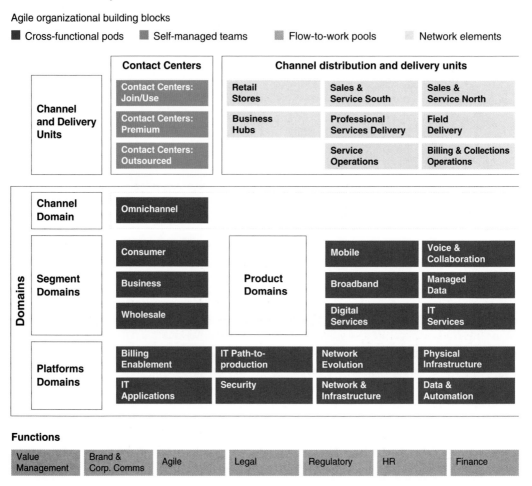

Channel and Delivery Units	Contact Centers		Channel distribution and delivery units		
	Contact Centers: Join/Use		Retail Stores	Sales & Service South	Sales & Service North
	Contact Centers: Premium		Business Hubs	Professional Services Delivery	Field Delivery
	Contact Centers: Outsourced			Service Operations	Billing & Collections Operations

Domains

Channel Domain	Omnichannel				
Segment Domains	Consumer	Product Domains	Mobile	Voice & Collaboration	
	Business		Broadband	Managed Data	
	Wholesale		Digital Services	IT Services	
Platforms Domains	Billing Enablement	IT Path-to-production	Network Evolution	Physical Infrastructure	
	IT Applications	Security	Network & Infrastructure	Data & Automation	

Functions

Value Management	Brand & Corp. Comms	Agile	Legal	Regulatory	HR	Finance

EXHIBIT 14.9

One of the most difficult tasks when implementing an enterprise-wide model is to clarify how the organization creates value, and where and how agile can make a difference (for example, to enable working across functions). An enterprise-wide agile operating model is not for every company. We believe it can be successfully adopted by companies where customer centricity, collaboration, and resource deployment flexibility are a performance differentiator beyond technology-intensive applications.

Notes

1. Somesh Khanna, Nadiya Konstantynova, Eric Lamarre, and Vik Sohoni, "Welcome to the Digital Factory: The answer to how to scale your digital transformation," McKinsey.com, May 14, 2020, https://www.mckinsey.com/capabilities/mckinsey-digital/our-insights/welcome-to-the-digital-factory-the-answer-to-how-to-scale-your-digital-transformation.

2. Rag Udd, "Pushing the velocity of value with digital factories," *BHP*, May 4, 2020, https://www.bhp.com/news/prospects/2020/05/pushing-the-velocity-of-value-with-digital-factories; Will Hernandez, "Why Scotiabank is building 'digital factories',"" *American Banker*, October 18, 2019, https://www.americanbanker.com/news/why-scotiabank-is-building-digital-factories#:~:text=We%20wanted%20to%20build%20replicable,could%20make%20really%20good%20software.

3. Tanya Chhabra, "Amazon business model | How does Amazon make money?," Feedough, February 21, 2023, https://www.feedough.com/amazon-business-model/; Bianca Chan and Carter Johnson, "JPMorgan is adding 25 'mini-CEOs' as part of a massive plan to overhaul its 50,000-strong tech organization and pivot the bank to operate more like a startup," *Business Insider*, April 15, 2022, https://www.businessinsider.com/insider-jpmorgans-massive-shift-product-oriented-tech-operating-model-2022-4.

4. Oliver Bossert and Driek Desmet, "The platform play: How to operate like a tech company," McKinsey.com, February 28, 2019, https://www.mckinsey.com/capabilities/mckinsey-digital/our-insights/the-platform-play-how-to-operate-like-a-tech-company.

5. See "ING's agile transformation," *McKinsey Quarterly*, January 10, 2017, https://www.mckinsey.com/industries/financial-services/our-insights/ings-agile-transformation; "All in: From recover to agility at Spark New Zealand," *McKinsey Quarterly*, June 11, 2019, https://www.mckinsey.com/industries/technology-media-and-telecommunications/our-insights/all-in-from-recovery-to-agility-at-spark-new-zealand; "2020 Financial and ESG Report," Walmart (Mexico), December 31, 2020, https://informes.walmex.mx/2020/en/pdfs/2020_Financial_and_ESG_Report.pdf.

Chapter 15

Professionalize product management

Getting good players is easy. Getting them to play together is the hard part.

—*Casey Stengel*

While implementing an agile operating model requires companies to develop multiple capabilities (as described in Chapters 13 and 14), two deserve a closer look because of their importance: product management and customer experience design (which is tackled in Chapter 16). A crucial difference between many tech companies and their peers in other sectors is the degree to which they have embedded these capabilities – along with a software engineering culture and use of data and analytics – into how they work.

Building product management depth is usually one of the core reskill-ing goals in a digital and AI transformation. There are two primary roles: the product owner, who leads pods, and the senior product owner, who leads a group of pods or a domain. Product owners are absolutely indispensable because they combine crucial operational and strategic skills, including: understanding business needs, having an intense understanding of the customer, and having a solid grounding in technology (see Exhibit 15.1).

The skills of a great product owner

Customer-experience grounding	Market orientation	Business acumen	Technical skills	Soft skills
Ability to design customer-centric experiences throughout the customer decision journey	Ability to deeply understand market trends, partner ecosystems, and competitive strategies	Comfort with business strategy, portfolio prioritization, go-to-market, pricing, tracking key performance indicators and financial metrics	Ability to go deep on technology trends, architectural questions, stack control points, roadmaps, and managing the development life cycle	Ability to lead teams, communicate with diverse groups, and influence change throughout the organization

EXHIBIT 15.1

Many have described this role as a "mini-CEO" in terms of the breadth of responsibilities and skills required. For this reason, product management is quickly becoming the new spot for top business talent rotations, and a place where many current tech CEOs cut their teeth.

But too few companies have the right product management capabilities in place. Some 75% of business leaders in a McKinsey analysis responded that product management best practices aren't being adopted at their companies, that product management is a nascent function within their organization, or that it doesn't exist at all.[1]

In their words: Moving to a product management world

For us, the biggest challenge historically has been moving from a financial product world to a product management world. A person who knows everything about deposit accounts, credit cards, or loans may have a great understanding of the intricacies and requirements of a particular product. That doesn't mean that person's always the best product manager or product owner when it comes to working with an agile scrum team and delivering that product to market or grooming a backlog or setting priorities. It's an evolution.

We've seen some of those people embrace it, have tremendous career pivots, and become fantastic product managers. But like anything else, you've got to be a student of the game, you've got to learn, and you've got to be open to learning. Those who have embraced that opportunity have done really well. But we've also had to hire, because you also have to bring examples into the organization for others to learn from. It's also important to understand diversity of thought and culture.

—Ken Meyer, Truist's chief information and experience officer

Working closely with domain leaders and user experience designers, product owners have total accountability for the entire lifecycle of the product, from gathering customer insights to engineering the solution to adoption. The product owner is responsible for delivering a specific set of clear OKRs, which they assess and review during QBRs, where priorities can pivot. They know how to guide the development of tech-intensive solutions, ensure that agile pods work on the right customer/user problems, and innovate solutions to these problems. Importantly, product owners are responsible for their entire backlog, including basic maintenance tasks like bug fixes, rather than creating new product features. This ensures their accountability for the quality of the products created, and helps reduce technical debt.

Finding someone with the breadth of skills needed for a product manager can be difficult, so consider how to provide the right level of support. In the case where the product owner is less comfortable with deep-tech topics, for example, it's a good idea to staff the pod with strong senior engineers to support him or her.

Career paths and professional development

Professionalizing the product management function includes creating roles and levels, corresponding pay grades, and certifications. One particular area of focus is developing a specific career path with expanding responsibilities – not having this career growth program can lead to promising product owners leaving. As with tech-specific career paths, discussed in Chapter 12, your product owner career path should look different from the managerial track, and should clarify specific responsibilities and capabilities needed (see Exhibit 15.2).

How many levels there are in the career path will depend on the product management maturity and technical profile of the business, and it will inevitably vary across companies – some companies have as many as 10 levels. The names and responsibilities for roles vary – particularly between the tech sector and other sectors – but generally, introductory roles (e.g., product owner, associate product manager) manage and prioritize a team's backlog based on the business goals, team constraints, and stakeholder expectations. These people help determine what the agile team should be working on.

More senior roles (chief product officer, senior director, vice president) have broad responsibility for the business's most important products or set of products. They set strategy across the portfolio of products and have end-to-end accountability for the whole product lifecycle of all the products. Their teams can be as large as 5,000 people and some will report directly to the CEO.

Advancement along the product owner career path should be clearly defined, with specific skills between roles clearly communicated. Exhibit 15.3 shows a sample progression of business skills for a product owner.

Product management expert and managerial career tracks

CAREER PATHS

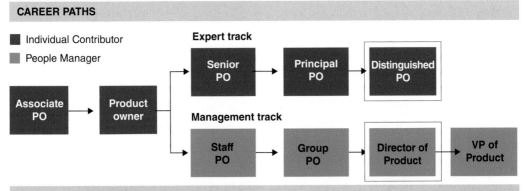

ROLES AND RESPONSIBILITIES

	Expert track: Distinguished PO	Management track: Director of Product
Scope of responsibility	Works on cutting-edge technologies, products, or customer experiences	Works on managing profitability across a flagship product or product group (or journey)
	Works on flagship or strategic products facing severe competition	Leads work on multiple features or products, by providing vision and managing performance
	Works on strategic products important for critical customers (B2B) leaders, and pod members	
Organizational influence	Able to rally support from senior leadership across functions on new product experience vision and ideas	Able to rally support from senior leadership across functions
	Able to build and lead a rockstar cross-functional team	Able to manage a budget to deliver on specific projects and ideas
	Sought by other POs and colleagues as a mentor and educator	Able to build, coach, and performance manage a team of POs
	Helps in recruiting, retaining, and coaching fellow POs and engineers	Coaches fellow POs and other colleagues on best practices
		Responsible for recruiting, retaining, and coaching POs
Market influence	Presents thought leadership and is a published author on technical topics	Serves as the external face of the product/product group
	Develops strong relationships with ecosystem – OSS developers, partners, etc	Develops relationships with strategic partners, influencers, and customers
	Communicates product vision to customers and partners with ease, and brings on early adopters	Communicates product vision to customers and partners with ease
		Able to attract the best talent by creating a compelling employee value proposition

EXHIBIT 15.2

Product Owner: Skills framework

Critical skills for POs

CUSTOMER EXPERIENCE	**Design thinking:** Take empathetic and design-led approach to problem solving and decision making	**Customer centricity:** Focus on learning from customer needs and pain points to drive value	**User engagement and feedback:** Regularly engage end users to elicit and implement feedback
MARKET ORIENTATION	**Industry and competitor trends:** Aware of relevant market and technology trends, informing product strategy		**Driving Innovation:** Drive innovative ideas, and provide input for business development
BUSINESS ACUMENT	**Product vision and roadmaps:** Develop product vision and iterative roadmap based on user needs **Go to Market:** Assist with GTM plan for effective product growth and adoption		**Prioritization:** Maintain prioritized backlog of work, and define smart goals focused on value of users **Impact tracking:** Define and track outcome metrics that align to product strategy and business goals
TECHNICAL SKILLS	**Technology planning and execution:** Devise feasible solutions with experts for MVP and releases **Risk management:** Manage risk, engaging others to align on outcomes and business needs		**Ways of working:** Make right trade-offs with teams for continuous improvement **Backlog management:** Create and manage backlog with team(s) for user needs
PRODUCT LEADERSHIP	**Effective execution:** Own, drive and prioritize user-centric product outcomes collaboratively **Communication:** Manage stakeholder and sponsor communications **Inspire and Influence:** Be a thought leader who generates followership through ideas		**People development:** Build high performing team culture through passion, trust, collaboration **Collaboration:** Co-create features and facilitate alignment on dependencies across teams to drive value

SAMPLE SKILL PROGRESSION – USER ENGAGEMENT AND FEEDBACK

DEVELOPING	PROFICIENT	EXPERT
Ability to collect and consider some feedback, without paying attention to ideas that throw a plan offtrack	Regular interactions with customers and end users, with some data analysis feeding back into backlog	Close and consistent collaboration with end users and designers from product idea origination to operational deployments – ensuring validated customer insights impact the backlog

EXHIBIT 15.3

Given the importance of understanding the industry and the business itself, product owners are often sourced internally from marketing, operations, R&D, and IT. In fact, technical people who have an interest in business make good candidates for product-management roles. Too often, however, companies pick either a project manager or someone from the business without previous product-management experience to fill this role, with little training or support.

It is not easy training a good product owner. It takes time, support, and practice – product management is a craft that must be learned over years. Some product owner bootcamps lasting about eight weeks can offer intense instruction to build specific skills (e.g., how to design customer surveys, how to create OKRs, how to write a press brief and FAQ for a planned product, etc.). The best programs combine classroom learning with immersive training that simulates real-world customer problems.

Exhibit 15.4 shows how one bank approached a training for 300 product owners. They conducted the program in three three-month waves, with 100 product owners in each one. Product owners had the opportunity to put into practice what they'd learned in a cap-stone project, supported by hands-on coaching. This training included about 20 hours of training over four classroom forums and another 20 hours of capstone learning with the support of a product owner coach.

These types of product-oriented programs can be helpful to pro-vide a foundation of skills, but on their own aren't enough. We often see people emerge from these skill-building programs only to plunge back into a business-as-usual work environment where they can't use their new skills. You will need to ensure teams use the same artifacts (e.g., tools and templates), have the same under-standing of what a product owner is responsible for, and use similar review processes during QBR meetings to create a true product management craft.

Field & Forum product management upskilling program

Example for a US financial institution

	FORUM 1 **Discovery phase**	**FORUM 2** **Viability phase I**	**FORUM 3** **Viability phase II**	**FORUM 4** **Build phase**
Learning goal	Understanding problem space and defining product vision	Empathizing with the user and defining the "How" (innovative and not incremental)	Communicating value and engaging with customers and engineers	Converting product idea into execution
Forum learning	**5 hours** Understanding problem space and market opportunity • Market requirements document • Competitive analysis Defining product vision • Press release and frequently asked questions • Business model canvas • Roadmap	**5 hours** Portfolio prioritization (data-backed) Understanding user and key unmet needs • User persona (includes methods of research) • As-is journey Defining how we want to solve the unmet need • To-be journey • Prototype	**5 hours** Defining and measuring success • Product success metrics • Objectives and key results Communicating and engaging with customers • Positioning statement • Product one-pager • Customer pitch deck Converting product idea into requirements • Product requirements document	**5 hours** Overview of Build phase & continuous development approach Minimum Viable Product mindset Ongoing refinement and prioritization • Product backlog Leadership development — Influencing w/o authority Demo day overview and objectives
Field training	**Field capstone project** (20 hours) Cohorts of ~100 PM; Program executed ~3 months			
Core PO skills	Market orientation Business acumen Customer-experience grounding	Business acumen Customer-experience grounding Technical skills	Business acumen Customer-experience grounding Soft skills Technical skills	Soft skills Technical skills Business acumen

EXHIBIT 15.4

The skills and capabilities of product owners will need to evolve. Product owners of the future, for example, will be analytics gurus. They will be able to quickly spin up a data cluster in the cloud, pull usage data, analyze the data, and draw insights. They will be adept at applying machine-learning concepts and tools that are specifically designed to augment the product owner's decision making.

We anticipate that most modern product owners will spend at least 30% of their time on external activities like engaging with customers and the partner ecosystem. Such engagement will not be limited to consumer products – as the consumerization of IT continues, B2B product owners will directly connect with end users rather than extracting feedback through multiple layers of sales intermediaries.

Note

1. Chandra Gnanasambandam, Martin Harrysson, Jeremy Schneider, and Rikki Singh, "What separates top product managers from the rest of the pack," McKinsey.com, January 20, 2023, https://www.mckinsey.com/industries/technology-media-and-telecommunications/our-insights/what-separates-top-product-managers-from-the-rest-of-the-pack.

Chapter 16

Customer experience design: The magic ingredient

When you start to develop your powers of empathy and imagination, the whole world opens up to you.

—Susan Sarandon

You can do the planning, the developing, the hiring, and the investing, but if the customer – either internal or external – doesn't want to use the digital solution you've created, none of that matters. This tension – between what users need and what companies want to launch or know how to build – is what makes customer experience design an essential ingredient in your digital and AI transformation, with the power to drive innovation, adoption, and value.[1]

Every company wants to be customer centric. They all want to offer products, experiences, and services that customers or users love. Those who really stand out on this front have created disproportionate value. Our research shows that design-driven companies had much higher revenue growth and higher TRS growth over a five-year period than their peers.[2] User experience design, as it's most often referred to, acts like a magic ingredient added to a digital recipe.

That value is as real for B2B companies as it is for B2C ones. We have found that in heavy industrial settings, user experience (UX) design is just as important in having front-line operators adopt new digital solutions. Any company that is serious about its digital and AI transformation will need to build up a UX design capability in the following four ways.

Hire great designers first

Don't postpone hiring designers. Some companies prefer to focus their budget on only hiring hard-core engineers. That's usually a mistake. After a year of development, they find out that customers/users are not adopting the solution they developed because its usage is clunky.

Start with a small nucleus, perhaps 5–10, CX designers and build from there. We have found that great customer experience designers can be hired from other industries, design firms, or even out of graduate schools. Increasingly, top schools are offering MBA programs that incorporate design thinking.

Know what you are looking for. Designers are not all the same. Design roles have tended to cluster around four competencies (see Exhibit 16.1). Before hiring and building up your design capability, be clear about what competencies you really need.

Different design competencies

	CORE COMPETENCIES	CORE METHODS*
Service design	Skilled in analytical parsing of root causes and secondary effects from a frontstage and backstage delivery of a product or service Can think systematically, i.e., systems thinking – seeing components as part of a larger whole Ability to negotiate between business, technical, and user needs and goals to achieve satisfactory solution	Business model canvas Blueprints, ecosystem maps Feature prioritization matrix Problem-solving frameworks Leading design workshops Tools: Figma, Sketch, Adobe Creative Suite
Design research	Skilled in conducting qualitative research, e.g., contextual interviews, diary studies, longitudinal work studies, etc. Ability to field surveys and conduct usability testing Versed in best practice methods to ensure valid results and synthesis of insights Awareness and increasing knowledge of analytics and other quantitative research methods	Interview guides Surveys Personas Journeys, workflow maps Pathway analysis, with analytics Tools: Dovetail, UserTesting.com
UX design	Skilled in human-centered design, predominantly for digital solutions but also inclusive of service design Able to develop coherent solutions that address user needs and accords to best practices	Experience concepts, interaction models Information architecture, navigations Wireframes Prototypes Tools: Figma, Sketch, Adobe Creative Suite
Visual design	Skilled in compositional balance, color theory, iconography, etc. Masters visual design patterns and systems, including but not exclusively brand architecture Skilled in visual system development and documentation best practices	Brand expressions and extensions Mood boards, asset libraries Interaction design frameworks Omnichannel design patterns Visual design Tools: Adobe Creative Suite, Sketch, Invision

* Core methods are not exhaustive

EXHIBIT 16.1

Invest in a CX-design development process

The CX-design approach can neatly be defined as a two-part process: design the right thing, then design the thing right.

Designing the right thing is about figuring out what users want. Designers spend time with users to identify needs in ways no quantitative or marketing survey can. Solid customer insights gathered firsthand by observing users in their own environments can be a powerful way to uncover both functional and emotional needs. Use data for sure, but don't forget the "empathy" side of the equation.

An increasing array of methodologies exist to conduct consumer research, but they require a clear view of which tool can best service which purpose (see Exhibit 16.2).

The way designers capture insights about customers' unmet needs is evolving rapidly. You will want to make sure that your design team has an excellent mastery of those techniques.

Designing the thing right – the second part of the process – can only happen when a firm understanding of both the customer need and the problem to solve is in place. Don't be tempted to jump ahead. Prototyping without understanding and aligning on the first part of the process inevitably leads to delays.

The process goes through five stages, as outlined in Exhibit 16.3. At each of these stages, designers will leverage a suite of design tools to create their end products. The tooling suite must be standardized to drive team productivity and work product reuse.

In the early stages of this process, it is crucial to make ideas tangible as early as possible. For this reason, we recommend starting with a "quick and dirty" low-fi option, often mockups on a piece of paper. Then rapidly test these with real customers, and iterate toward ever more sophisticated versions, such as fake apps, before settling on a working product for engineers to develop. While this process might

Range of research methods to gather customer feedback

● Natural use of product   ■ Scripted (often lab-based) use of product

▲ Decontextualized/not using product   ◆ Combination/hybrid

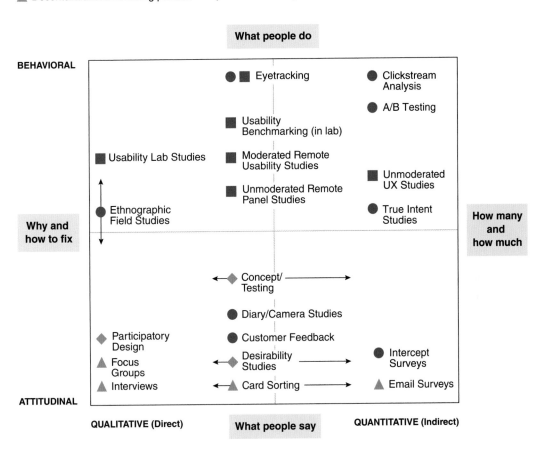

QUALITATIVE

Answers the "Why"

Deep understanding of user behaviors and emotional needs

Uncovers needs users don't even know

Observation-based; ability to co-create with users

QUANTITATIVE

Answers the "How Many and How Much"

Quantify data and generalize results from a sample of population

Opinion-based and validates hypotheses or solutions with statistically reliable data

EXHIBIT 16.2

seem time consuming, it almost always results in faster development (because the teams know exactly what to build) and better outcomes (because the user gets what they want).

Process and tools to go from design to development

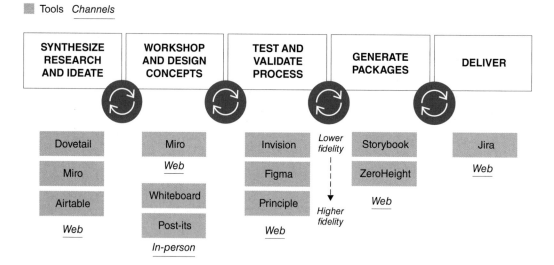

EXHIBIT 16.3

Tools like Figma, which allow for much faster prototyping to test highly functional products or services without having to write code, are heralding a tech-driven acceleration in design. New low-code/no-code and generative AI technologies like GPT-4 will also rapidly change the complexion of this development process. Drag-and-drop functionality that automatically generates code in the background is reducing development time from weeks to days, or days to hours. This will increasingly give experience design teams more time to test and refine their products and services.

One hurdle we often see companies hit during this prototyping process is the excessive focus on delivering features and functionality when developing the MVP (minimum viable product). This focus can lead to a prototype working as expected but the user not having a good experience with it. Development pods instead should focus on developing a "minimal lovable product" that focuses on how much the end user actually enjoys using the product or service. As an example, this might mean that rather than narrowing down the arrival windows that a service operator might offer (to install cable, for example), the company would focus on contacting the customer with an alert when the service person is nearby, which the customer appreciates more.

This focus on meeting user needs leads to greater adoption of the products or services created, simpler applications and experiences, a substantial reduction of low-value features, and better financial performance.

Make UX design part of your teams from the very beginning

CX and design experts need to be core parts of agile pods from the very beginning. Too often, however, a business sponsor will think they know the customer needs and so believe they don't need designers until much later in the development process. This is a mistake. Best-in-class organizations deliver great customer experiences by embedding design into every aspect of the product or service development.

Designers guide development processes by, for example, ensuring customer input throughout sprints, driving concepting, creating core experience artifacts, such as personas and user journeys (the series of interactions to achieve an end), and ensuring the team uses them throughout product development. They map each customer journey with a focus on identifying pain points and potential sources of delight rather than starting with "copy and paste" technical specs from the last product.

Link every part of CX design to value

The best companies are deeply focused on connecting customer experience to value. As teams develop journey maps, they identify and link the points in those journeys with key business performance metrics and the value it generates. For example, improving a bank's customer care interactions within a customer journey will result in happier customers, and therefore lower churn. This type of analysis enables designers to home in on where the greatest differences in value lie.

These metrics aren't for show. You should assess design performance with the same rigor you use to track revenues and costs. Companies can now build design metrics (such as satisfaction ratings and usability assessments) into product specifications, just as they include requirements for grades of materials or target times to market.

Notes

1. See "Driving business impact through customer centricity and digital agility," McKinsey.com, July 30, 2021, https://www.mckinsey.com/capabilities/mckinsey-digital/our-insights/driving-business-impact-through-customer-centricity-and-digital-agility.
2. Benedict Sheppard, Hugo Sarrazin, Garen Kouyoumjian, and Fabricio Dore, "The business value of design," *McKinsey Quarterly*, October 25, 2018, https://www.mckinsey.com/capabilities/mckinsey-design/our-insights/the-business-value-of-design.

Getting Ready
Section Three

The following is a set of questions to help you home in on the right actions to take:

Is the C-suite aligned on the operating model to enable hundreds of pods to deliver digital innovations?

Are the OKRs for each pod aligned to business priorities?

Are "control functions" (e.g., finance, legal, regulatory) part of your agile process along with business and technology?

In what way are your financial and governance processes aligned to serve a more agile operating model?

How are you measuring the advances in speed and agility that your organization is making?

How many of your teams and solutions are led by a high-quality product owner?

Are your customer experience and design experts part of your agile teams, and are they involved early enough in the process?

Technology for Speed and Distributed Innovation

Building a technology environment that empowers the entire organization to digitally innovate

At its simplest form, the objective for technology is to make it easy for your pods to constantly develop and release digital and AI innovations to customers and users. Achieving this requires building a distributed technology environment where every pod can access the data, applications, and software development tools they need to rapidly innovate and deliver secure, high-quality solutions.

Recent and maturing technology advances – including the thoughtful use of APIs to decouple applications, the availability of developer tooling, the selective migration of high-value workloads to the cloud, and the automation of infrastructure provisioning – can create this distributed environment.

Those of you who do not come from a tech background may be tempted to skip this section. Don't! You need to know the basics about technology to be an effective leader in the digital world. While this section does dig into some of the specifics of a fast-evolving technology landscape, it also highlights the most important issues and topics to understand to be an effective digital leader.[1]

Seven broad capabilities are needed to build a technology environment that can support a digital transformation:

Chapter 17: Decoupled architecture for development flexibility and operational scalability. The overarching design principles and choices to build a decoupled architecture that will enable your pods to innovate by minimizing dependencies - say hello to APIs.

Chapter 18: A more surgical and value-backed approach to cloud. Focus on meaningful business domains when migrating your applications to the cloud so you can ensure the maximum ROI of your cloud investment.

Chapter 19: Engineering practices for speed and high-quality code. The automation of software development and deployment is fundamental to building and releasing high-quality software.

Chapter 20: The tools to make your developers highly productive. Build a developer platform to make it easy for all your engineers to be productive and avoid tool proliferation.

Chapter 21: Delivering production-grade digital solutions. Creating the conditions for secure, controlled, and scalable production environment through automation.

Chapter 22: Build in security and automation from the start. Automating security checks throughout the software development process. This is what accelerates overall development velocity and ensures that all digital solutions are secure and robust.

Chapter 23: MLOps so AI can scale. AI/ML models are 'living organisms' that require monitoring and constant data retraining. That's why MLOps automation tooling is needed to scale AI.

Note

1. Thomas Elsner, Peter Maier, Gerard Richter, and Katja Zolper, "What CIOs need from their CEOs and boards to make IT digital ready," McKinsey. com, December 1, 2021, https://www.mckinsey.com/capabilities/ mckinsey-digital/our-insights/what-cios-need-from-their-ceos-and-boards-to-make-it-digital-ready; Steve Van Kuiken, "Boards and the cloud," McKinsey.com, November 18, 2021, https://www.mckinsey.com/ capabilities/strategy-and-corporate-finance/our-insights/boards-and-the-cloud.

Chapter 17

Decoupled architecture for development flexibility and operational scalability

We shape our buildings; thereafter they shape us.

—Winston Churchill

A platform architecture supports systems of engagement (front end) and systems of record (back end) as well as the data and analytics needed to develop solutions and drive the digital and AI transformation. The best architectures provide flexibility, stability, and speed so that agile pods throughout the organization can build the solutions needed to deliver the digital roadmap. The key concept here is that a distributed and decoupled architecture is needed to enable teams to assemble modular and reusable components (see Exhibit 17.1).

Four foundational shifts to upgrade architecture for digital

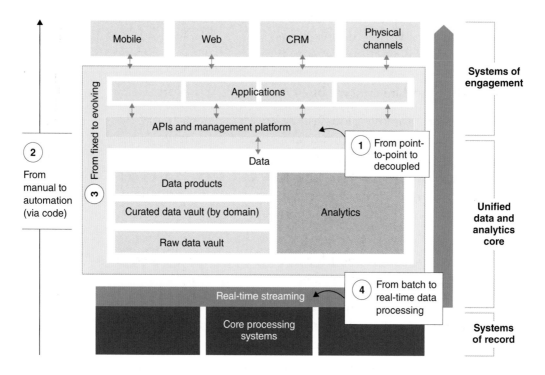

EXHIBIT 17.1

An enterprise architecture team decides on the overarching architecture design philosophies and choices for all agile pods within the enterprise, as well as the engineering practices those agile pods need to follow.

Enabling this kind of architecture requires you to embrace the cloud as your technology foundation (more on this in Chapter 18) and drive the following four key shifts in how it operates:

From point-to-point to decoupled

From an architecture perspective, decoupling (literally separating connections between points in one system and another) enables an organization to evolve its applications independently from one another, thus improving the organization's agility and ability to scale. The following two techniques are used for decoupling.

Adopt API-based interfaces, but manage proliferation

Application programming interfaces (APIs) allow pods to expose their data and application functionalities to other pods within the enterprise or externally to customers or partners. APIs essentially enable breaking down large monolith applications into microservices. This shift is a fundamental cornerstone to enable hundreds of pods to innovate without constantly running into dependencies with other pods.

Jeff Bezos at Amazon is famously known for a memo that changed Amazon and the world of software[1]. In essence, it said:

- All teams will expose their data and functionality through service interfaces (i.e., APIs) and teams must communicate with each other through these interfaces.
- There will be no other form of interprocess communication allowed: no direct linking, no direct reads of another team's data store, no shared-memory model, no backdoors whatsoever. The only communication allowed is via service interface calls over the network.
- It doesn't matter what technology they use. HTTP, Corba, Pubsub, custom protocols – doesn't matter. Bezos doesn't care.
- All service interfaces, without exception, must be designed from the ground up to be externalizable. That is to say, the team must plan and design to be able to expose the interface to developers in the outside world. No exceptions.
- Anyone who doesn't do this will be fired.

APIs simplify integration between applications by shielding development teams from the complexity of different layers, which speeds time to market and reduces the chance of causing new problems in existing applications. These interfaces also allow for easier replacement of individual components as requirements change.

Given these advantages, however, companies tend to create too many APIs. The often-massive proliferation of APIs is as disadvantageous as the propagation of web services and even point-to-point interfaces in legacy architectures. Minimize the number of APIs and optimize their use. APIs are absolutely key to decoupling, but they need to be managed.[2]

The presentation and usability of APIs are crucial to being able to take advantage of their benefits. Use a management platform (often called a gateway) to create and publish APIs, implement usage policies, control access, and measure usage and performance. This platform also allows agile pods to search for existing APIs and reuse them rather than build new ones. Put in place standards, guidelines, and a taxonomy to ensure consistent creation and use of APIs.

One pharma company, for example, set up an internal "data marketplace" for all employees via APIs to simplify and standardize access to core data assets, rather than relying on proprietary interfaces. The company gradually – over 18 months – migrated its most valuable existing data feeds to an API-based structure and deployed a management platform to expose the APIs to users. This architecture for enterprise data enabled significant acceleration in the development and deployment of analytics- and AI-based innovations.

In their words: An API transformation

"[We first prioritized our APIs by structuring] the existing services we had on our enterprise service bus (ESB) in standard banking domains, such as customer and product. We also prioritized certain nonbanking

APIs as "common" or "channel engagement," such as campaigns, offers, and optical character recognition (OCR) functionalities.

We then prioritized the services based on relevance for our transformation—that is, when we would need to decouple each IT platform to drive the modernization—as well as on their level of complexity. Based on these criteria, we could better understand what the overall effort of "API-zing" our IT architecture would be. Then we started to outline the operating model and governance, in addition to detailing the API taxonomy, standards, and guidelines. Last, we decided on the technology solution for the API management platform and other relevant components and started the first proof of concept.

We outlined the importance and potential of APIs for both technology and business to our management and dedicated a significant part of the budget to it. We had initial funding that was sufficient to lay the technological foundation, define the required standards and policies, and migrate all our services from the legacy ESB to microservices accessible via our standard APIs. We now have roughly 800 microservices available.

This foundation allowed us to establish three agile squads that worked only on building APIs in the different domains. We kick-started our API effort by running several API awareness sessions in IT, and we also spread awareness among our business colleagues to help our employees understand the opportunities.

To drive API adoption, it was crucial to implement a user-friendly developer portal with good documentation and sufficient search functionalities. We looked for best practices across the globe. Moreover, we invested in training our developers to familiarize them with the developer portal and with the API guidelines and standards right from the beginning. We wanted to lay the right foundations so we could easily scale when the time was right.

After initial small successes with the internal use cases and some external ones, the business demand grew significantly. They wanted additional APIs—and they wanted them quickly, so we created an agile budgeting and prioritization process to cater to the increased demand.

One of our biggest challenges was to get the right talent to drive our API approach. Completely redesigning the integration architecture, setting up an API management platform and developer portal, and continuously prioritizing the initial API backlog are very complex tasks. On the one hand, we needed experienced engineers who knew the technological details, and on the other hand, we needed experienced product owners to ensure a laser focus on the right priorities.

In the beginning, there were several concerns about being able to build up the required talent in Dubai, since tech talent is not readily available. However, we managed to do it through a balanced combination of hiring and developing our existing talent. One key element to our success was establishing dedicated learning journeys for the different roles we needed with a combination of internal and external courses as well as certification programs.

Later on in our journey, we faced the challenge of increasing the productivity of our agile API squads. When we started, it was acceptable for our teams to deliver one API in two-to-three-week sprints. However, to follow our roadmap, we needed to increase our productivity dramatically. We leveraged DevOps automation tools to optimize the integration and maintain continuous deployment and delivery and doubled our API output."

—Saud Al Dhawyani, chief technology officer, Emirates NDB

Leverage a cloud-based data platform

A data platform "buffers" transactions outside of core systems. It pools data for analytically intensive applications and enables asynchronous data usage. Such buffers can be provided via a data lake or a distributed data mesh, which is an ecosystem consisting of best-fit platforms created for each business domain's expected data usage and workloads (see Chapter 26 on data architecture).

In a more advanced data architecture, there is further buffering with the creation of data products that enable high-quality data and simplified consumption (see Chapter 25 on data products).

Exhibit 17.2 provides an overview of a modern application architecture implemented by a medical device manufacturer for its consumer application. The front door gateway controls inbound traffic and ensures security. The API layer resolves which application services are being requested. The cloud-based data platform is organized as bulk data storage in the data lake and more curated data products ready for user or application consumption (e.g., customer data, medical product, and location data to ensure compliance with local regulations).

Exhibit 17.3 shows the detailed schematic illustrating how the architecture was put together. It is usually at this level of detail that solution architects and full-stack engineers would typically engage. This architecture was built in Azure with the addition of best-in-class and/or open-source tools. It should be straightforward to do the one-to-one mapping between Exhibits 17.2 and 17.3. All business leaders should understand their solution architecture at the level of Exhibit 17.2 while architects and engineers should master this at the level of Exhibit 17.3.

From manual to automated via code

The cost of manually provisioning infrastructure, or manually building and deploying software, cannot be underestimated. Not only is this process slow and cumbersome, but it is also error prone. To eliminate these issues, leading companies implement infrastructure automation and software delivery automation:

Automate infrastructure provisioning

Using infrastructure as code (IaC) enables agile pods to provision cloud environments and infrastructure, storage, and any other services they need in a repeatable, cost-effective, and reliable manner. Explicitly code all infrastructure specifications in configuration files to create a "single source of truth." This also creates a useful trail of all changes, and simplifies reversions if needed.

Modern application architecture[1] – overview

Example of consumer application architecture for a global medical device company

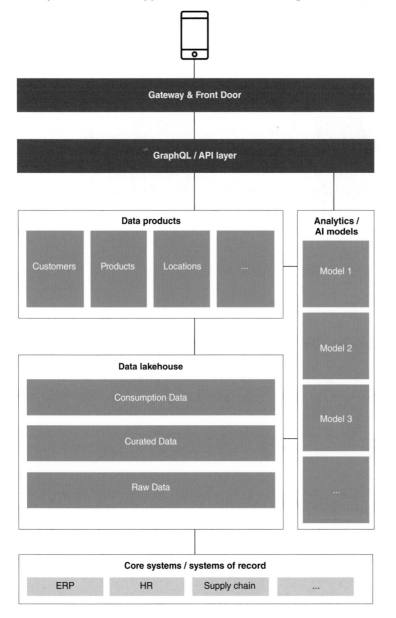

Gateway & Front Door
Controls traffic and adds security

GraphQL/API platform
Resolves what services to call to return exact data needs

Data products
Each data product has its own storage and scaling capacities, allowing the data needs to scale/evolve

Data lakehouse
Data from core systems and Apps get stored in data lakehouse. This then follows a process of cleansing and structuring the data for consumption

Analytics/AI models
Advanced analytic/AI models generate insights for the app to consumer

Core systems/ systems of record
Systems that run core business operations of the company

1. Serverless, microservices with Data lakehouse storage and Data Science capabilities

EXHIBIT 17.2

Modern application architecture – detailed schematic

Example of consumer application architecture for a global medical device company

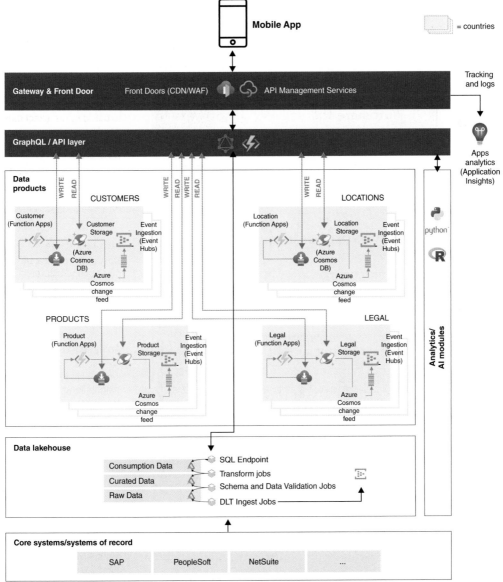

Companies need to be aware of local regulations when deciding on where data is housed

EXHIBIT 17.3

To promote code reuse and avoid duplication, enforce the creation of blocks of code when writing infrastructure scripts. Create a simple and user-friendly way to catalog these high-quality code blocks in a single place and make them easy for developers to find (see Chapter 20). Examples of IaC code blocks in Google Cloud Platform (GCP) could include setting up a Cloud Asset Inventory service that provides visibility into resources to monitor, analyze, and understand all assets across projects. Another example is setting up a Compute Engine, a service to be able to provision high-performance virtual machines inside a virtual private cloud.

Automate the delivery of software to production

Automating the building, testing, validation, and deployment of software is such an important topic that we dedicate an entire chapter to discussing how this is done (see Chapter 19).

From fixed to evolving

There are many similarities between the construction industry and computing industry – however, the notion of having a perfect, pre-planned architecture before any development occurs is not one of them. The technology changes at a rapid rate. The technology and architecture that support your organization will evolve over time so building in the necessary flexibility is essential. The idea is to be able to introduce new data, analytics, and software development tools without having to change everything.

Make this shift by moving toward a modular architecture that uses best-of-breed and, frequently, open-source components that can be replaced with new technologies as needed without affecting other parts of the architecture. Practically, this requires developing clear standards to prevent the proliferation of tools that have more or less the same functionality, and having well-designed interfaces between components to minimize variability and complexity resulting from system dependencies.

The enterprise architecture team should not sit in an ivory tower away from agile pods but work closely with them to understand needs and adapt standards over time. This requires enterprise architects to talk to agile pods about the business implications of technology decisions. Hire enterprise architects who understand both these cutting-edge components and tools, and what it takes to deliver modern software.

From batch to real-time data processing

The costs of real-time data messaging and streaming capabilities have decreased significantly, paving the way for more mainstream use. These technologies enable a host of new business applications. For example, transportation companies can inform customers as their taxi approaches with accurate-to-the-second arrival predictions; insurance companies can analyze real-time behavioral data from smart devices to individualize rates; and manufacturers can predict equipment issues based on real-time sensor data. While unit costs for real-time processing continue to fall, overall costs can be substantial for large data sets so it's important to be thoughtful about which digital solutions really require this kind of capability.

When approaching real-time data processing, you need to decide on the standard for messaging between applications (i.e., messaging platform) and the standard for streaming data. Messaging platforms provide a way for digital applications to publish messages, where applications that subscribe to them can then act on them as they are received. There is an abundance of options for messaging platforms at the enterprise level (e.g., Apache ActiveMQ, Apache Kafka, RabbitMQ, or Amazon Simple Queue Service). Deciding on a standard messaging platform enables digital applications to send and receive discrete messages in a decoupled way without tying those applications together.

Streaming is typically used for analytics or real-time data processing. There are different kinds of streams, e.g., sensors or stock reports, and each one should have its own standard. For example, in fraud detection, streaming can help you analyze and interpret a group of transactions versus each individual transaction (see Exhibit 17.4). As with messaging platforms, there is an abundance of options for streaming at the enterprise level (e.g., Kafka, Amazon Kinesis, Apache Spark, or Apache Flink).

Messaging vs. streaming

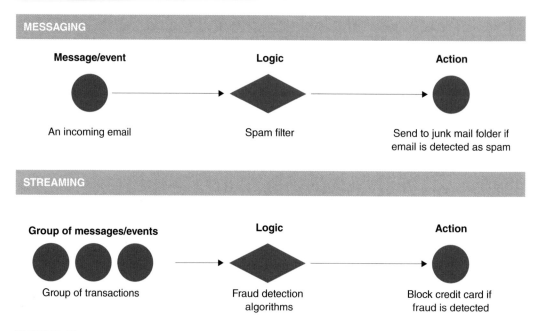

EXHIBIT 17.4

The enterprise architecture team should decide early on with the agile pods what capabilities are needed for messaging and streaming within the organization. Standardization early on will allow agile pods to collaborate more effectively.

Notes

1. Augusto Marietti, "The API Mandate: How a mythical memo from Jeff Bezos changed software forever," Kong, May 23, 2022, https://konghq.com/blog/enterprise/api-mandate.
2. Sven Blumberg, Timo Mauerhofer, Chandrasekhar Panda, and Henning Soller, "The right APIs: Identifying antipatterns of API usage," McKinsey.com, July 30, 2021, https://www.mckinsey.com/capabilities/mckinsey-digital/our-insights/tech-forward/the-right-apis-identifying-antipatterns-of-api-usage.

Chapter 18

A more surgical and value-backed approach to cloud

Revelations are found in clouds.

—*Serge King*

How much cloud migration work should you undertake as part of your digital transformation? That is a tough question, and one made harder by an often-limited understanding of cloud economics and effective migration strategies. The truth is that results from large-scale cloud migration efforts have too often fallen short of promises and, in many cases, led to surprisingly high investments and drawn-out implementations.[1]

Successful integration of the cloud into digital and AI transformation requires an approach based on where the value is.[2] In other words, which business domains have you decided to prioritize on your digital roadmap and what cloud migration approach – if any – will you require for the existing applications in these domains? A more surgical approach to cloud gets to the value faster.

Reimagine the business domain and underlying tech concurrently

Most of the value the cloud generates comes from increased agility, innovation, and resilience provided to the business rather than a lower-cost hosting replacement for traditional infrastructure as found in a data center.

Starting with your priority business domains, be sure to reimagine the domain *and* the underlying technology concurrently. This allows you to develop a clear view of the applications that you need to migrate to get the most value while avoiding the trap of migrating a bunch of applications that are too disconnected to fully exploit the benefits of the cloud.

For example, an insurer that wanted to redesign its customer-onboarding journey launched two workstreams: one that reimagined and simplified the entire onboarding process, and another that modernized the underlying technology in the cloud. The two teams, working together, were able to modernize the omnichannel platform and technology in the cloud, which enabled them to transform what had been a set of disparate, paper-based, channel-specific processes into a seamless, digitally-enabled omnichannel experience.

As you build the technology roadmap for your priority domains, clarify the architectural choices for each of the digital solutions on that roadmap all at once (versus piecemeal). This will provide you with a comprehensive understanding of dependencies and the optimal sequencing to get to value.

Exhibit 18.1 provides a simple framing of the most common architectural choices and related cloud engineering considerations. These can range from leaving the application "as is," to migrating it to the cloud, to retiring it.

Typical architectural options for building digital solutions

Typical architectural options	Banking examples	Engineering considerations
Build new cloud-native application	Build mobile credit card onboarding application with fewest clicks possible	Provide data to flow from core systems to onboarding app and credit analytics
Use core system application "as is" (with a wrapper)	Use "KYC — Know your customer" application in core banking system	Use API to access KYC system application and ensure real-time performance needs
Build new cloud-native features to replace part of a core system application	Build new credit decisioning engine to replace core system credit risk assessment	Build new credit decisioning engine with access to customer data in real-time
Migrate and refactor core system application to cloud to enhance performance innovation	Migrate and refactor entire credit risk assessment application to cloud to accelerate time to market	Decide on best migration option (see cloud migration options)
Change entire core system to enhance performance and reduce unit cost	Change entire core banking system to reduce unit cost and enable broad new suite of features	Run legacy and new core system in parallel and establish data migration strategy

Increasing complexity (vertical label, left axis)

EXHIBIT 18.1

Determine cloud dispositions and migration approach

If a given solution needs to migrate to the cloud (as opposed to being retired or replaced with an SaaS solution), the secondary decision is whether to "rehost" the application to the cloud, to "refactor/rearchitect," or something in between, like "replatforming" (see Exhibit 18.2).

Six options for disposition/migration of legacy applications

1 **Retire**
Applications that are no longer useful and can be retired within the next 1–2 years

2 **Repurchase**
Application that is end-of-life from a technical or business perspective and needs to be replaced with a cloud-native SaaS[1]

3 **Rehost ("lift and shift")**
Application that is lifted and shifted to cloud to quickly implement a larger legacy migration thus enabling exiting of data centers

4 **Replatform**
Change of application platform in order to achieve some tangible benefit without changing core architecture

5 **Refactor/Rearchitect**
Change of architecture, adding features, scale, or performance that would otherwise be difficult to achieve in current app environment

6 **Retain**
Applications that are not ready to be migrated or whose migration does not make sense in terms of benefits

1. If replacing an application, you may build a bespoke application or configure an SaaS application depending on SaaS market maturity and business needs

EXHIBIT 18.2

- **Rehosting** ("lift and shift") involves migrating the application to the cloud with no/limited code or architecture changes. This is an option that businesses choose to make quick progress. But experience shows that simply lifting and shifting applications to the cloud does not generate much value. You need to replatform or refactor applications to take advantage of the benefits of the cloud.

- **Replatforming** involves making relatively easier changes compared to rearchitecting such as changing the data layer interactions and driving value quickly by leveraging some cloud-native capabilities.

- **Refactoring/rearchitecting** involves moving to the public cloud and rearchitecting to take advantage of cloud-native capabilities. While this requires code changes and investments, it is often the best option if the applications need to be significantly enhanced to meet the new business requirements.

Leading organizations usually follow a mix of approaches for their business domain application. Often rehosting or replatforming is the first step in the modernization journey to get value quickly (reduction in costs and some cloud capabilities) before rearchitecting. However, it is critical to assess and modernize at once all relevant applications of the business domain and not take a piecemeal application-by-application approach, which will tend to be more costly.

Migrating applications often requires remediating security and compliance fixes, and optimizing systems in the cloud. Migrating and then optimizing later can help break through the gridlock many companies have experienced with their cloud programs. But this approach requires accepting that some applications may cost more in the short term and offer less performance.

> ### Selecting a cloud service provider
>
> Avoid having individual teams choose their own cloud service provider (CSP). Leaving it to agile pods to independently decide what services to use will eventually lead to fragmentation, complexity, and lack of collaboration throughout the organization. Skills, in many cases, will not be transferable between CSPs. Similarly, the enterprise architecture team should consider what services should be standardized to avoid complexity and technical debt (i.e., what database services or messaging technologies should the enterprise adopt as a standard?). Each CSP offers hundreds of native services and marketplaces that provide access to an ecosystem of third-party services.

Build the cloud foundation

Many cloud efforts fail to scale because companies have not invested in building a solid cloud foundation. You will need a handful of highly-capable cloud architects to build these foundational elements well:

1. **Base cloud capabilities.** These capabilities include network connectivity and routing; centralized firewall and proxy capabilities; identity standardization; enterprise logging, monitoring, and analytics (ELMA); shared enterprise services; golden-image (or primary-image) pipelines; and compliance and security enforcement. Companies can build base capabilities once and reuse them across all isolation zones.

2. **Isolation zones.** Isolation zones (sometimes called landing zones) are cloud environments where applications live. Each zone contains CSP services, identity and access management (IAM), network isolation, capacity management, shared services specific to that isolation zone, and change control where one or more related applications run. Isolation zones provide redundancy in case a zone crashes. You therefore want to have more than one isolation zone to create redundancy but not so many that you create complexity.

   Aligning on the number of isolation zones is a critical decision. With a single isolation zone, configuration changes to support one application can unintentionally affect others. Going to the other extreme – one isolation zone for each application – prevents the efficient deployment of configuration changes, requiring the same work to be carried out across many isolation zones.

3. **Application patterns.** These are code artifacts that automate the secure, compliant, and standardized configuration and deployment of applications with similar functional and nonfunctional requirements. Application patterns can be responsible for configuring shared resources, standardizing deployment pipelines, and ensuring quality and security compliance. Examples of application patterns include data-processing patterns such as SQL DB, NoSQL DB, data mart/warehouse; web apps such as a static website or three-tier web app; APIs, etc. The number of patterns needed to support the inventory of applications should be small, therefore maximizing ROI. For example, one large bank successfully used just 10 application patterns to satisfy 95% of its necessary use cases.

These foundational elements enable a potential eightfold acceleration in the pace of cloud migration and adoption, and a 50% reduction in migration costs over the long term.[3]

Build up your FinOps capability

The most efficient cloud economics is about paying for capacity only when you need it, rather than paying for capacity you don't use. You achieve this by choosing the cloud services that best match the current workload requirements. This can lead to savings on cloud spend of up to 20%.

Top-performing enterprises develop this capability by bringing together technical, financial, and sourcing talent to create FinOps teams to manage cloud spend. This team needs to identify the business's compute and network needs, often using advanced analytics to help forecast demand, then translate the needs into optimal cloud offerings and pricing arrangements. They use cloud tools to create automated dashboards to track cloud usage and reallocate resources to optimize spend. The FinOps team also tracks enterprise-wide cloud spend to ensure financial discipline.

The cloud is a huge force multiplier. You will need cloud capabilities to digitally transform but that doesn't necessarily mean having to migrate all workloads. A top-notch team of cloud architects and FinOps experts can navigate the necessary choices and tradeoffs (and pay for themselves many times over).

Notes

1. Abhi Bhatnagar, Bailey Caldwell, Alharith Hussin, and Abdallah Saleme, "Cloud economics and the six most damaging mistakes to avoid," McKinsey.com, May 3, 2022, https://www.mckinsey.com/capabilities/mckinsey-digital/our-insights/cloud-economics-and-the-six-most-damaging-mistakes-to-avoid.
2. Aamer Baig and James Kaplan, "Five steps for finding value in the cloud," *CIO*, February 2, 2022, https://www.cio.com/article/304106/5-steps-for-finding-value-in-the-cloud.html; See "Seven lessons on how technology transformations can deliver value," McKinsey.com, March 11, 2021, https://www.mckinsey.com/capabilities/mckinsey-digital/our-insights/seven-lessons-on-how-technology-transformations-can-deliver-value.
3. Aaron Bawcom, Sebastian Becerra, Beau Bennett, and Bill Gregg, "Cloud foundations: Ten commandments for faster – and more profitable – cloud migrations," McKinsey.com, April 21, 2022, https://www.mckinsey.com/capabilities/mckinsey-digital/our-insights/cloud-foundations-ten-commandments-for-faster-and-more-profitable-cloud-migrations.

Chapter 19

Engineering practices for speed and high-quality code

Engineers turn dreams into reality.

—*Hayao Miyazaki*

It used to be that releasing new software was like releasing a major new car model: years of design, engineering, and rigorous testing, often followed by a big marketing event and a launch party. But better methods and tools have come to the fore – including the increasing advantages of open source software – allowing development teams to progress through the different phases of their software development and release new features quickly and iteratively. This has changed the game – every company now needs to become a software company.[1] At the heart of this revolution is the automation of the software development lifecycle (SDLC), the focus of this chapter (see Exhibit 19.1).

Software development life cycle (SDLC)

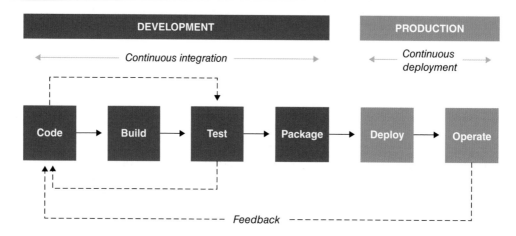

EXHIBIT 19.1

Automation of the SDLC allows agile teams to make small changes, validate quickly (through rapid feedback mechanisms), test frequently, and iterate continually – a stark contrast to the pervasive approach where teams make large changes in batches during release windows, then release to production. Due to the size of those changes, and the number of things that are changed, any number of issues could possibly arise and slow the agile pod's ability to iterate quickly.

Netflix created a cloud-based IT architecture that allows its developers to launch hundreds of software changes a day. Its website comprises hundreds of microservices hosted in the cloud, and each service is developed and maintained by a dedicated team. Developers don't need to request resources from the IT operations team; instead, they can automatically build pieces of code into deployable web images. As those images are updated with new features or services, they can be integrated with Netflix's existing infrastructure using a custom-built, web-based platform on which infrastructure clusters are created. Testing is carefully done in the production environment with a subset of users.

Once the web images are live, a load-balancing technology routes part of the traffic to them from older versions. Automated monitoring ensures that if something goes wrong with the deployment of new images, traffic is routed back to older versions, and the new images are rolled back. Because of this level of automation, Netflix can deploy new code into its production environment within hours, where most companies would need months.[2]

While Netflix might represent a more highly evolved state than most companies need, any modern software development could use these techniques. Underpinning these successful "small-and-fast" engineering practices through the SDLC are the following three needs:

Ground rapid software delivery in DevOps

DevOps seeks to apply the principles of lean manufacturing to the way organizations deliver software into users' hands. DevOps is a shorthand way of saying, "We are going to bring all the people that develop applications together with all the people that operate and secure those applications into integrated working teams." To be clear, operations doesn't go away; it becomes part of development.

By now, many companies have heard of DevOps and are *attempting* to adopt it. But many still struggle to implement DevOps at scale, tending to think of it as a tool or an expert that's added to existing teams. To implement DevOps, you will need to adopt three principles and associated practices:

1. **Flow.** Accelerate the delivery of work from development so that it arrives speedily and efficiently into users' hands. Start by mapping out the value stream across the SDLC, i.e., what steps are involved to code, build, test, package, and deploy software in the environment. This is a manual process initially. Next, identify the time it takes between steps, and any *manual* processes that engineers follow through the SDLC. For example, this could identify that engineers in an agile pod have to ask another team

to do some work on their behalf. Finally, systematically reduce or remove any manual steps that have been identified, by automating (see below for CI/CD). Start with the steps that are the largest time sinks as a way of prioritizing this effort.

2. **Feedback.** Enable multiple feedback loops across the SDLC value stream to help agile pods diagnose issues as they arise, so they can be addressed readily. This is done by building dashboards to visualize the value stream, taking live input from various steps in the SDLC.

3. **Continuous learning.** Create a culture of sharing lessons, learning, and continuous improvement. Periodically review and seek improvements throughout the SDLC, ensuring pods can efficiently deliver software into users' hands without having to endure manual processes.

Companies will typically create a DevOps team to carry out this specialized work. That team will also work with the different pods to train them and ensure consistent adoption.

With a firm foundation in DevOps, companies are extending those capabilities into other code development practices such as DevSecOps, MLOps, and DataOps (see Exhibit 19.2). The spirit of these capabilities is to continuously push automation, machine learning, and data management tasks to increase development velocity, improve security, and reduce cost.

- **DevSecOps** embeds security into the development and release process rather than having it come at the end. As with DevOps, companies can increase the frequency of software releases from quarterly to weekly, or even daily, without compromising their risk posture. Getting security and compliance right from the outset is imperative as companies' growing dependence on digital technologies makes them more vulnerable to cyberattack.[3] In many cases, DevSecOps has replaced DevOps and the two are used interchangeably. We explore the topic of security in depth in Chapter 22.

- **MLOps** builds on DevOps, but for machine learning (ML) and AI models. Any company that tries to develop, maintain, and improve hundreds of ML/AI models in production understands the challenges in ensuring that prediction models are stable and accurate, and well calibrated against an evolving data environment. That's where MLOps comes in. We explore MLOps in detail in Chapter 23.

The family of xOps practices

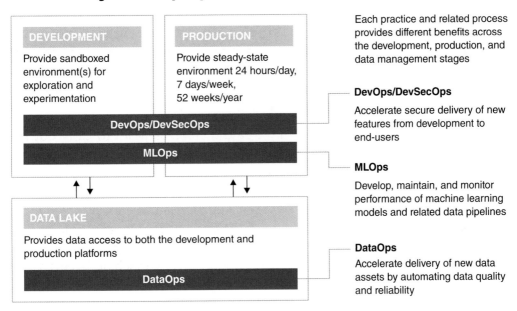

EXHIBIT 19.2

- **DataOps** is also a relatively new and rapidly growing field. It's essentially a capability to accelerate the delivery of new data assets and update existing ones while also boosting data quality. We explore DataOps in Chapter 26.

Improve quality through coding standards and code maintainability

As the number of agile pods increases and the code they generate multiplies – the typical smartphone app has 50,000 lines of code – it has become imperative for organizations to focus on code standards. The CEO of an electric vehicle manufacturing company includes code quality on his dashboard.

With an absence of focus on code standards, the time it takes to make changes to code increases, the code becomes more complex, engineers become increasingly frustrated, and tech debt increases.

Technical debt: What it is and how to measure it

With the great array of digital solutions and teams supporting a digital transformation, there is a significant risk of creating technical debt. Technical debt is the "tax" companies pay on any development to redress technology issues. The tech debt comes from the accumulation of poor coding practices, such as taking shortcuts, submitting badly written code, making temporary fixes (that inevitably become permanent), and implementing one-off solutions. Technical debt hidden in the architecture can spring surprises that make projects run over budget and miss deadlines. With too much tech debt, much of IT employees' time is spent managing complexity rather than thinking innovatively about the future.

Tech debt continues to rise in the majority of organizations we examined. Furthermore, almost half of firms that completed modernization programs were unsuccessful in reducing technology debt. Bringing clarity to the issue requires tech leaders to quantify this problem in cost/benefit financial terms. Essentially this is a matter of understanding the cost of the time lost by developers dealing with issues resulting from tech debt (i.e., the interest) versus the costs of paying down the tech debt itself (i.e., the principal).

Developing the cost-benefit analysis is no trivial task. First, the only way to get that detail is at the application level. Second, companies need to understand what type of tech debt they're dealing with (we've identified 11 different types).[4] These are the drivers of the tech debt, so knowing what type they are is necessary to then know how to remediate each one. Tech debt in data, for example, is different from tech debt resulting from the infrastructure. Third, companies use this analysis to develop a cost-benefit analysis that highlights which applications provide the biggest payoffs in terms of addressing their tech debt.

We have found that companies in the 80th percentile in terms of keeping tech debt low have revenue growth that is 20% higher than those in the bottom 20th percentile.

Good code quality has dozens of characteristics, including testability, reliability, reusability, portability, and maintainability. Ensuring high code quality requires that you:

Choose and use a version control system for all code

Version control and its disciplined use are core enablers of high-performing development pods. Organizations use version control to store infrastructure as code (IaC) scripts; applications source code; and any configuration, tests, and deployment scripts. It enables reproducibility and traceability – two key requirements that organizations struggle with, especially those companies with many onerous manual processes.

Version control systems include Git, CVS, SVN, and many others. These systems also provide important capabilities such as code auditing and they empower agile pods to look closely at how vulnerabilities may have entered the system and make the necessary fixes.

Decide on which software framework to use

A software framework provides guidelines for writing code for a specific goal. For example, if the goal is to create web applications, and the language is JavaScript, frameworks such as React or Angular can be effective. If the goal is to produce microservices that are lightweight and have good error reporting, then Python or TypeScript can be good options. Similarly, there are software frameworks, such as Kedro, for writing data pipelines, and machine learning models.

Software frameworks enforce a way of organizing code and make it easier to reuse code functionalities, which enables faster development.

Ensure consistency in the way code is written

A code linter is a static code analysis tool used to flag programming errors, bugs, stylistic errors, and suspicious constructs. Different code languages often have their own tools (GitHub's Super Linter supports multiple languages). The Python programming language, for example, has tools such as Pylint, while the JavaScript programming language has tools such as JSLint. These tools can be run by agile pods to verify that the code they are producing adheres to consistent quality standards.

Decide on a testing framework to verify code

Agile pods use a test framework to write unit tests for the code they are writing. Different programming languages support their own test frameworks: the Python language has pytest or unittest, while the JavaScript programming language has Jest. Regardless of the test framework chosen (there are many), the key is standardizing on the framework and ensuring that all pods use it.

There are different types of testing that engineers in agile pods write (see Exhibit 19.3).

For solutions where reliability and performance are especially important (e.g., e-commerce site, compliance, regulations), consider a separate site reliability engineer function, or SRE, to work on performance and reliability scripts. While DevOps engineers focus on solving development pipeline problems, site reliability engineers solve operational, scale, and reliability problems. SRE teams are highly skilled engineers who focus on solving issues for a specific period of time, then move on to another solution.

Minimize code complexity

It is imperative to ensure that code complexity is kept to a minimum. A code metrics framework analyzes code using various mathematical techniques, essentially to measure how complex it is. Various third-party products, such as SonarQube, look at code stored in a version control system to understand its complexity and report on its health. These tools (some opensource, some paid) also look for vulnerabilities in the code, or vulnerabilities in the dependencies used by the code.

Testing strategies – definitions

↑	**Penetration testing**	Verifies robustness of an application to cyber attacks
	Regression testing	Ensures that existing software applications are not adversely impacted when a new functionality is added
	Performance/ Load testing	Ensures working condition of application under varying conditions by simulating multiple users accessing the application concurrently
Increasing cost and time for testing	**Acceptance testing**	Ensures that the application works correctly from a user's perspective
	End-to-end (system) testing	Ensures entire application as a whole behaves as expected
	Integration testing	Verifies the communication paths and interaction between components to detect interface defects
	Unit testing	Tests individual units (modules, functions, classes) in isolation from the rest of the application

EXHIBIT 19.3

Automate document generation for compliance

Documentation of code and APIs is necessary in some industries before the code is put into production. Many languages provide a mechanism to embed documentation within the code itself (as comments). Tools can then scan the code and generate the documentation automatically into a human-readable form. This documentation can be stored within source control alongside the code and used as an audit of the code at that moment in time.

Generating documentation from code is preferable to having developers manually write it because it's more time efficient and also more accurate (although a developer will still need to validate that the documentation is 100% accurate). For some industries, this documentation can help compliance and regulators "sign off" on what is being released to production.

Instill end-to-end automation through continuous integration and continuous deployment (CI/CD)

As software becomes more complex, apparently simple changes can have unintended side effects. The complexity can increase when several developers across several different teams work on the same software. Continuous integration/continuous deployment (CI/CD) is an approach that addresses this issue. Here is a brief overview of the CI/CD process (see Exhibit 19.4 for an example):

Continuous integration (CI) addresses the problem of coordinating and validating software changes in development in an automated way to ensure high quality. Multiple tools exist to implement CI.

At one global pharma company, an agile pod developing new API functionality configured CircleCI as their CI tool of choice. The life cycle of the code is described below:

1. Engineers in an agile pod made code changes, which then were stored into GitHub (version control).

2. CircleCI detects the code changes made in version control.

3. CircleCI validates that the code conforms to standards by running Pylint (a linting tool).

4. CircleCI validates that the code has the correct behavior by running tests associated to the code – in this case, using Pytest.

5. CircleCI validates that the code conforms to quality standards by running code metrics – in this case, using SonarQube.

6. Documentation for the code is autogenerated using a tool – in this case, using Sphinx (an open source tool that extracts documentation from code and generates human-readable documentation for the web).

7. CircleCI packages code that has passed into a modular building block that it stores in a package repository – in this case, the package is stored in a container (Docker) and stored in Amazon ECR (a storage for Docker images managed by Amazon). Containers allow applications to run in any environment though should be used judiciously.

Python code pipeline – continuous integration and deployment – example

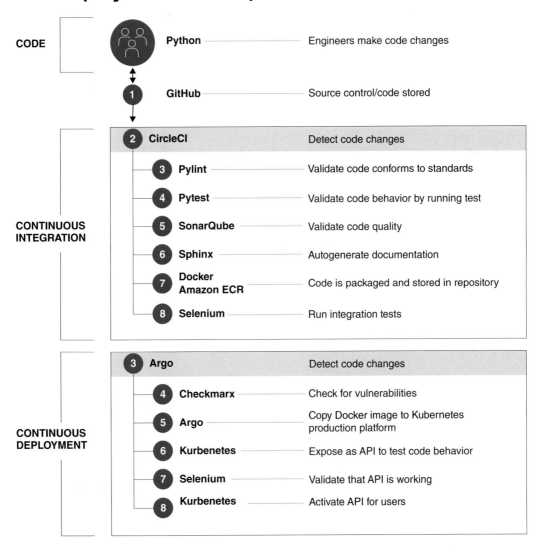

EXHIBIT 19.4

8. CircleCI then runs any integration tests, validating that the new modular building block works when integrated with all other software, and any other changes made by other team members – in this case, using Selenium (an open source web automation tool for writing tests in an automated fashion).

Because this entire process is automated and runs frequently (as code is changed), it gives developers fast feedback on the quality of the code, and confidence that high-quality software is being released.

Continuous deployment is the next process step and is a natural extension of CI. It takes the software that successfully passed all the CI steps and delivers it to production, removing any manual steps in the process, so the software is automatically available to end users.

The pharma company referenced above chose the Argo CD tool to deploy to production (a Kubernetes cluster). The company's process covered the following steps (see Exhibit 19.4. Note that the following enumeration is different from the exhibit for clarity).

1. Argo CD detects a change in GitHub (version control) made by continuous integration (indicating something new to deploy).

2. Argo CD validates the package for vulnerabilities using Checkmarx, which was used to detect security attack vectors in the package or code that has been written. This is an additional step to ensure that what is put into production is safe to run in production.

3. Argo CD then copies from Amazon ECR the Docker image to the production Kubernetes platform. A Kubernetes platform simplifies container management and makes applications more portable.

4. Argo CD then ensures that this new container has a private API that can be used to test that the behavior of the package is working correctly.

5. Argo CD asks Selenium (a testing tool) to validate that the API is behaving correctly.

6. Finally, if everything is okay up to this point, Argo CD can use one of its strategies for exposing the API to the end users in a safe way that does not disrupt any users using the API.

In this way, the deployment of a CI/CD pipeline helped the pharma company decrease deployment time from hours to just 10 minutes while substantially reducing technical debt and security risks.

A disciplined CI/CD approach is what makes it possible to consistently release reliable, high-quality software in days (even hours) instead of months or quarters. In essence, CI/CD is a pipeline where new software features move through different steps from the initial coding to release to users in a production environment.

Notes

1. Chandra Gnanasambandam, Janaki Palaniappan, and Jeremy Schneider, "Every company is a software company: Six 'must dos' to succeed," McKinsey.com, December 13, 2022, https://www.mckinsey.com/capabilities/mckinsey-digital/our-insights/every-company-is-a-software-company-six-must-dos-to-succeed.
2. Oliver Bossert, Chris Ip, and Irina Starikova, "Beyond agile: Reorganizing IT for faster software delivery," McKinsey.com, September 1, 2015, https://www.mckinsey.com/capabilities/mckinsey-digital/our-insights/beyond-agile-reorganizing-it-for-faster-software-delivery.
3. Santiago Comella-Dorda, James Kaplan, Ling Lau, and Nick McNamara, "Agile, reliable, secure, compliant IT: Fulfilling the promise of DevSecOps," McKinsey.com, May 21, 2020, https://www.mckinsey.com/capabilities/mckinsey-digital/our-insights/agile-reliable-secure-compliant-it-fulfilling-the-promise-of-devsecops.
4. Vishal Dalal, Krish Krishnakanthan, Björn Münstermann, and Rob Patenge, "Tech debt: Reclaiming tech equity," McKinsey.com, October 6, 2020, https://www.mckinsey.com/capabilities/mckinsey-digital/our-insights/tech-debt-reclaiming-tech-equity.

Chapter 20

The tools to make your developers highly productive

If you give people tools, and they use their natural abilities and their curiosity, they will develop things in ways that will surprise you very much beyond what you might have expected.

—*Bill Gates*

GitHub famously tried to empower its own engineering teams to use local laptop environments (on macOS) for many years. It found that despite its efforts, local development environments remained brittle. Innocent changes could render a local environment useless and waste hours of valuable time to recover. Breakages due to inconsistent local environment configurations were common. GitHub addressed these challenges by moving to virtual environments that are standardized, have preloaded tools, and have access to any data needed.

As an organization scales and moves from five agile pods to 20, 100, or even 1,000+ development pods, it should move to self-service (sandbox) environments, which are self-scaling and provide all the modern and standardized tools that agile pods need to develop solutions. This will avoid the need for burdening IT with requests to provision infrastructure and tools while allowing teams to develop code that works in a production environment.

A special engineering team – sometimes called a developer platform team – implements the tools and technologies that enforce the standards provided by the enterprise architecture team. This team also provides user-experience-focused tools to streamline agile pods, helping them to focus on delivering value quickly, versus getting bogged down in how to manage and maintain infrastructure and tooling.

In their words: Revamping how to create services in the cloud

We realized that we needed to take a completely new approach to how we managed and offered services on cloud. We laid out three principles that we were going to abide by:

- *The services we offered to development teams had to be fully standardized and automated . . . so there would be no more custom/ad hoc requests.*
- *Any services we offered on cloud had to be compliant from a security, privacy, and regulatory perspective from day one. So, no more one-off exceptions or manual workarounds. Not only that, any applications built on top of these services also had to be compliant from day one.*
- *Lastly, we had to come up with a creative way to educate our development teams on how to build their applications using these services; for far too long, they had been used to giving custom requests to the infrastructure team.*

That was the genesis of what we call today our Atlas platform. We developed a plan that looked at the most desired cloud services and created a product that templated most of the services and ensured that they are built to fit together. We've also ensured that they are secured together and connect to all of our back-end security logging systems.

To do that, we paused our cloud infrastructure team entirely and brought in a product owner who partnered with us to completely change how we were looking at the cloud. We then retrained the staff around the concept of building a product that app development could pull and consume in a self-service way, rather than just building infrastructure. The final product, Atlas, allows the app-development team to start by pulling the code into its continuous-integration and continuous-deployment (CI/CD) pipeline. It provisions itself.

—Martin Christopher, former senior vice president and chief information officer of CUNA Mutual Group

There are two elements to creating an effective development environment, as discussed next.

Flexible and scalable development sandboxes

It used to be that a team could take weeks, sometimes months, to request, create, and access a development environment. This is no longer the case. Development environments, or "sandboxes," can be created in minutes or hours at the most via infrastructure as code (IaC) automation. This rapidly enables agile pods to provision their "own" development sandbox (see Exhibit 20.1). Each team gets its own sandbox within the broader cloud environment, with standardized tools, dedicated memory and compute capabilities, as well as access to data (either test data, which is copied automatically, or, in some cases, access to a subset of production data).

Example of a developer platform

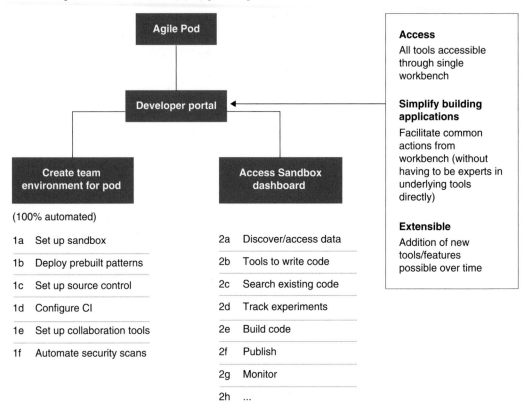

EXHIBIT 20.1

Running IaC scripts that can create these environments in seconds or minutes can be a bit daunting to some engineers. What if there are elements within those scripts you want teams to be able to configure, such as memory, or compute, or even the applications to preload? Developing an effective self-service sandbox capability that can address multiple needs has led to the rise of internal developer platforms (IDPs), a light user interface (UI) layer that abstracts all the complexities of provisioning infrastructure, security, and tooling but also provides a single user experience (UX) to configure those environments.

Case example: Spotify tackles developer productivity

As Spotify scaled to many agile pods, and the technology the company used became more complex, it recognized that not all its engineers were well versed in using those technologies, such as Terraform for infrastructure, GCP/AWS/Azure CLIs for various cloud providers, GitLab CI for version control, Prometheus for monitoring, Kubernetes and Docker for containers, and many more tools. This became more complicated because different agile pods needed different tooling to address developing back-end APIs, front-end mobile applications, etc.

To address the challenge, Spotify built a UX tool called Backstage (which it has since open-sourced). Backstage removed the need for engineers to learn the myriad technologies and tools. Instead, engineers could click a button in a simple web portal to add more compute to the machine they were working on, or access debug logs. Over time, Spotify has added additional features to help agile teams discover libraries, applications, and services that other agile pods developed – to empower the pods to move faster – all from a one-stop portal, thus simplifying and improving the developer experience.

At our firm, our platform engineering team built a custom, light, self-service developer web portal called Platform McKinsey to empower hundreds of McKinsey agile teams to build digital and AI products without worrying about the underlying infrastructure or tools. The web portal does two things (see Exhibit 20.1):

1. Acts on a team's request for a sandbox environment by taking the following steps automatically:

    a. Set up the sandbox with the right access controls for the team members, and the right tools.

    b. Set up any version control needed, so the team does not need to do this manually.

    c. Set up any collaboration tools, like wikis, where the team can collaborate, and keep its product/project documents.

    d. Set up and configure the CI tool, so the team can focus just on its product.

2. Presents the team with all the tools they need to develop products through a web portal, including:

    a. Tools to discover and access data

    b. Tools to write code

    c. Tools to search for non-confidential code that has already been written by other teams (to save time through reuse)

    d. Tools that allow them to track experiments (particularly important for developing machine learning models)

    e. Tools to see the status of the CI build (i.e., have any code changes affected the quality of the overall product?)

    f. A simple way to publish code to production with a click of a button

    g. Tools to monitor the health of the solution they are building in development and production

Within their sandboxes, each team can flex memory and compute capacity individually. This is particularly important when developing analytics and data products where there is an element of experimentation involved in the development process, such as determining the right algorithm or the right volume of data to process.

Modern and standardized tooling

Within the sandboxes, engineers need access to modern and standardized tools. Those tools are used across the SDLC to develop, test, package, and store code that agile pods are creating (before being deployed). Many cloud service providers have also started to package up tools that can be used as part of their platform-as-a-service (PaaS) offering.

There are five basic categories of development-related tools that are important for any agile pod developing digital solutions. It should be noted that the choice of tools in the first two categories below depends heavily on what product the agile pod is building (e.g., front-end, back-end, API, data-pipeline, or model).

1. **Developer tools.** These are tools used for experimentation and building code, which also includes integrated development environments (IDEs). Tooling here depends on the language (i.e., Python, R, JavaScript, etc). Good developer tools will provide syntax checking and code validation as well as allowing multiple engineers to collaborate and work on the same file at the same time.

2. **Software packaging tools (for production).** For a working solution that needs to package multiple blocks of code, such as webpack that packages js, css, and html, that code needs to relate to other versions of other code around it, and other dependencies. This allows developers to modularize software better and release updates more easily.

3. **Package storage tools.** These are tools to store code packages. Tools like Nexus, Docker Hub, and JFrog Artifactory can store packages that are ready for production.

4. **Software development tools.** These tools provide integration and access to version control and continuous integration for agile pods using a sandbox environment without worrying about how to configure and set up. This enables the team to focus on delivering high-quality software.

5. **Monitoring tools.** Sandbox environments need to be monitored to make sure they are running properly and not burning cash (e.g., many tools licensed with no users, or people using the infrastructure to mine bitcoin off the clock – yes, this happens). Examples of such tools include Grafana and Graphite.

The developer platform team provides a set of standardized common tools that all sandboxes can take advantage of. Some developers like to pick tooling they are comfortable with. Organizations should take a core/common/custom approach, that is, define what is "core" and cannot be deviated from; what is "common," that is, optional to use and provided to all; and what is "custom," which is purchased/downloaded/installed for a particular user or pod. The latter should only be done when there's a real business value associated with doing so.

Chapter 21

Delivering production-grade digital solutions

Until we have established reliability, there is no sense at all in wasting time trying to make the thing go faster.

—*Carroll Smith*

Transformative data products, AI models, and digital user journeys have got to be deployed to the people or applications that use them in a setting where it counts, like sales transactions, supplier management, and pricing decisions. Production environments need to be reliable and available. The reliability of this production environment is far more important than a discovery and development environment.

The platform engineering team is the one that creates this environment for all agile pods to deploy their products to. The team is responsible for the design, building, and governance of the infrastructure, the underlying tech stack, and the services, including integration with downstream systems. The environment conforms to the standards set out by the enterprise architecture team and should not be created manually but follow standard engineering practices. Whatever code agile pods want to deploy into a production environment must be deployed via the strict continuous deployment process.

There are three important aspects to creating a reliable and effective production environment, as discussed next.

Aim for a high degree of control and auditability

Given that the production environment serves business-critical applications, there needs to be a high degree of control and auditability. This is not only for reliability reasons, but also compliance, i.e., SOC 2, ISO 27001, PCI, etc. This capability should focus on two areas (see Exhibit 21.1):

1. **The production environment itself,** specifically how the environment has been configured, what security policies have been applied, what (limited) users have access, what incoming (ingress) access is allowed, and what outgoing (egress) access is allowed, etc. By specifying these production concerns within IaC scripts, and storing within version control, organizations can have full visibility into, and be able to audit changes made to, the environment. Changes to the environment can only be made by the platform engineering team and are only made using CI/CD.

2. **What runs within the environment,** specifically how a deployed application or API is scheduled to run, who can deploy it, etc. Agile pods apply continuous deployment to ensure that what ends up in production is auditable and easily reversible. By ensuring that the entire state of the environment is specified as code within

version control, code can be rolled back to the previous state of the environment, if needed.

Control and auditability of the production environment

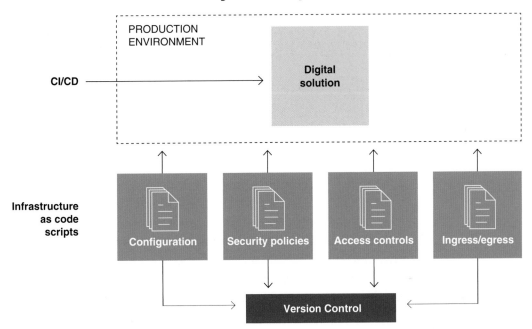

EXHIBIT 21.1

Ensure the environment is secure, scalable, and available

To make sure that the production environment can meet the needs of the digital transformation, it needs to provide three capabilities:

1. **Security.** Most data that is stored or transferred within the production environment needs to be encrypted. Encryption ensures that only authorized users or applications can access the data using a key. Cloud service providers provide managed services that manage keys, i.e., AWS Key Management Service, Azure Key Vault, or Google Cloud Key Management Service.

Direct access to the environment should be limited and audited. Each cloud service provider has rich access controls, such as IAM.

2. **Scalability.** The underlying infrastructure should be able to scale up as required depending on demand. Cloud providers have this kind of scaling capability, but companies need to set up specific services to detect the load on applications that may need to be scaled. For example, Amazon provides AWS Auto Scaling, which monitors applications for load and scales capacity to maintain performance. Companies need to clearly think through which services they use, because each one has its own set of dependencies.

3. **Availability.** While cloud service providers are resilient and reliable, their environments can suffer outages. Ensuring that there is an ability to switch from one geography to another without interruption is important. There are many mechanisms to do this, including having a separate landing zone or secondary production environment running in another geography, i.e., a mirror production environment. The secondary production environment uses the same IaC as the primary production environment. Companies need to set up monitoring to look for failures, and upon detecting one, switch from the primary environment to the secondary one.

Incorporate monitoring and observability

Monitoring sounds like a dry topic, but it is important and often misunderstood. Companies need a good way to understand the health and activity of the infrastructure, environment, the solutions they have built, and the users of those applications. Monitoring is based on knowing what you are looking for so you can define dashboards to surface warnings when something that you are looking for happens:

1. **Application monitoring.** The solutions that agile pods are developing themselves need monitoring for reliability purposes, but also to capture feedback and telemetry on how business users

are interacting with a solution. Tools such as Datadog, New Relic, or Dynatrace are commonly used.

2. **Cloud and infrastructure monitoring.** This covers what data is going in and out of your cloud, who is using it, and what the performance is like. Tools such as New Relic or Zabbix can be used. For example, if you are using traditional virtual servers in the cloud, then understanding their behavior and load is important, especially when diagnosing application performance issues. Virtual servers usually have fixed sizes, so spikes in load can affect performance and responsiveness for end users. Monitoring the reliability of the flow of data and the quality of data is a less mature space. In addition to the tools mentioned previously, other tools do exist, such as monitoring tools within Azure Data Factory that can look at the ingestion of data.

Note that there is no single monitoring tool that enables organizations to understand the end-to-end flow of information. For production purposes, a platform engineering team needs to figure out the tools it needs to ensure not only that the environment is reliable, but that it is also able to diagnose issues quickly if they happen. Exhibit 21.2 shows the performance monitoring dashboard for McKinsey's Corporate Finance Analytics solutions. These solutions are accessible by clients through a web interface or APIs.

The dashboard, written with New Relic tooling, provides typical application performance information that a solution development team would want to monitor. The upper part of the dashboard tracks the response time provided to users, including Adpex scores (a ratio of satisfied requests versus total requests). The middle part helps the development team zoom-in on the features (or transactions, in this case) that are least responsive and thus guides the cloud and software engineers on the priority features to improve. Lastly, the bottom part helps optimize cloud storage and compute usage over time by better matching workload elasticity needs with the cloud service purchased.

Sample monitoring dashboard for a digital solution

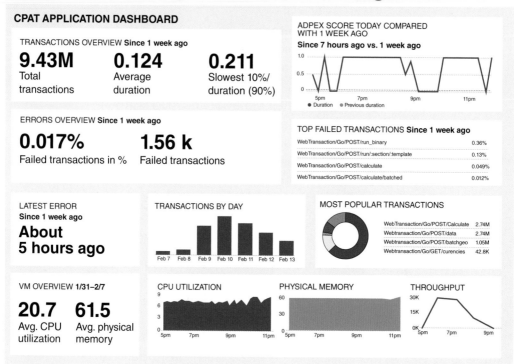

EXHIBIT 21.2

Every live digital solution should have a monitoring dashboard that tracks the most important user experience and performance characteristics of the solution.

Chapter 22

Build in security and automation from the start

Treat your password like your toothbrush. Don't let anybody else use it, and get a new one every six months.

—Clifford Stoll

Almost all security breaches in the cloud stem from human error and misconfiguration, rather than from attacks that compromise the underlying cloud infrastructure.[1] Cloud requires secure configuration of applications and systems. In addition, traditional cybersecurity mechanisms have not been designed to operate at the tempo required. As a result, companies must adopt a new security approach built around automation.[2]

Shift left on security

"Shift left on security" is a software industry movement to inject security earlier into the SDLC, as opposed to leaving it to the last step (see Exhibit 22.1). There are two rationales for this.

First, it is quicker for development teams to address security concerns while code is being written. Any security concern can be addressed by an agile pod then and there in the process, without waiting for it to be detected later (often by a completely different team). The cycle time for detecting and addressing problems is drastically reduced.

Second, each step of the SDLC adds security checks at that moment in time. For example, in the coding step, checks can be made for vulnerabilities in third-party components used in the development. If a vulnerability is detected, it would enable the team to look for alternative third-party components to use as a workaround.

Making this shift starts with mapping out the manual controls and governance processes used for managing risk and security throughout the SDLC – for both infrastructure and applications. This includes any risk and security reviews. Once this is done, look for tools and technologies that can be used to minimize or eliminate manual (human) controls. For example, using IaC (that is stored within source control) provides the additional benefit of being able to use tools to analyze for security vulnerabilities or misconfigurations before it is used by other teams. Static code analysis on IaC can ensure that no vulnerabilities exist within the infrastructure code (e.g., tfsec, checkov). Similarly, many teams use modular and reusable open-source components to build these solutions. While open source has many benefits, it can also introduce security vulnerabilities that can become embedded in those digital solutions. You can identify and remediate these vulnerable components early in the SDLC using tools such as Synk.

Improving security by "shifting left"

From: Leaving security to last – Security check after deployment of software

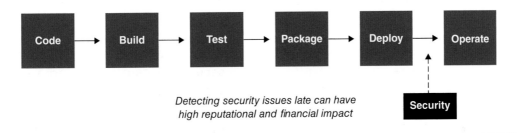

Detecting security issues late can have high reputational and financial impact

To: "Shifting left" on security – Security checks and procedures are embedded in every step of the SDLC

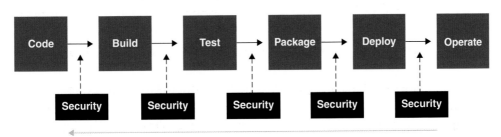

Earlier remediation can help avoid catastrophic problems later

EXHIBIT 22.1

Embed security into the SDLC using DevSecOps

Implementing the "shift left" approach requires DevSecOps, which embeds security into the DevOps approach. That means integrating security experts into DevOps teams and implementing security measures throughout the SDLC process. Automation is a core tenet of this approach. Within the same end-to-end CI/CD process, the platform engineering team embeds tools to validate and address security risks (see Exhibit 22.2). The goal is to move to 100% automation of security checks over time.

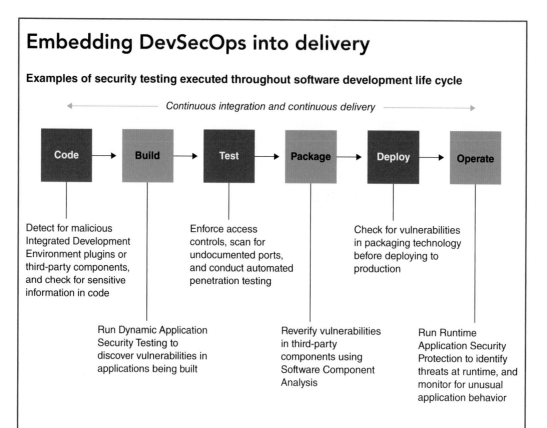

Embedding DevSecOps into delivery

Examples of security testing executed throughout software development life cycle

← ———————— *Continuous integration and continuous delivery* ———————— →

Code → Build → Test → Package → Deploy → Operate

Detect for malicious Integrated Development Environment plugins or third-party components, and check for sensitive information in code

Enforce access controls, scan for undocumented ports, and conduct automated penetration testing

Check for vulnerabilities in packaging technology before deploying to production

Run Dynamic Application Security Testing to discover vulnerabilities in applications being built

Reverify vulnerabilities in third-party components using Software Component Analysis

Run Runtime Application Security Protection to identify threats at runtime, and monitor for unusual application behavior

EXHIBIT 22.2

Implementing security checks in CI/CD:

1. **Code**

Using tools like Synk, check to detect if any malicious integrated development environment (IDE) plugins have been installed by developers that introduce vulnerabilities within the code. Check if any sensitive secrets are being stored within source control (e.g., using git secrets from AWS, or even the built-in secret-scanning tools that some source control systems have available, such as GitHub secret scanning). Finally, run static application security testing (SAST), which analyzes the code that is written. This is language-dependent; for IaC, a tool like tfsec can be used, while for Python code, a tool like semgrep can be run.

2. **Build**

    Run dynamic application security testing (DAST), which looks for vulnerabilities in applications being built. Tools such as appcheck or the open-source OWASP Zed Attack Proxy tool can be used. Run interactive application security testing (IAST), which looks for vulnerabilities while the digital application is running. Tools such as Synopsys or Veracode can be used.

3. **Test**

    Check if traditional access controls of the digital application are enforced. Look for whether access controls (roles or policies) are enforced and restrict access appropriately. Check if undocumented ports are open (apart from the ports that are needed and protected).

4. **Package**

    Reverify that any vulnerable third-party components have not been introduced by using software component analysis (SCA).

5. **Deploy**

    Recheck any vulnerabilities that may have been introduced before deploying to production. This could be in the packaging technology (e.g., Docker) or looking within the package using SCA.

6. **Operate**

    Run a runtime application security protection (RASP), which looks within a digital application's internal data to identify threats at runtime. Monitor for unusual application behavior using traditional monitoring/observability tools such as Datadog.

In their words: The right mindset and the shift left

Security can feel overbearing, but we have a very collaborative relationship. We have what we call a "security maven" program to train and certify people on security throughout our business, be they developers, product owners, or engineers. They also have sponsors in the security team, and when they do projects and find things that need fixing, they present their work to senior management, and we celebrate those wins. What that does is embed that skill set within our teams, because you can't be everywhere.

We've also been trying to "shift left" by building security in the initial designs of everything we're building on the cloud. Because cloud moves so fast, if you don't shift left, you've missed the opportunity, and then you're just cleaning up constantly.

—Casey Santos, Asurion CIO

The implementation of security automation should be part of the mandate of the DevSecOps team as it develops the CI/CD pipeline, including training the pods to use it.

Notes

1. Arul Elumalai, James Kaplan, Mike Newborn, and Roger Roberts, "Making a secure transition to the public cloud," McKinsey.com, January 1, 2018, https://www.mckinsey.com/capabilities/mckinsey-digital/our-insights/making-a-secure-transition-to-the-public-cloud.
2. Jim Boehm, Charlie Lewis, Kathleen Li, Daniel Wallance, and Dennis Dias, "Cybersecurity trends: Looking over the horizon," McKinsey .com, March 10, 2022, https://www.mckinsey.com/capabilities/risk-and-resilience/our-insights/cybersecurity/cybersecurity-trends-looking-over-the-horizon.

Chapter 23

MLOps so AI can scale

Building advanced AI is like launching a rocket. The first challenge is to maximize acceleration, but once it starts picking up speed, you also need to focus on steering.

—Jaan Tallinn

For AI/ML to make a sizable contribution to a company's bottom line, organizations must scale the technology across the organization, infusing it in core business processes, workflows, and customer journeys to optimize decision making and operations in real time. This is particularly difficult with AI/ML models because they are "living organisms" that change with the underlying data. They require constant monitoring, retraining, and debiasing - a challenge with even a few ML models but simply overwhelming with hundreds of them.

Defining key terms

Artificial intelligence (AI) covers the broad concept of creating smart intelligent machines.

Machine learning (ML) is a subset of artificial intelligence. It's a method that "learns" from data to improve performance on some set of tasks.

Deep learning is a subset of machine learning. It uses vast volumes of data and complex algorithms to train a model.

In recent years, massive improvements in ML tooling and technologies have dramatically transformed ML workflows, expedited the application life cycle, and enabled consistent and reliable scaling of AI across business domains. With all these new capabilities, however, the key point to remember is that effective ML operations (MLOps) requires a focus on the full set of application development activities rather than just focusing on the models themselves. We estimate that as much as 90% of the failures in ML development come not from developing poor models but from poor productization practices and the challenges of integrating the model with production data and business applications, which keep the model from scaling and performing as intended. Effective productization requires developing an integrated set of components to support the model (or, often, set of models) such as data assets, ML algorithms, software, and user interface.[1]

MLOps is really a set of practices that are applied across the lifecycle of an ML model (see Exhibit 23.1):

Data: Building systems and processes that continuously collect, curate, analyze, label, and maintain high-quality data at scale for ML applications.

Model development: Professionalizing model development to ensure that high-quality algorithms can be explained, are not biased, perform as expected, and are continuously monitored and regularly updated using fresh data.

Data and model pipelines: Maximizing the business value and reducing the engineering overhead by delivering integrated application pipelines that accept data or events, process and enrich them, run the model, process the results, generate actions, and monitor the different components and business KPIs.

Productizing and scaling: Enhancing the data processing and model training components to run at scale, including adding tests, validation, security, CI/CD, and model retraining.

Live operations: Actively monitoring resources, performance, and business KPIs.

This is an ongoing process requiring you to build robust engineering and ML application practices to continuously develop, test, deploy, upgrade, and monitor the end-to-end AI applications. MLOps builds on the DevOps engineering concepts and end-to-end automation touched upon earlier, to address AI's unique characteristics, such as the probabilistic nature of ML outputs and the technology's dependence on the underlying data.

When companies embrace MLOps best practices, it can dramatically raise the bar for what can be achieved. It's the difference between experimenting with AI and transforming your company's competitive position with AI. Effective MLOps relies on implementing four key practices:

1. **Ensure data availability, quality, and control to feed the ML system**

   ML models are dependent on data. Without high-quality data, and available data, the ML models will not be accurate or usable. So, you need to implement data quality checks. Tools are now available to assess data quality and detect anomalies to find errors. This is useful in high-throughput scenarios such as monitoring financial transactions.

   To ensure data availability to feed the ML models, you will need to extract from raw data the features that will drive the ML model.

AI/ML model lifecycle

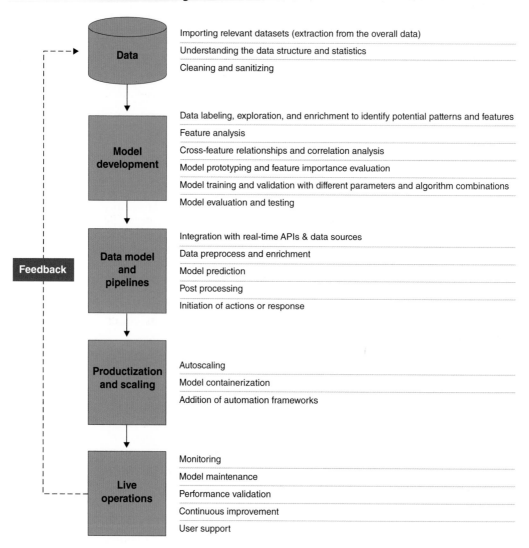

Data
- Importing relevant datasets (extraction from the overall data)
- Understanding the data structure and statistics
- Cleaning and sanitizing

Model development
- Data labeling, exploration, and enrichment to identify potential patterns and features
- Feature analysis
- Cross-feature relationships and correlation analysis
- Model prototyping and feature importance evaluation
- Model training and validation with different parameters and algorithm combinations
- Model evaluation and testing

Data model and pipelines
- Integration with real-time APIs & data sources
- Data preprocess and enrichment
- Model prediction
- Post processing
- Initiation of actions or response

Productization and scaling
- Autoscaling
- Model containerization
- Addition of automation frameworks

Live operations
- Monitoring
- Model maintenance
- Performance validation
- Continuous improvement
- User support

Feedback

EXHIBIT 23.1

These features are the fuel for ML models. For example, barometric pressure is measured by atmospheric sensors, but the feature in a weather-forecasting model is the change in barometric pressure. A feature store is a central vault for these features. Feature stores manage, maintain, and monitor features, ensuring that the fuel needed for ML models is consistently available.

2. **Provision tooling to optimize ML development**

Writing reproducible, maintainable, and modular data science code is not trivial. Software frameworks such as Kedro (using Python) aim to make it easier. They borrow concepts from software engineering – including modularity, separation of concerns, and versioning – and apply them to ML code.

Data scientists like to experiment, trying different data/features and different algorithms to develop a model that satisfies a business outcome. These experiments need to be stored somewhere, along with any associated metadata (e.g., the features that were used, or any additional model configuration that was used). Tools such as MLflow and MLRun provide model governance and an ability to reproduce these experiments, and also track which experiment have yielded a better business outcome.

3. **Implement an ML delivery platform to automate as much as possible**

Moving from small-scale data science exploration and model development to large-scale production often involves code refactoring, switching frameworks, and significant engineering work. These steps can add substantial delays or even result in the failure of the entire solution.

It is crucial to design and implement a continuous ML application delivery platform. This platform should execute scalable and automated pipelines for processing data, training, validation, and packaging of high-quality models for production. In addition, the ML platform should deploy the online application pipelines that incorporate the trained model, run data pre- or post-processing tasks, integrate with the data sources and other applications, and collect vital data, model, application, and business metrics for observability.

4. **Monitor model performance to drive continuous improvement**

ML models are not like software. When software is deployed to production, the deployed software should work as expected (as long as there has been a focus on quality and rigorous testing). On the other hand, ML models are "trained," which means that people need to monitor how each model works and adjust it to improve outcomes over time. Similarly, ML models are sensitive to real-world data conditions and can degrade over time, which is why it is important to monitor them to ensure they are behaving correctly.

For example, when we were locked down during the worldwide pandemic, customer behaviors changed overnight. ML models that had been trained on historical customer spending patterns (pre-pandemic) were no longer able to make effective predictions, such as models recommending a customer should visit a restaurant, even though the restaurants were closed. This is why monitoring model performance and being able to rapidly diagnose the underlying reason for the variance are critically important.

Model monitoring should extend beyond looking for drift. It should also be validating data quality and conformance, and measuring model accuracy and performance against business KPIs. This more expansive view of monitoring is particularly important so that companies don't just fixate on model performance but assess how well it's helping the business.

MLOps is a fast-evolving field. As of the time of this writing, more than 60 suppliers offer different MLOps software tools ranging from turnkey platforms to niche tooling.

Case example: Cutting AI application development times

An Asian financial services company was able to reduce the time to develop new AI applications by more than 50%. It created a common data layer on top of source systems that provided high-quality, ready-to-use data products for use in numerous customer-centric AI applications.

The company standardized data management tooling and processes to create a sustainable data pipeline, and created assets to standardize and automate time-consuming steps such as data labeling and data lineage tracking. This was starkly different from the company's previous approach, in which the teams structured and cleaned raw data from source systems using disparate processes and tools every time an AI application was being developed. This approach had contributed to a lengthy AI development cycle.

Note

1. Jacomo Corbo, David Harvey, Nayur Khan, Nicolas Hohn, Kia and Javanmardian, "Scaling AI like a tech native: The CEO's role," McKinsey .com, October 13, 2021, https://www.mckinsey.com/capabilities/ quantumblack/our-insights/scaling-ai-like-a-tech-native-the-ceos-role.

Getting Ready
Section Four

The following is a set of questions to help you home in on the right actions to take:

Do you have a technology environment that can attract and inspire modern cloud-native talent?

How many pods are able to develop and directly release new versions of their digital solutions to customers/users?

What is your release cycle time (and are you sure you're measuring it correctly)?

How do you know you are building well/responsibly, not just fast?

What's the ratio of foundational investment versus new functionality you need to succeed and do you have a process for making it happen?

What proportion of your engineering development uses the continuous integration/continuous delivery approach?

What proportion of your workloads are on the cloud, and what should the target be?

How well is your security function integrated into the development process, and automated?

Are your AI/ML models currently in production well calibrated? How do you know?

Embedding Data Everywhere

What it takes to make data easy to consume across the organization

In established companies, data is often a source of frustration. In our experience, as much as 70% of the development efforts of an AI-based solution are composed of wrangling and harmonizing data. Many of these issues can be traced back to legacy, siloed systems so it's critical to architect data thoughtfully for easy consumption and reuse; otherwise, scaling becomes challenging. The goal is to have clean, relevant, and available data so that agile pods can use it to make better decisions and build better data-enabled solutions.

The core unit for achieving this goal is the data product – a set of data elements that are curated and packaged in such a way that any team or application across the organization can easily consume it.[1]

What data products do you need and what data elements should they contain? That question is always the first place to start, and answers should be guided by your digital roadmap to focus your efforts on the highest-value data.

To enable the easy development of data products, top companies put in place a solid data architecture that lets data efficiently "flow" from where it's sourced to where it's used. They also deploy a federated data governance model in which business leaders act as sponsors for the data and data products they own. This section will show you how to turn your data into a competitive advantage.[2]

Chapter 24: Determine what data matters. Assess which parts of your data estate need fixing based on what value they can create, and develop a plan for how to bring them up to a useful standard of readiness.

Chapter 25: Data products: The reusable building blocks for scaling. Realize both the near- and long-term value from data investments, by managing it like a product. Dedicated teams make these data products easy for any pod to securely consume.

Chapter 26: Data architecture, or the system of data "pipes." Solve for both the BI (business intelligence) and AI (artificial intelligence) needs of your organization in building your target data architecture. Use existing reference architectures to cut back on implementation complexity.

Chapter 27: Organize to get the most from your data. Clarify data governance and ensure you have the right data talent and tools so you can continuously improve the state of your data.

Notes

1. Veeral Desai, Tim Fountaine, and Kayvaun Rowshankish, "How to unlock the full value of data? Manage it like a product," McKinsey.com, June 14, 2022, https://www.mckinsey.com/capabilities/quantumblack/our-insights/how-to-unlock-the-full-value-of-data-manage-it-like-a-product.
2. Veeral Desai, Tim Fountaine, and Kaybaun Rowshankish, "A better way to put your data to work," *Harvard Business Review*, July–August 2022, https://hbr.org/2022/07/a-better-way-to-put-your-data-to-work; "The data driven enterprise of 2025: Seven characteristics that define this new data-driven enterprise," McKinsey.com, January 28, 2022, https://www.mckinsey.com/capabilities/quantumblack/our-insights/the-data-driven-enterprise-of-2025?linkId=150307929.

Chapter 24

Determine what data matters

It is a capital mistake to theorize before one has data.

—Sherlock Holmes

A data strategy defines what data you need and how to make it ready to deliver on your business priorities. The output is a plan to clean that data and make it easily accessible.

Identifying and prioritizing data

Start by identifying the data needed to deliver on the digital solutions and underlying use cases prescribed in the digital roadmap. The roadmap will often identify data needs at a high level, but those have to be translated into specific data needs.

Defining key terms

Data element: Basic unit of information that has a unique meaning, e.g., customer name, customer address, product name, date.

Data domain: Conceptual grouping of related data, often used to organize both data governance efforts and data architecture.

Data product: A high-quality, ready-to-use set of data that people across an organization can easily access and use. It is usually a subset of a data domain.

In almost every case, you'll find you have more data than you need to get started. Prioritize data domains based on their importance to the business in enabling the digital roadmap, as well as other considerations such as risk and regulatory requirements.

This prioritization exercise should also extend to the data elements within each data domain to identify what matters most. For example, within the customer data domain, there may be hundreds or thousands of data elements like customer name, address, and credit card number. Identify the elements that are the most important to deliver on the use case (typically that's ~10–15% of all the data elements) and focus most of your effort on them.

For one US-based insurance company looking to offer enhanced property protection advice to its clients, this prioritization process meant focusing on catastrophe and safety data, (e.g., disaster risk data from the National Oceanic and Atmospheric Administration, the United States Geological Survey, and the Federal Emergency Management Agency), and asset market data like historic property price, purchase history, and neighborhood indices (see Exhibit 24.1).

From business domains to data elements

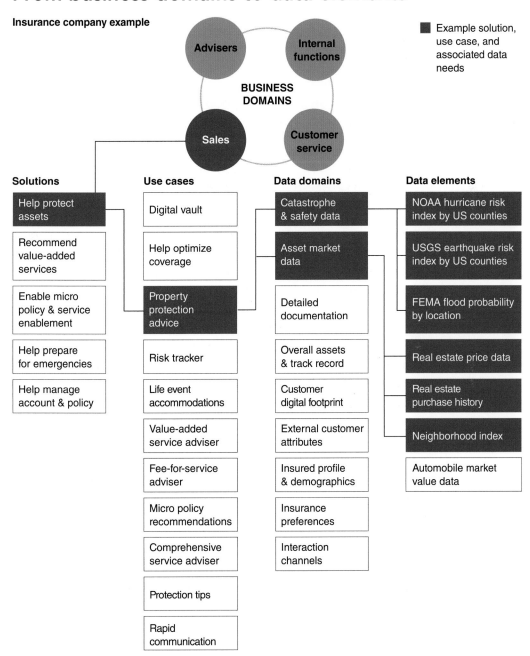

Insurance company example

BUSINESS DOMAINS

- Advisers
- Internal functions
- Sales
- Customer service

■ Example solution, use case, and associated data needs

Solutions	Use cases	Data domains	Data elements
Help protect assets	Digital vault	Catastrophe & safety data	NOAA hurricane risk index by US counties
Recommend value-added services	Help optimize coverage	Asset market data	USGS earthquake risk index by US counties
Enable micro policy & service enablement	Property protection advice	Detailed documentation	FEMA flood probability by location
Help prepare for emergencies	Risk tracker	Overall assets & track record	Real estate price data
Help manage account & policy	Life event accommodations	Customer digital footprint	Real estate purchase history
	Value-added service adviser	External customer attributes	Neighborhood index
	Fee-for-service adviser	Insured profile & demographics	Automobile market value data
	Micro policy recommendations	Insurance preferences	
	Comprehensive service adviser	Interaction channels	
	Protection tips		
	Rapid communication		

EXHIBIT 24.1

Assessing data readiness

It's not uncommon that the data needed for a solution can be of poor quality. This creates the classic "garbage in, garbage out" issue where poor-quality data undermines digital and AI transformation progress. Before fixing or cleaning the data, you need to identify what's wrong with it by thoroughly assessing it (sometimes called "interrogating the data"). The nine dimensions of assessing data quality are shown in Exhibit 24.2.

Nine dimensions to assess data quality

1 Accuracy
Degree to which data should match the agreed source

2 Timeliness
The timescale within which the data should be refreshed, and the acceptable systems "lag" when values change

3 Consistency
Extent to which identical data must have the same value wherever it is stored or displayed

4 Completeness
Extent to which field must be populated, and the required breadth, depth, and history exist

5 Uniqueness
Extent that data should be uniquely stored in one place, and be unique for one customer

6 Coherence
Extent to which data definitions remain similar over time so historic data has the same context

7 Availability
Extent to which current and historic data is available for analysis

8 Security
Extent to which data is held securely, subject to access restriction, and recoverability

9 Interpetability
Extent to which clear definitions for data are in place—enabling easy understanding

EXHIBIT 24.2

Assessing data against these dimensions involves three steps for each data element. First, given known and likely future business needs for the data, define a set of data quality rules. For example, take the data element "customer address": A rule relevant for many B2C organizations is "customer address is accurate."

Second, for each rule, set a target that meets business needs. For example, the target accuracy rate for "customer address is accurate" could be >95%. Higher accuracy is important if a company is shipping a customer a package, but less critical if the company is offering digital services. Avoid making changes to targets that are outside of scope, as they drive back-end data governance efforts.

Third, measure the quality of the data and report performance against the defined data quality rules. Most companies use software packages (e.g., Talend Open Studio, Ataccama ONE, Informatica Data Quality) to measure performance against rules and run broader scans to uncover data quality issues. Regardless of whether software is used or not, the process to define data quality rules and targets remains critical.

When done well, this process can uncover a range of issues, including inaccurate data values that result in wrong calculations, different definitions across business units that result in data being improperly used, and latency in data integration resulting in data missing a deadline for reporting.

One of the biggest issues companies run into during this process is that data quality assessment and cleanup efforts can be time consuming and expensive, although we are seeing AI tools emerging to help with this step. For this reason, it's important to focus on the most important data for your priority use cases. At the insurance company referenced in Exhibit 24.1, for example, it was important to have data that was less than three months old and easily available while also meeting stringent privacy and confidentiality requirements. But it didn't need to be 100% accurate. Or in the case of a real estate company, the data recency was critical but only in the New York and Los Angeles markets.

Developing a minimum viable product (MVPs) with less-than-perfect data can be successful if the right critical mass of data is in place and the team is clear on the value they're going after. Additionally, companies are increasingly turning to machine learning and AI tools such as Talend, Trillium Quality, Sypherlink, Syncsort, and AI4DQ[1] to clean up existing data (although some problems will always require a degree of manual effort, such as aligning product hierarchies across regions for consistent global reporting).

In many cases, it's possible to improve the quality and type of data a company has through a process called "data enrichment." You can use multiple avenues to improve what you have, such as sourcing data externally or adding new sources for data (e.g., sensors, websites). Data enrichment is continuous. Practically, this means your business and functional leaders should report back on their plans to improve their data assets over time and make the investments required. A good idea is to make this reporting a part of your yearly planning effort.

Developing the data roadmap

Once the priority set of data and its current readiness are well understood, the next step is to create the data roadmap. This essentially becomes the plan for sequencing the work needed so that the data can support the digital solutions identified in the strategic roadmap. This work is crucial for identifying and allocating the necessary resources to ready the data.

In our experience, you will be working at three different levels in parallel:

Level 1 focuses on creating data pods that will take on the specific job of ensuring readiness of priority data elements and building the consumption pathways for that data (more on this in the next chapter).

Level 2 is on developing the data pipes and storage architecture that will serve your priority data domains and the ones that follow (see Chapter 26).

Level 3 lays the foundation for healthy data governance to ensure that all your data cleaning and conditioning efforts are not wasted by ensuring that future data is collected correctly (see Chapter 27).

Note

1. AI4DQ is a QuantumBlack AI by McKinsey product.

Chapter 25

Data products: The reusable building blocks for scaling

Data is a precious thing and will last longer than the systems themselves.

—Tim Berners-Lee

To realize both the near- and long-term value from data investments, manage data like a consumer product. A data product delivers a high-quality, ready-to-use set of data that is formatted in such a way that people and systems across an organization can easily access and apply to different business challenges. For example, a data product could provide a 360-degree view of an important entity, such as customers, employees, product lines, or branches. One emerging area is the use of a data product as the core of a digital twin, which replicates the operation of real-world assets.

More about digital twins

A digital twin is a virtual representation of a physical asset, person, or process. Fueled by the wealth of data produced by embedded sensors and IoT devices, enabled by telematics, and driven by AI models that continuously train themselves, digital twin technology is rapidly becoming an important component in digital and AI transformations.

Digital twins have two primary parts: emulators and simulators. Emulators are data products that fuse disparate datasets to monitor real-life systems. Emulators offer the ability to capture, store, and replay data at scale (e.g., monitoring outages in a network operation, exposing bottlenecks on a manufacturing line). Simulators, on the other hand, are software applications that are anchored in real-life data that allow companies to experiment with hypothetical "what-if" scenarios such as rerouting inventory through a logistics network and modifying the design of an engine.

The most mature data-driven organizations have begun to combine those two elements to develop digital twins that alert, analyze, predict, and retrain themselves continuously. This approach allows the data to be enriched over time, enabling further simulations or use cases that result in a digital twin that can solve many business problems with significant ROI.

Successful digital twin applications are emerging. A classic example of, a digital twin is a 360-degree view of customers, including all the details that a company 's business units and systems collect about them—for example, online and in-store purchasing behavior, demographic information, payment methods, and interactions with customer service. AI use cases leveraging the twin could include customer churn propensity models or a basket of the next products a customer would be likely to buy.

Alternatively, the twin might replicate the operation of real-world assets or processes (such as an entire factory production line or critical pieces of machinery) and generate information on average equipment downtimes or the average time for completing a

product assembly. AI use cases could include predictive maintenance and process automation and optimization.

Successful digital twin projects require dedicated, multidisciplinary
agile teams including data scientists, data engineers, designers,
developers, and domain experts working in unison to target
specific applications.[1]

This represents a fundamental shift in the way companies think about
and manage data (see Exhibits 25.1 and 25.2).

In this way, data products are the secret sauce for scaling. The benefits of this approach can be significant. New business use cases
can be delivered as much as 90% faster. Total cost of ownership,
including technology, development, and maintenance costs, can
decline by 30%. And finally, risk and data governance burden can
be substantially reduced.

Data products incorporate the wiring necessary for different business
systems, such as digital apps or reporting systems, to "consume" the
data. Each type of business system has its own set of requirements
for how data is stored, processed, and managed; we call these "consumption archetypes."

Examples of data products

A data product that represents a 360-degree view of a telecom-
munications network takes in network sensor data (e.g., data from
cell towers, homes, or fiber) and descriptive data (e.g., network
element specs, or consumer and cost data) and creates a digital
representation of the whole network. The data product enables
a variety of operational and consumer experience use cases – for
example, assessing what would happen to customer experience
if a given part of the network went down, and defining network
improvements to lessen this impact.

For example, a data product for investments focused on environ-
mental, social, and governance (ESG) performance would bring

together asset details such as carbon intensity, external ESG ratings, and portfolio holding data to understand overall investment exposure to that asset. The data product allows an asset manager to calculate how ESG-friendly their organization's current and potential future investment products are, and highlights actions the organization needs to take to meet its external commitments (e.g., to achieve net-zero carbon impact).

The legacy data setup in many organizations can be complex and inefficient

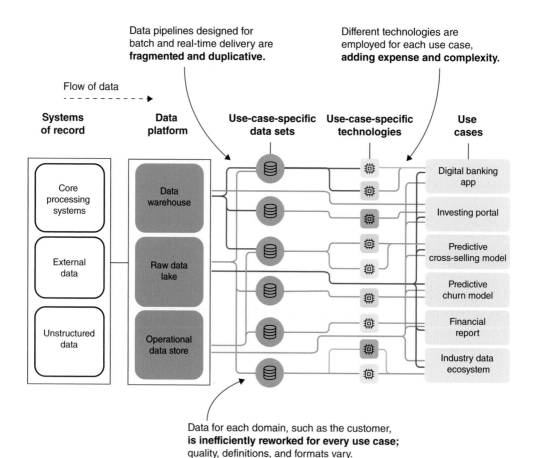

Data pipelines designed for batch and real-time delivery are fragmented and duplicative.

Different technologies are employed for each use case, adding expense and complexity.

Flow of data

| Systems of record | Data platform | Use-case-specific data sets | Use-case-specific technologies | Use cases |

Data for each domain, such as the customer, **is inefficiently reworked for every use case;** quality, definitions, and formats vary.

Source: Veeral Desai, Tim Fountaine, and Kayvaun Rowshankish, "A Better Way to Put Your Data to Work," *Harvard Business Review*, July–August 2022

EXHIBIT 25.1

A data product approach results in standardization that saves time and money

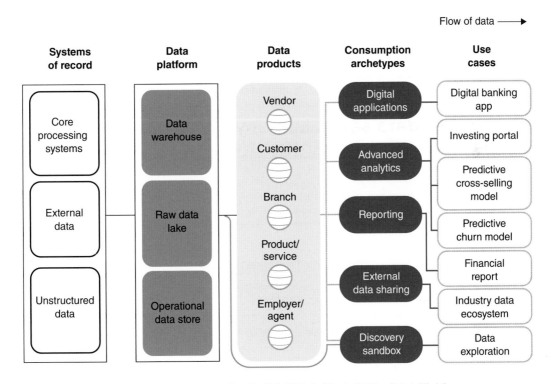

Source: Veeral Desai, Tim Fountaine, and Kayvaun Rowshankish, "A Better Way to Put Your Data to Work," *Harvard Business Review*, July–August 2022

EXHIBIT 25.2

While an organization might have hundreds of use cases on its roadmap, it typically consumes data in one of five ways, which we call consumption archetypes (see Exhibit 25.3). Data products built to support one or more of these consumption archetypes can easily be applied to multiple business applications with similar archetypes.

Not every data element should be packaged in a data product. Only focus on those that have a high degree of reusability across different use cases. For example, in a customer-360 data product, perhaps information about the geolocation of the customer's buildings is needed as part of a solution to assess safety risk, but this information has no use for other solutions. In this case, it makes more sense to capture the data directly from the data platform or the source systems with a custom data pipeline built just for that need.

Consumption archetypes for data products

ARCHETYPE	REQUIREMENTS	EXAMPLE USES
Digital applications	Specific data cleaned and stored in a particular format and frequency (e.g., delivering access in real time to event streams of GPS or sensor data)	A marketing trends app or vehicle tracking app
Advanced analytics systems	Data cleaned and delivered at a certain frequency and engineered to allow processing by machine learning and AI systems	Simulation and optimization engines
Reporting systems	Highly governed data with clear definitions – managed closely for quality, security, and changes – aggregated at a basic level and delivered in an audited form	Operational or regulatory compliance dashboards
Discovery sandboxes	A combination of raw and aggregated data	Ad hoc analysis for exploring new use cases
External data-sharing systems	Adherence to stringent policies and agreements about where the data sit and processes for managing and securing data	Banking systems that share fraud insights

Source: Veeral Desai, Tim Fountaine, and Kayvaun Rowshankish, "A Better Way to Put Your Data to Work," *Harvard Business Review*, July–August 2022

EXHIBIT 25.3

Building data products requires investments. You need to select them judiciously.

Identifying data products that generate value

Building data products is an essential requirement for digital and AI transformations. While there is a wide variety of data products that firms could build, doing so can be expensive and time consuming, so it's crucial to develop a clear view of the specific data needs as described in the previous chapter. In many cases, companies will shortchange this process, relying on an imprecise understanding of the data set needed or an incorrect view of the digital solution requirements. This can lead to buying a data set or investing millions for a large team and months of work that doesn't actually create much value.

Understanding the business need for a given data product boils down to a sharp analysis that answers the following questions:

- Is the data product unique? Similar data may already exist in the organization or in the marketplace.
- Is the product relevant to the people and systems who will ultimately use it? For real estate, that might mean a company has great data, but only for certain markets that their marketing team and customers don't care about.
- What does "good" look like? Be clear about what the minimum bar for quality is. For example, for commercial real estate data, it might be important to have data within a month for priority markets, whereas other markets might not need such recent data. Similarly, it's important to define how precise the data needs to be. In this same real estate example, does the data need to be at the block, neighborhood, or ZIP code level?
- How many use cases can this data product support, and what is the value of those cases? Data products should serve multiple use cases so that the asset has the greatest use. For many companies, that can be a customer-360 product that multiple teams – marketing, sales, R&D – can use to develop their own products and solutions.

The goal of this process is to narrow the options and identify the data elements that are distinctive, valuable, and shared. With this in place, companies can set targets of what data products to actually build, put together a plan for building them, and hire the right types and number of people.

Setting up data product pods

Data products require dedicated pods and funding. Each data product should have a (data) product owner and a cross-functional pod that is funded to build and continually improve the product and enable new use cases. The data product owner has multiple duties: setting direction, understanding the opportunities and the needs across the organization and clients, optimizing investment value, developing and leading execution against a roadmap, managing dependencies, and measuring success.

Each pod is made up of four to eight people with specific skillsets, which will vary based on the nature of the underlying data and how the product will be used (see Exhibit 25.4). It is best practice to bring business people into the pod to provide the user perspective (including feedback), which helps improve the products and identify new use cases. It may also make sense to include legal, compliance, and risk subject matter experts to develop compliant and socially responsible data products.

In the construct of the operating model, data pods are often part of data platforms because they produce a service that gets used by customer/user-facing pods (read more on platforms in Chapter 14).

The chief data officer should establish standards and best practices for how pods document data provenance, audit data use, and measure data quality. These standards should also cover how the necessary technologies should fit together for each consumption archetype so they can be reused across data products. A center of excellence is often helpful for developing these practices and patterns.

To confirm that their products meet end-user needs and are continually improving, data product teams should measure the value of their work. Relevant metrics may include the number of monthly users for a given product, the number of times a product is reused across the business, satisfaction scores from surveys of data users, and the return on investment of the use cases enabled.

Example of a pod that develops data products

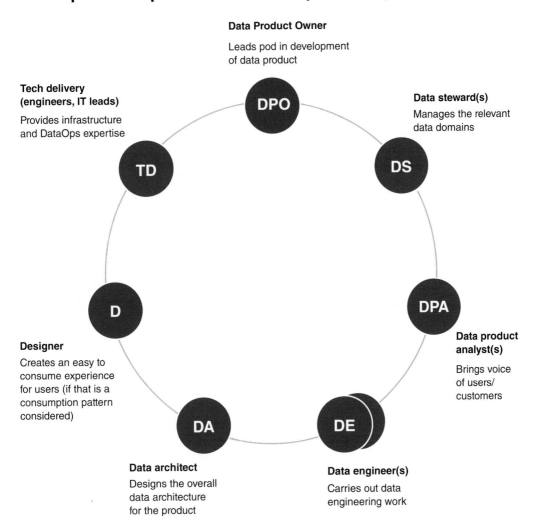

Data Product Owner

Leads pod in development of data product

Tech delivery (engineers, IT leads)

Provides infrastructure and DataOps expertise

Data steward(s)

Manages the relevant data domains

Designer

Creates an easy to consume experience for users (if that is a consumption pattern considered)

Data product analyst(s)

Brings voice of users/ customers

Data architect

Designs the overall data architecture for the product

Data engineer(s)

Carries out data engineering work

EXHIBIT 25.4

Because quality issues can erode end-user trust and usage, data product teams closely manage data definitions (for instance, whether the definition of customer data is limited to active customers or includes active and former customers), availability, and access controls that meet the right level of governance for each use case. To confirm data integrity, they work closely with data stewards who own data source systems (see Chapter 27).

Developing data products

The process of developing data products is iterative, requiring pods to continuously test and adapt the product until it's ready for use. It normally takes three to six months to build an MVP version of a data product. From this point, the team iterates on the product based on user feedback (internal or external).

At the highest level, data product pods work through an iterative process of defining requirements for data, deciding what data to use and getting it in good shape, and then sharing that curated data through a variety of potential consumption archetypes. For example, the data product could offer an API to enable easy access and consumption, providing direct integrations with key operational systems. It could also provide a set of dynamic dashboards with embedded analytics to enable business decisions. See Exhibit 25.5 and the following example for a best-practice six-step process to develop a data product.

Data product development approach

"6S" data product recipe – example

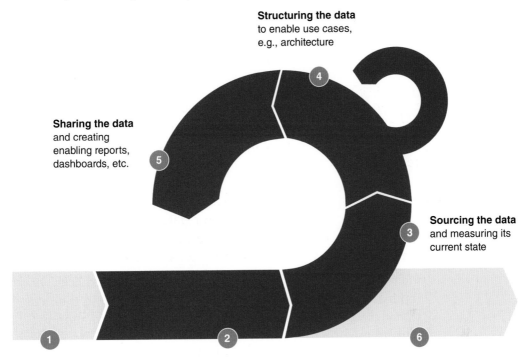

Structuring the data to enable use cases, e.g., architecture

Sharing the data and creating enabling reports, dashboards, etc.

Sourcing the data and measuring its current state

Scoping where to focus development to create value

Upfront planning – "Sprint 0" to develop the product backlog

Selecting the data to curate over time

Agile sprints to iteratively develop the product

Steering the product by confirming roles and processes

Develop plan for next release

EXHIBIT 25.5

Case example: A credit card company creates a "single source of truth" about their customers

A large global credit card issuer had nearly 200 different applications managing customer data. Each of these applications cost an average of $300,000 per year to maintain. Worse, this proliferation of applications led to challenges with regulators, who asserted that the applications didn't have a consistent "source of truth" for customer information to assess risk and other factors.

To address this issue, the company mapped its use cases to data products and assigned a value to each one. In this way, they identified and developed eight specific customer data products (e.g., Customer 360, Merchant 360), which had the added benefit of uncovering new ways to support their applications. They built a set of shared assets (e.g., data lake, data catalog, shared repository of analytics code), which reduced the effort required to maintain their environment, helped deliver new capabilities quickly, and reduced the complexity of staying compliant. Having their customer data in order enabled them to provide information to all parts of the business from a single source. In the end, they saved an estimated $300 million a year in cost while providing better service and better compliance.

Note

1. Joshan Cherian Abraham, Guilherme Cruz, Sebastian Cubela, Tomás Lajous, Kayvaun Rowshankish, Sanchit Tiwari, and Rodney Zemmel, "Digital twins: From one twin to the enterprise metaverse," McKinsey .com, October 2022, https://www.mckinsey.com/capabilities/mckinsey -digital/our-insights/digital-twins-from-one-twin-to-the-enterprise -metaverse.

Chapter 26

Data architecture, or the system of data "pipes"

The script is a blueprint for the film. There are very few bad scripts that make good movies.

—Topher Grace

If you think of data as water, then data architecture is the system of "pipes" that deliver water from where it's stored to where it's used. Data architecture is the master environment to manage where data is stored, transformed, analyzed, and consumed by users or applications. Without sound data architecture, companies struggle, as data is often spread and trapped across dozens of data silos (e.g., legacy core systems).

When well implemented, data architecture leads to the ability to build reusable and high-quality data products more quickly and put data within easy reach of teams. This leads to better results for decision making, better intelligence in customer-facing applications and better internal access to, and control of, the data.[1]

In their words: A data platform to enable agility

For most companies, the traditional approach to managing IT has been to build a budget around big application projects. Most customers are realizing they need to go to a more agile model, where the applications they develop are modular; they're smaller. That move toward an agile model is really helped by having a data platform that can support different applications.

Once you build an independent data platform, you can make application development much more agile. The platform has to be metadata based so you can actually understand and have a true catalog of data. It doesn't have to store all the data. It's just a place where the data gets processed into the right applications. That creates an abstraction layer.

Think of the supply of data coming from back-end systems and older systems, which can only move so fast. And the consumption of data is changing much more rapidly. By creating an abstraction layer through the data platform, you are enabling new applications to move much faster without having to create point-to-point connections.

—Anil Chakravarthy, President, Digital Experience Business, Adobe

Data architecture archetypes

There are five archetypical data architectures to build a modern data platform (see Exhibit 26.1). Each of these is built on cloud-based scalable storage offered by leading cloud service providers, but the database and data access technologies built on top of this are different.

The data platform must serve the needs of AI-based digital solutions you aspire to build, but it must also meet the needs of business intelligence (BI) use cases such as creating management reports and monitoring operations. This duality continues to be reflected in the way companies build their data platform with both the data lake

Data architecture archetypes

CLOUD-NATIVE DATA LAKE

Centralized serverless architecture leveraging object storage and compute which can scale independently

Optimized for (very) large-scale data marts for SQL analytics and modern AI/ML applications

Flexible foundation to add capabilities (e.g., DWH, real-time) but beginning to be seen as "legacy" architecture

CLOUD-NATIVE DATA WAREHOUSE

Highly scalable and agile SQL-driven platform with independently scalable storage and compute

Implements modern data transformation driven by SQL or UI-centric ETL tools (e.g., dbt, Matillion)

Very good performance on vast majority of enterprise analytical workloads

Very well supported by tooling and required SQL skills are plentiful among data users, analysts, and data experts

LAKEHOUSE

Combines benefits of Data Lake and DWH into an integrated platform for analytics (e.g., BI, SQL) and AI/ML use cases

Leverages nextgen storage technologies (e.g., Delta Lake or Iceberg) supporting ACID transactions on top of object storage

Handles the most complex batch data jobs and high-volume streaming data (e.g., IoT)

Less mature tooling but rapid pace of technical innovation

DATA MESH

Emerging archetype; fundamental departure from centralized IT and data functions

Decentralized architecture approach focused on data products fully owned by business domains

Data products are curated for quality, cataloged, and accessed via well-defined data services

Data products are built leveraging any of the data architecture archetypes defined above

DATA FABRIC

Emerging strategy for creating a unified data environment across the Enterprise's data landscape

The Fabric is stitched together through metadata into a secure, unified data management layer

Meant to solve multicloud scenarios for heterogeneous data sources and infrastructure

No existing tooling currently enables a true Data Fabric, it must rather be built in-house

EXHIBIT 26.1

archetype (for AI) and the cloud-based data warehouse archetype (for BI) coexisting. These have been the two dominant archetypes for the past decade. In the early 2020s a new archetype emerged – the lakehouse – that seeks to unify the data tech stack to serve both BI and AI needs.

The last two archetypes listed in the previous exhibit have recently emerged to address the trend to decentralize data management (data mesh) and the need of large corporations to manage data across multicloud environments (data fabric).

We describe below what each archetype is best suited for, and its limitations:

The data lake is the simplest archetype and has well-understood reference architectures available across all major cloud platforms. It is best suited for data science workloads, especially for handling unstructured data, and is a good starting point for organizations that are just beginning to dip their toes into advanced analytics and AI/ML, and so need a simple architecture that can scale with their needs.

Until recently, data lakes have resided on-premises in the form of the complex Hadoop platform. Cloud is a game changer here, where Hadoop's core capabilities are delivered through scalable and robust data services managed by the cloud provider in the form of object storage (e.g., S3, ADLS), Spark (e.g., AWS Glue, Azure Synapse Analytics), and a distributed query engine (e.g., Amazon Athena, BigQuery).

The downside of this architecture is that it is unsuitable for typical SQL-heavy BI analytics workloads, is engineering-heavy, and tends to result in centralization of data, which can eventually become a bottleneck for the organization.

The cloud-native data warehouse (e.g., Snowflake, Synapse, BigQuery) is the dominant design to create BI for operational and management reporting, and custom BI reports. This architecture radically simplifies the tech stack to quickly deliver sophisticated business intelligence and analytics capabilities. This design puts SQL at the center of data engineering work, which can still be orchestrated into modern, well-tested data pipelines, using

DBT, a data transformation tool. This architecture is especially attractive for cloud-native organizations and large organizations migrating to cloud.

The main disadvantage of this architecture is that it doesn't yet support advanced analytics and AI/ML development very well. SQL is also not always the most effective approach for high-complexity data workflows. Lastly, its ease of use can also lead to an explosion of amateur use that, if not carefully governed, can end up slowing down value creation rather than accelerating it.

The lakehouse is an innovation by Databricks that combines the capabilities of the data lake and the data warehouse into a single integrated platform. It represents a major step forward in capabilities compared to the data lake, especially when handling large-scale structured data, without any detriment to unstructured data-handling capabilities (e.g., ACID[2] transactions, real-time support, data versioning, data management, SQL support).

Despite the expanded set of capabilities, it requires significant engineering skills to develop for and manage cost effectively. It makes most financial sense for large data sets (100+ GB scale). All major cloud providers and new niche players like Tabular (Apache Iceberg), Onehouse (Apache Hudi), and Dremio (Arctic) are pushing lakehouse archetype forward, confirming the lakehouse as a modern data architecture pattern, not just the proprietary design of a single vendor.

The data mesh is a decentralized approach to data that seeks to unlock the next phase of growth for large organizations that have achieved a high degree of maturity in their data capabilities and struggle to meet exploding demand.

In the data mesh approach, data is delivered as curated, reusable data products under the direct ownership of business domains (e.g., marketing and sales, regional operations, a manufacturing plant) that use data tooling provided by IT. A mesh emerges as multiple domains build their own data capabilities and source data from one another, preferably using data federation tools as a common data service layer to minimize unnecessary data movement. Domains are responsible for their own data, which means they must fix data availability and quality issues for themselves and other domains sourcing their data through the mesh.

The decision to move to a data mesh can easily evolve from the data lakehouse as it has more to do with your data operating model than the choice of data technologies. For most organizations starting with highly centralized data and IT capabilities, and low business data maturity and ownership, the data mesh journey may not be a good fit. However, data mesh is not an all-or-nothing proposition. Large organizations may find benefits in operating in a hybrid model where the most mature business domains onboard into the data mesh model, owning their data and building data products to meet their needs, while less mature domains continue to leverage centralized data expertise.

The data fabric is a modernized, centralized approach to data, the "yin" to data mesh's "yang." What distinguishes the data fabric is the promise of greatly accelerated and cheaper integration through virtualization to connect data sources to the data fabric without unnecessary data movement. This solves a challenge faced by large organizations operating in multicloud environments. While the data fabric archetype has great future potential, the capabilities needed to automatically link and integrate data across a large, complex organization are only beginning to emerge. As of the time of this writing, it may be too early to consider the data fabric archetype.

The selection of an archetype needs to take into consideration your current cloud journey and your digital roadmap. If you foresee having many AI-intensive applications in addition to your baseload BI applications, consider a data lakehouse. On the other hand, if your digital roadmap points to many BI-intensive applications, consider building a cloud-based data warehouse.

Cloud versus on-premises data infrastructure

Leveraging cloud infrastructure from major public cloud providers can be a significant accelerator for successful implementation and low-cost operation of large-scale data capabilities. Cloud-native services offer massive benefits in terms of the productivity of your data teams, which are no longer forced to manage overly complex data systems and can instead focus their time on the delivery of the use cases that drive business value.

Numerous cloud-native data technologies have emerged to facilitate building digital and AI-based solutions. The journey to enable modern cloud-based data capabilities is constantly getting easier, putting technologies that were once differentiators within the reach of every company.

Some organizations opt to build capabilities on-premises or via a hybrid of on-premises and cloud. Two issues typically drive this decision: concerns around using cloud for highly sensitive data or critical workloads, or a belief that the organization can design and build modern data capabilities that are comparable to those of cloud providers.

Keeping up with the pace of innovation and capabilities of cloud providers is challenging, so opting for an on-premises or hybrid approach is usually only pursued by large organizations with a history of technology innovation. But beware. Success requires cutting-edge in-house engineering skills, investments in building and maintaining modern data centers, and the commitment to sustain these investments over the long term. Modern cloud platforms usually require smaller investments and deliver a regular stream of innovation that organizations will have trouble matching, especially for AI workloads where innovation is especially fast and where infrastructure needs are the most complex.

Deciding on data capabilities and adopting reference architectures

Each architecture described in this chapter involves a set of necessary capabilities such as event streaming, data warehouses, and data APIs that let data efficiently "flow" from where it's sourced (at the bottom of Exhibit 26.2) to where it's used (at the top of Exhibit 26.2). Which data capabilities you need depends on the use cases. The challenge is that there are literally hundreds of data technologies that have emerged to help build and operate a data architecture. This situation reflects the rapid pace of innovation in this field, but it also makes the selection and integration of these data technologies more complex.

Organizations commonly view their data architecture implementation as a multiyear "waterfall" project that maps out each phase from building a data lake and pipelines to implementing data-consumption tools, tackling each phase only after completing the previous ones. You can realize faster results by taking an approach guided by your digital roadmap, and adopting a reference architecture – a set of technologies proven to work well together to deliver on your chosen archetype.

In this approach, your lead data architect will first develop a high-level target of the data capabilities needed – a version of Exhibit 26.2 – focused on building a "minimum viable data architecture" to meet the needs of your priority digital solutions (including both BI- and AI-intensive solutions). This data capability map will help build alignment on what's needed and provide a good benchmarking framework when analyzing the current-state architecture. While a lead data architect owns this assessment, the input of data consumers, data managers/administrators, and data product and application owners who can speak about required technical capabilities is critical.

Data capabilities

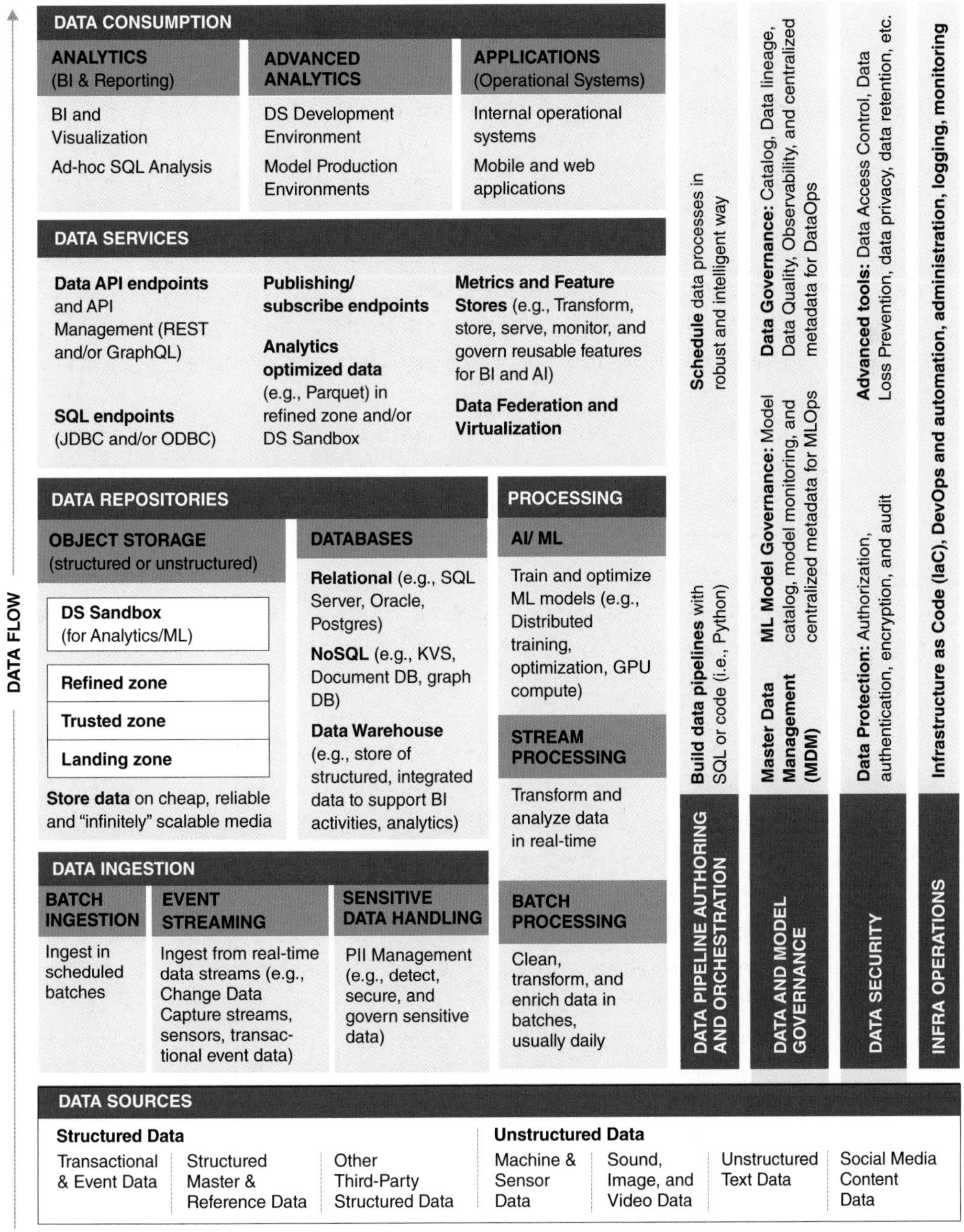

The exhibit is organized as a layered stack with "DATA FLOW" as a vertical arrow on the left side.

DATA CONSUMPTION

ANALYTICS (BI & Reporting)	ADVANCED ANALYTICS	APPLICATIONS (Operational Systems)
BI and Visualization	DS Development Environment	Internal operational systems
Ad-hoc SQL Analysis	Model Production Environments	Mobile and web applications

DATA SERVICES

Data API endpoints and API Management (REST and/or GraphQL)	Publishing/ subscribe endpoints	Metrics and Feature Stores (e.g., Transform, store, serve, monitor, and govern reusable features for BI and AI)
SQL endpoints (JDBC and/or ODBC)	Analytics optimized data (e.g., Parquet) in refined zone and/or DS Sandbox	Data Federation and Virtualization

DATA REPOSITORIES / **PROCESSING**

OBJECT STORAGE (structured or unstructured)	DATABASES	AI/ ML
DS Sandbox (for Analytics/ML)	Relational (e.g., SQL Server, Oracle, Postgres)	Train and optimize ML models (e.g., Distributed training, optimization, GPU compute)
Refined zone	NoSQL (e.g., KVS, Document DB, graph DB)	
Trusted zone		STREAM PROCESSING
Landing zone	Data Warehouse (e.g., store of structured, integrated data to support BI activities, analytics)	Transform and analyze data in real-time
Store data on cheap, reliable and "infinitely" scalable media		

DATA INGESTION

BATCH INGESTION	EVENT STREAMING	SENSITIVE DATA HANDLING	BATCH PROCESSING
Ingest in scheduled batches	Ingest from real-time data streams (e.g., Change Data Capture streams, sensors, transactional event data)	PII Management (e.g., detect, secure, and govern sensitive data)	Clean, transform, and enrich data in batches, usually daily

Vertical bands (right side):

- Schedule data processes in robust and intelligent way
- Build data pipelines with SQL or code (i.e., Python) — **DATA PIPELINE AUTHORING AND ORCHESTRATION**
- Data Governance: Catalog, Data lineage, Data Quality, Observability, and centralized metadata for DataOps
- ML Model Governance: Model catalog, model monitoring, and centralized metadata for MLOps
- Master Data Management (MDM) — **DATA AND MODEL GOVERNANCE**
- Advanced tools: Data Access Control, Data Loss Prevention, data privacy, data retention, etc.
- Data Protection: Authorization, authentication, encryption, and audit — **DATA SECURITY**
- Infrastructure as Code (IaC), DevOps and automation, administration, logging, monitoring — **INFRA OPERATIONS**

DATA SOURCES

Structured Data			Unstructured Data			
Transactional & Event Data	Structured Master & Reference Data	Other Third-Party Structured Data	Machine & Sensor Data	Sound, Image, and Video Data	Unstructured Text Data	Social Media Content Data

EXHIBIT 26.2

Once you have selected the data capabilities you need and established the buildout sequence, the selection of specific data technologies can start. This is where a reference architecture matters. In general, the core technology components will be determined by the archetype selected and your chosen cloud service provider (CSP). Exhibit 26.3 shows the technology selection for a lakehouse architecture built using Databricks on Azure. In this specific instance, the design maximizes the use of Databricks' features. An alternative design could have maximized open-source software to minimize vendor lock-in, reduce cost, and/or secure best-of-breed capabilities. Similar lakehouse architectures exist for the other cloud environments.

In summary, don't reinvent the wheel but instead adopt a proven reference architecture to accelerate your design and minimize your implementation risks.

Case study: A retail bank moves its data architecture to the cloud

A rapidly growing retail bank in Asia had embarked on a program to adopt cloud to modernize its data and analytics capabilities as part of a digital transformation. They prioritized a customer-360 "super-mart" data product to support both business intelligence and AI use cases. But they had an on-premises Hadoop data platform that could only support a few reporting use cases despite several years of development, a highly centralized IT function, and no data APIs.

To achieve compliance with banking cloud regulations and a desire to take advantage of cloud innovation, the bank realized it needed to build a hybrid platform (on-premises and public cloud), use cloud-neutral tools to avoid lock-in to the selected cloud provider, and be cloud-native by leveraging tools that could be readily deployed either on-premises (e.g., Kubernetes) or in the cloud with minimal or no change. They also needed the customer-360 super-mart to handle 100GB+/day data volumes, hundreds of concurrent analytics users, and support easy connections to operational systems (e.g., B2C mobile app) via APIs.

The team decided to build out a hybrid open-source-based data lake leveraging Kubernetes on premises and a cloud service provider for cloud, using the same cloud-native OSS tooling (e.g., Python/Spark/Airflow/Parquet on S3) for both. Data from the bank's operational systems was ingested into a common landing zone on premises and was then anonymized and sent to the cloud to build data products and support analytics use cases. Non-anonymized data remained on premises to comply with regulatory reporting. Data APIs were developed to mediate access to the customer 360 data product. A data federation tool (e.g., Dremio, Trino) served as a common SQL access layer that could span across on-premises and cloud-based data sets.

The data platform and customer-360 data product was built in about 10 months with a dramatic increase in use-case deployment and processing speeds. For one use case, this approach helped increase data processing speeds by 50% and allowed the model to deliver more insights and generate more impact (>$100,000/day of value).

Best practices for designing a data architecture

Start small. If there are many data capabilities you don't have, define a minimum viable architecture to meet the highest-priority needs and start there. Build and deploy a minimum viable architecture that delivers the specific data components required for each desired use case. For example, a mid-sized asset management company defined a cloud-based data platform and stood up an initial version that they could use to begin structuring data in the course of just a few months.

Reference architecture: Lakehouse using Databricks on Azure

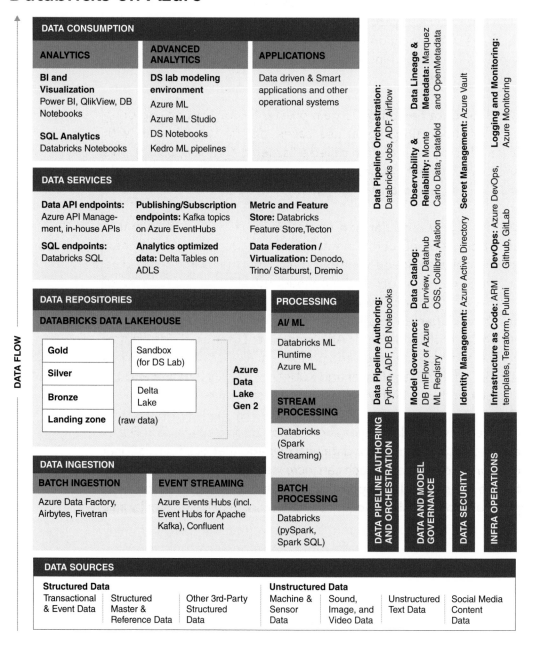

EXHIBIT 26.3

Drive maturity across the entire data lifecycle rather than over-investing in just one stage of the data flow. The architecture will only be as strong as the weakest component. For example, if real-time data flow and processing is needed, only investing to enable real-time data ingestion will not be sufficient – the data will flow in rapidly and then be hindered by batch processes in the warehouse or other points.

Build for data flexibility. To gain greater flexibility when exploring data or supporting digital use cases, design data models with fewer physical tables (often called a "schema-light" approach). This approach makes it easier to explore data, offers greater flexibility in storing data, and reduces complexity by simplifying data queries.

Build a highly modular and evolutionary data architecture that uses best-of-breed components, which can be replaced with new technologies as needed without affecting other parts of the data architecture. Focus on data pipeline- and API-based interfaces to simplify integration between disparate tools and platforms. Build out an API management platform (often called an API gateway) to create and publish data-centric APIs, implement usage policies, control access, and measure usage and performance. Analytics workbenches such as Amazon SageMaker and Kubeflow simplify building end-to-end solutions in a highly modular data architecture.

Build a semantic data layer aligned with business data domains as a single source of truth for data and manage that as a foundational data product. This approach can increase data quality and reliability for the benefit of all. Graph databases are ideal for this purpose, in particular for digital applications that require massive scalability and real-time capabilities, and for data layers serving AI applications. Graph databases offer the ability to model relationships within data in a powerful and flexible manner.

Notes

1. Sven Blumberg, Jorge Machado, Henning Soller, and Asin Tavakoli, "Breaking through data-architecture gridlock to scale AI," McKinsey .com, January 26, 2021, https://www.mckinsey.com/capabilities/ mckinsey-digital/our-insights/breaking-through-data-architecture-gridlock-to-scale-ai; Antonio Castro, Jorge Machado, Matthias Roggendorf, and Henning Soller, "How to build a data architecture to drive innovation – today and tomorrow," McKinsey.com, June 3, 2020, https://www.mckinsey.com/capabilities/mckinsey-digital/our-insights/ how-to-build-a-data-architecture-to-drive-innovation-today-and-tomorrow.
2. ACID refers to the properties of transaction: atomicity, consistency, isolation, and durability. ACID transactions provide the highest possible data reliability and integrity by ensuring that data never falls into an inconsistent state because of an operation that only partially completes.

Chapter 27

Organize to get the most from your data

Chaos in the midst of chaos isn't funny, but chaos in the midst of order is.

—Steve Martin

The data operating model is the overall approach for how the organization should manage data. It has four primary components: organization, talent and culture, tooling and DataOps, and governance and risk (see Exhibit 27.1).

Some companies worry that building up this capability can seem like developing another bureaucracy or is perhaps only relevant to large banks. But in our experience, getting this data governance and operating model right is absolutely pivotal to becoming a data-intensive enterprise. It's easy to neglect having a strong operating model when you're dealing with one or two data use cases since you can often get away without it. But getting value from hundreds if not thousands of use cases is simply impossible without an effective and well-organized operating model. By developing clarity in these areas, companies can avoid the conflicts, confusion, and delays that typically hamper efforts around data.[1]

Components of an effective data operating model

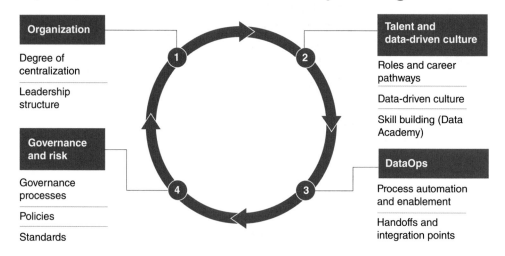

Organization

Degree of centralization

Leadership structure

Governance and risk

Governance processes

Policies

Standards

Talent and data-driven culture

Roles and career pathways

Data-driven culture

Skill building (Data Academy)

DataOps

Process automation and enablement

Handoffs and integration points

EXHIBIT 27.1

Organization

Many companies struggle with how they should organize for effective data management and analytics. Who should own data? Should we have a data organization? How should it link with the business? And with IT? Who should own data engineering? Should data privacy and compliance be separated? These questions are complex because data touches every part of the organization.

There are two central design decisions to make: the degree of centralization and what senior leadership roles and management forums are needed.

Degree of centralization

Some companies have primarily centralized models, with teams of data staff that serve the whole enterprise. Others have a primarily decentralized model, with each business unit and function developing capabilities to meet its own needs. Both models can work on a limited basis but are not generally responsive enough or able to scale to meet broader business needs.

Leading companies deploy a federated model where a central function (often referred to as the data management office or chief data office or enterprise data office) sets policies and standards, and provides support and oversight, while business units and functions manage data activities like running data governance day to day, defining and managing data products, and building data pipelines to enable consumption.

Striking the right balance between central and local responsibilities in this federated approach should happen at the functional level. Exhibit 27.2 describes the typical setup across data functional areas in a best-practice federated model.

Leadership structure and management forums

An increasingly large number of organizations have a chief data officer (CDO) or equivalent to lead the data functions. This leader often reports to the CIO, but this varies significantly depending on the broader organizational structure, needs, and goals for data (e.g., reporting to the COO, CRO, or, in some cases, even directly to the CEO). This role is sometimes merged with analytics leadership and called a chief data and analytics officer (CDAO). This is often done to ensure that data efforts are closely aligned to analytics use case delivery and impact. It is less common in industries with significant data-related regulation (e.g., banking) where data governance and data risk management have elevated importance.

Typical setup across data capability areas in a best-practice federated model

	Degree of centralization[1]	Where capa-bilities report	What the center provides[2]	What is delivered in federated manner
Data strategy	>50–75%	Chief Data Office	Enterprise data strategy, value assurance across BUs	Business unit-level data strategies, use cases, and opportunity and issue areas
Data product management	<25%	Chief Data Office	Data product standards, tooling, and playbook; management of some enterprise products	Management of the majority of data products, with cross-functional teams comprised of Business, Data, and Technology resources
Data architecture	>75%	Chief Data Office or IT	Enterprise data architecture, architectural guardrails and review	Ownership and management of source systems; identification of external data needs
Data engineering	25–50%	Chief Data Office or IT	Deep expertise, pooled capacity for use case enablement	Data engineering teams aligned to business areas (in particular as data maturity increases)
Data governance	<25%	Chief Data Office	Data governance policy and standards, metrics and dashboards, governance of some enterprise domains	Day-to-day management of data domains (e.g., metadata definition, data quality measurement and improvement)
Data operations	50–75%	Chief Data Office or IT	Data operations team that manages issues and data requests (e.g., for extracts, new datasets)	Remediation of issues unique to a business unit or requiring deep business expertise
Data risk (incl. data privacy)	>75%	Chief Data Office or Legal/ Compliance	Data risk taxonomy; interpretation of regulations; and policies, standards, and controls to manage risk	Business unit–specific risks and regulatory concerns. Business guidance on acceptable risk tolerance.
Data talent and culture	>75%	Chief Data Office or HR	Data capability building, talent strategy and management, and change management	Role modeling of target culture and behaviors. Input on resource performance. Business unit–specific capability building.

1. Typical % of FTE in the center
2. Usually in an Enterprise Data Office, but with some areas commonly owned by IT, Legal, Risk, and others

EXHIBIT 27.2

The scope of the CDO always includes data strategy and data governance. They also commonly have oversight over data product management, data architecture, data operations, data risk, and data talent and culture. The scale of the organization varies. For example, some large banks facing a high degree of regulatory scrutiny with a largely centralized model have data organizations with hundreds of staff. On the other hand, a moderately sized retail organization just getting started on its data and analytics organization may have fewer than 20 people in the function.

In the federated organizational model, it is important to establish forums to bring together teams and leaders across the enterprise to ensure alignment. Organizations typically do this at two levels: a data-domain-level forum and a senior-executive-level forum. The data domain forum is often led by the head of data governance (a direct report to the CDO) and brings together all of the data domain owners. This council monitors progress and issues across data domains, aligns on any changes in standards or direction (set by the CDO), and works to address roadblocks.

The senior-executive-level data forum is often chaired by the CDO and brings together senior leaders (often the CEO and direct reports) to set the strategy for data and make critical decisions on initiatives, people, and funding. They also address any unsolved issues from the data-domain-level forum.

Talent and a data-driven culture

New roles at the intersection of data and the business are needed to manage data well. Key roles include the data domain steward, data product owner, and data quality analyst (see Exhibit 27.3). In some cases, these roles can be filled with current employees given sufficient training and support. More technical roles like data architect, data engineer, and data platform owner are also critical (as described in Sections One and Three of this book).

Data-domain-aligned roles are often part-time responsibilities (especially data domain owners) or follow a "burst then sustain" model where a full-time role and a team are staffed for three to six months to rapidly establish the data domain (e.g., defining metadata, establishing data quality rules, remediating high-priority data quality issues). The domain is then managed by part-time coverage from the data domain owner and steward(s).

Key data roles

Category	Role	Responsibilities
Data-domain-aligned roles	Data domain steward	Drives data governance efforts for a given data domain, working to improve quality and usability of the data
	Data domain owner (sometimes called "data owner")	Is ultimately accountable for data quality in the domain. Must "sign off" that the data is accurate; often part-time responsibility, or follow a "burst then sustain" model
Data-product-aligned roles	Data product owner	Sets the direction and oversees the development of a data product – i.e., a minimum collection of data to solve a specific business need (often pulling data from multiple data domain areas)
Data-architecture-aligned roles	Data platform owner	Sets the direction and oversees the development of the data platform – i.e., the set of technologies that are used to enable consumption, manipulation, and analysis of data
	Data architect	Establish information architecture strategy for data and assist data engineer in ingestion process
Roles that span capabilities	Data engineer	Build reusable data pipelines, both to ingest data into the architecture and to structure data for domains, products, and use cases
	Data quality analyst	Measure data quality against business needs, identify issues, and propose and execute solutions to improve

EXHIBIT 27.3

DataOps tooling

DataOps uses agile principles and technology to reduce the amount of time it takes to develop new data assets and update existing ones while also boosting data quality. Like DevOps, DataOps is structured into continuous integration and deployment phases with a focus on eliminating "low-value" and automatable activities, such as automatically pushing data engineers' new code into production, or automatically checking data quality and monitoring performance. While leading companies are still shaping what true best-in-class DataOps looks like, it requires rewiring your process in three ways:

1. **Fully integrated** data operations activities as part of the pod at each phase of the solution lifecycle, including development, testing, deployment, and monitoring stages (versus being handled later in the process by a separate team).

2. **Maximum automation,** using dedicated DataOps pipelines and scripting to fully automate deployment as well as security and data risk controls, including relevant data privacy considerations. Release management is fully automated.

3. **Robust set of tooling** for automated testing, end-to-end data lineage, and automated infrastructure deployment, with full-scale monitoring.

Governance and risk

Data governance essentially functions as the "tollgate" that allows enterprises to accelerate innovation confidently while ensuring that data is reusable and meets relevant risk and regulatory requirements. Historically thought of mainly from a risk focus, modern data governance practices can also drive speed and scale (some organizations are even rebranding data governance to "data enablement" to emphasize this fact). Data governance establishes robust definitions for data, monitors and improves data quality, and helps focus efforts where there are the biggest data issues given business requirements. Data governance also helps ensure that data flowing into (e.g., from a third party) and out of (e.g., to clients) the organization is robust and appropriately protected.

The data management office should establish a data governance council consisting of data domain stewards across the organization, often with C-suite leaders involved. It should engage with the C-suite to understand its needs, highlight the current data challenges and limitations, explain the role of data governance, and align with ongoing business priorities.

The data management office should describe boundaries and accountabilities for the data domains and work with heads of the business to propose and confirm data domain stewards. These stewards drive governance efforts day to day by prioritizing data elements for clean-up, and establishing quality standards. They should understand the value they will generate in these roles and be armed with the skills they need, including an understanding of the relevant regulations and core elements of the data architecture.

It is important to create tangible ways to track progress and value creation. For example, measure the amount of time data scientists and business intelligence analysts spend finding, curating, or enabling data for priority digital solutions, or the dollar losses associated with poor-quality data and associated business errors.

Tracking impact metrics like these helps ensure the attention and continuing support of top management. These metrics should be fed into a simple dashboard that leadership can easily access, which will help pinpoint where data issues are happening and empower the organization to quickly address them. Exhibit 27.4 shows an example dashboard used by a large bank.

Leading organizations take a "needs-based" approach when it comes to governance, adopting the level of sophistication appropriate to their organization and then adjusting the level of rigor by data set. The design of their programs should align with the level of regulation they uniquely face and the level of data complexity.

Example of data governance framework and executive level dashboard

Global bank example   ● Issue ○ At risk ● On target ● Completed

FRAMEWORK		SAMPLE TRACKING METRICS				
Name	**Definition**	**Metric name**	**Metric Results**	**Trend**	**Data sponsor**	**Data leader**
Data Program progress	**Tracking progress of data governance program implementation**	**Percentage of Milestones Complete** by accountable team (owner)	● 96% *(47/49)*	⬆	John	Jason
		Percentage of Milestones at Past Due by accountable team (owner)	● 4% *(2/49)*	⬇	John	Jason
Data policy and standard compliance	**Measure of compliance for the data governance policies and standards**	Launch **data governance forums** required for business-as-usual data governance	● 100% *(10/10)*	⊖	Kate	Kate
Data quality	**Measure of data quality from business process and data provider perspective**	Number of **Open Data Defects**	○ **Open Data Issues** 243 of 27,671*	⬆	Kate	Kevin
Data skills and talent	**Measure of the state of skills and talent needed to deliver the data program**	Priority hiring at leadership and one level down **data roles filled**	● 87% *(94/108)* 95% *(103/108)*	⬆	Kate	Marvin
Data risk	**Tracking risk reduction within data use cases**	Percentage of **VaR** impacted by adjustments (rolling 3 months avg.)	● 69% *45% Target*	⬆	John	Susan
		Reduction of total **expense variances** within Use Case 1	● 21% ($12.1B) **Reduced** *29% Target Reduction*	⬇	John	Susan

EXHIBIT 27.4

For example, organizations can apply light governance for data that is used only in an exploration setting and not beyond the boundaries of the R&D team. Data masking may be appropriate to ensure privacy, together with strict internal nondisclosure agreements (NDAs). However, as soon as such data is used in a broader setting, such as in interactions with customers, stronger governance principles need to be applied.

Data governance tools and platforms help organizations keep track of all of their data, improve data quality, and manage master data, among other things. There is a wide variety of tools on the market, including both newer platforms (e.g., Alation, Tamr, data.world, Octopai, or erwin) and established solutions (e.g., Informatica and Collibra).[2]

A crucial element in this process is the need to establish guardrails for how data should (and should not) be used, and communicate them to their employees, clients, and other stakeholders. A data program should go beyond just following regulations to protect the privacy of customers and the use of their data. It should also focus on providing transparency about what data is collected and how, how the information is used, and whether those use cases are appropriate. This is further complicated when building AI models, and companies need to take special care to ensure that they do not inadvertently build bias into their models. In addition, companies should regularly review data and data usage through a lens of how they conform with shifting regulations and laws.

Consider establishing a data ethics board, a cross-functional committee composed of representatives across business, compliance and legal, operations, audit, IT, and the C-suite. (See more on digital trust in Chapter 31.)

Notes

1. Bryan Petzold, Matthias Roggendorf, Kayvaun Rowshankish, and Christoph Sporleder, "Designing data governance that delivers value," McKinsey.com, June 26, 2022, https://www.mckinsey.com/capabilities/mckinsey-digital/our-insights/designing-data-governance-that-delivers-value.

2. Metadata: "Metadata is information that describes various facets of an information asset to improve its usability throughout its lifecycle." Source: Gartner, "Data lineage includes the data origin, what happens to it, and where it moves over time. Data lineage gives visibility while greatly simplifying the ability to trace errors back to the root cause in a data analytics process." Source: Natalie Hoang, "Data lineage helps drive business value," Trifacta, March 16, 2017.

Getting Ready
Section Five

The following is a set of questions to help you home in on the right actions to take:

Are you focusing your data cleaning and conditioning efforts on the data domains and data elements that will drive value?

Do you understand which data products your organization needs to be successful?

Do you have dedicated data product teams?

Are you clear on where combining your internal data with external data will create competitive advantage?

How are you making data more accessible to more people in your organization and directly to your digital solutions?

Do you measure data consumption?

Do you have an operating model for managing data where all the key stakeholders are clear on their roles and objectives?

Who are the data stewards in your organization and what difference are they making?

The Keys to Unlock Adoption and Scaling

How to both get users to adopt your digital solutions and scale those solutions across the enterprise

Developing a good digital solution can be complex and difficult. But for all the effort and focus needed, it's just the first step. Getting customers or business users to adopt that solution as part of their day-to-day activities, and scaling it across your customer base, markets, or organizational units – each with its own particularities – is often the biggest challenge.

It's usually easier to get investments for developing a digital solution than it is for driving its adoption. But that's a guaranteed recipe for not seeing a return on your digital investments. As a rule of thumb, for every $1 you spend on developing a digital solution, plan to spend at least another $1 (and sometimes more, depending on the solution) to ensure full adoption and scaling. That additional $1 will go toward implementing process changes, user training, change management initiatives, and sometimes even paying severance if productivity gains are involved.[1]

The core challenge in driving both adoption and scaling is addressing at a sufficiently granular level the technical, process, and human issues that keep a great solution from delivering its full value.

This section focuses on the specific change management complexities encountered in digital and AI transformations (we will not cover general change management topics like communications). While we are addressing adoption and scaling toward the end of the book, you need to think through these challenges at the beginning of the transformation.

Chapter 28: Nail user adoption and underlying business model changes. Capturing value requires you to go beyond addressing user needs to changing the underlying business model - a critical discipline that many overlook.

Chapter 29: Design solutions for easy replication and reuse. Design a replication capability that makes it easy to share and reuse digital solutions across different customer segments, markets, or organizational units.

Chapter 30: Ensuring impact by tracking what matters. Effective tracking requires a tight performance management architecture that links OKRs to operational KPIs, as well as a strong stagegate tracking process supported with tooling.

Chapter 31: Managing risk and building digital trust. Beware of the new risks introduced by your digital and AI transformation into areas such as cybersecurity, data privacy, and AI biases. Manage them by embedding control functions in the development process.

Chapter 32: So, what about culture? Pay attention to the "digital" leadership attributes of your top 300 people, and invest in building skills across the enterprise.

Note

1. Michael Chui and Bryce Hall, "How high-performing companies develop and scale AI," *Harvard Business Review*, March 19, 2020, https://hbr.org/2020/03/how-high-performing-companies-develop-and-scale-ai.

Chapter 28

Nail user adoption and underlying business model changes

Any sufficiently advanced technology is indistinguishable from magic.

—*Arthur C. Clarke*

We often hear discouraged leaders make comments like: "We seem to be forever stuck in pilot purgatory," or "There's a lot of inertia and resistance to change here," or "The pod delivered a good solution but business would not adopt it." These complaints are typical results of what we might call "last mile" issues. These are the issues that crop up when a business wants to implement a solution it has developed, only to find out that the users don't want it or it doesn't work as intended.

> ### Defining adoption and scaling
>
> **Adoption:** The usage of digital solutions by employees and/ or customers
>
> **Scaling:** An approach for capturing the full benefit of digital solutions as they get rolled out across customer segments, markets, or organizational units

Resolving these issues requires resolve and sustained effort, yes, but most importantly a commitment to managing digital solutions through the entire process from development to adoption.

Take the example of Freeport-McMoRan, a global mining company that developed a family of solutions for optimizing set points in copper concentrators. Rather than simply delivering the solutions, the development team worked side by side with frontline users for eight months after the solutions were initially rolled out. They created check-ins every three hours, 24/7, bringing together operators, mill engineers, and metallurgists to discuss the set-point recommendations from advanced analytics models and make operational changes in real time.

This approach ensured that the frontline teams knew how to use the solutions, learned to trust them, contributed to improving them, and became true advocates. That level of focus through the entire end-to-end process paid off. In just one quarter, the throughput at one of the mines exceeded 85,000 tons of ore per day—10 percent more than the previous quarter—while its copper-recovery rate rose by one percentage point and its operations became more stable. (read more about this case in Chapter 33).

It's helpful to think about adoption in two parts. First is the adoption of the solution by customers or users who are the targeted beneficiaries of the solution. This is essentially about making sure the digital solution itself works as expected and that people are convinced and eager to use it. Second is understanding the impact of implementing that solution on other elements of the business and adapting them as needed.

Two-pronged user adoption

Creating customer or user adoption is both a user experience challenge and a change management challenge. If the digital solution is not designed to be what the user needs or it does not fit naturally into the user workflow, it will fail and no amount of change management will fix this. This is an iterative process with frequent test-and-learn cycles grounded in data about how end users interact with the solution (read more in Chapter 16 on customer experience and design).

If the solution improves that user experience, you may still need to drive a change management program to ensure that it is adopted. Change management is about influencing end users through a series of specific interventions so they actually use the solution. Those change interventions are captured in a well-established and proven influence[1] model built around four elements (see Exhibit 28.1):

1. Leadership engagement and role modeling by leaders and peers to demonstrate support, enthusiasm, and encouragement for the new solutions being rolled out.

2. A compelling change story for why a solution matters to end users, to customers, and to the company overall.

3. Measurement and performance metrics (leading and lagging performance indicators) to track intended behaviors and outcomes, and to reward accordingly with the right incentives.

4. Role-based training and skill building to ensure that users have the right knowledge and upskilling to employ a solution successfully.

Influence model in action

Example: Driving the adoption of a revenue management solution for an airline's cargo business for its 250 cargo sales reps

Leadership engagement and role modeling	Compelling change story and communications
Involve the head of the cargo business in key development milestones of the solution	Communicate in company newsletter the value of new revenue management solution for customers, airline, and employees
Showcase the solution at annual sales conference	

Role-based trainings and skill building	Measurement and performance
Train 250 cargo sales reps globally on how to use the new application	Measure adoption of solution through frequency of app usage
Provide on-call support for first 3 months of rollout	Include adoption measure in performance review of senior sales executives

EXHIBIT 28.1

An important consideration when designing a change effort is to package all relevant solutions into a single change intervention program for the end user (versus going multiple times to the same end user to get them to use each different solution). For example, if an airline cargo salesperson needs to understand how to use three new solutions: one for assessing available cargo capacity, one for optimizing the pricing of this available capacity, and a third one for billing customers, it makes more sense to package all of these solutions into a single change intervention program. That's one of the reasons digital and AI transformations are more effective when an entire domain is transformed at once versus implementing piecemeal solutions or use cases.

Business model adaptation

Many companies treat a digital solution like adding an ingredient to a recipe and expecting the dish to taste better. A more accurate analogy is that deploying a solution is like putting an addition on a house. It won't work unless the house's foundations, walls, electrical, and plumbing systems are also changed to support the addition. This goes far beyond training people on how to use a new tool. It requires companies to break down all the interdependencies related to the solution itself and determine the implications for how the business model will operate in the future.

This system-level innovation is becoming better understood, especially in the context of implementing AI-based decisioning.[2] Exhibit 28.2 exemplifies business model shifts we have frequently observed in our work.

An insurance company, for instance, developed an analytics solution to help agents upsell customers on policies. For this solution to work in the field, however, changes needed to be made to the pricing algorithm, field force incentives, distribution model, customer engagement model, and metrics and performance indicators. Working through these changes involved creating a future-state business model and updating the full range of related business processes to enable the solution to deliver its full value.

In essence, this is about working with all the relevant upstream and downstream functions across the business (distribution, supply chain, marketing, sales, etc.) to identify critical changes in process, performance management, organization, and skills required for the digital solution to capture its full value. This kind of broad cross-functional impact is the nature of digital and AI transformations and a distinguishing feature compared to any other type of transformation. That's why CEO or division head involvement is needed to drive the cross-functional alignment (read more on this in Chapter 7).

Exhibit 28.3 shows an example of how a commercial airline that was implementing a new set of revenue management solutions for its cargo business on its passenger airlines captured the range of upstream and downstream issues.

Business model shifts created by introduction of new digital solutions

Examples

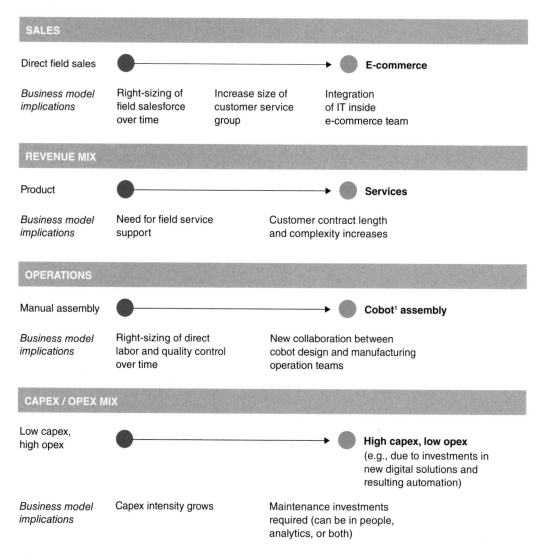

SALES

Direct field sales ●━━━━━━━━━━━━━━▶ ● **E-commerce**

Business model implications

| Right-sizing of field salesforce over time | Increase size of customer service group | Integration of IT inside e-commerce team |

REVENUE MIX

Product ●━━━━━━━━━━━━━━▶ ● **Services**

Business model implications

| Need for field service support | Customer contract length and complexity increases |

OPERATIONS

Manual assembly ●━━━━━━━━━━━━━━▶ ● **Cobot¹ assembly**

Business model implications

| Right-sizing of direct labor and quality control over time | New collaboration between cobot design and manufacturing operation teams |

CAPEX / OPEX MIX

Low capex, high opex ●━━━━━━━━━━━━━━▶ ● **High capex, low opex**
(e.g., due to investments in new digital solutions and resulting automation)

Business model implications

| Capex intensity grows | Maintenance investments required (can be in people, analytics, or both) |

1. Cobot: a collaborative robot that is capable of learning multiple tasks so it can assist human beings, versus an autonomous robot, is hard-coded to repeatedly perform one task, work independently, and remain stationary

EXHIBIT 28.2

End-to-end process impact assessment

Airline example

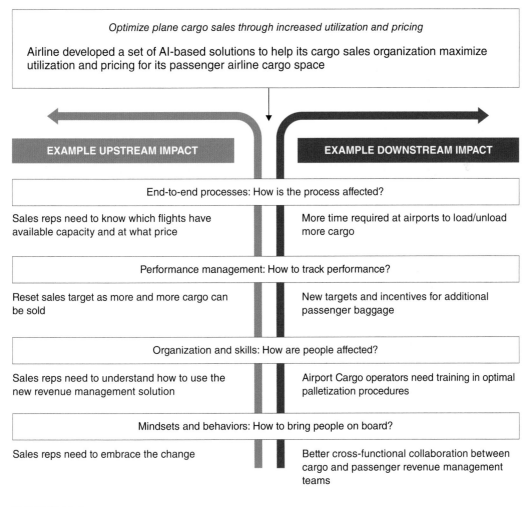

Optimize plane cargo sales through increased utilization and pricing

Airline developed a set of AI-based solutions to help its cargo sales organization maximize utilization and pricing for its passenger airline cargo space

EXAMPLE UPSTREAM IMPACT

EXAMPLE DOWNSTREAM IMPACT

End-to-end processes: How is the process affected?

Sales reps need to know which flights have available capacity and at what price

More time required at airports to load/unload more cargo

Performance management: How to track performance?

Reset sales target as more and more cargo can be sold

New targets and incentives for additional passenger baggage

Organization and skills: How are people affected?

Sales reps need to understand how to use the new revenue management solution

Airport Cargo operators need training in optimal palletization procedures

Mindsets and behaviors: How to bring people on board?

Sales reps need to embrace the change

Better cross-functional collaboration between cargo and passenger revenue management teams

EXHIBIT 28.3

The objective is to anticipate as many of these issues up front as possible, but the reality is that identifying all the relevant choke points both upstream and downstream is difficult. Some of this will invariably happen when the solution is in the field and people can see how it actually works. The process of adoption is, therefore, iterative and requires constant review and refinement.

Establishing an adoption team

The level of adoption support can vary greatly depending on the complexity of the solution, the size and geographic dispersion of the end-user base, and the magnitude of the underlying change to the business model. As a general rule, the domain leader is accountable for the successful implementation of the solution. It is their responsibility to mobilize the right resources to support the adoption effort.

In cases where adoption is particularly complex and requires long-term support, consider building an adoption team. An adoption team comprises people with a variety of skills, including change management and communications. This team works in an agile fashion and is involved early in the development, where it can highlight adoption issues and evaluate the needs for adoption support.

With those needs clearly articulated, the team identifies the relevant goals, toolsets, and technologies – some reused from other projects, and others created anew to support the launch and full adoption of the solution.

Case example: An insurer builds an adoption team

A leading insurance company took a portfolio of more than 15 digital and analytics solutions and drove adoption across a national field force of 2,300+ agents, 150+ field leaders, and 300+ reps, resulting in over $250 million of top-line impact generated within the first 24 months of execution.

The company invested in a dedicated adoption team comprising the domain leader and a broad range of required skill sets from across the organization – e.g., communications, change management, legal and compliance, and training.

The team packaged a coherent set of digital and analytics solutions that were ready to be introduced into the business. The foundation of the adoption plan was in the influence model – ensuring that the adoption of the new solutions was smooth (through training), compelling (with the help of field champions, leadership role modeling, and communications), and measured (by tracking success metrics and collecting feedback).

Notes

1. Scott Keller and Colin Price, *Beyond Performance* (Hoboken, NJ: Wiley, 2011).
2. Ajay Agrawal, Joshua Gans, and Avi Goldfarb, *Power and Prediction* (Boston: Harvard Business Review Press, 2022).

Chapter 29

Design solutions for easy replication and reuse

Often when you think you're at the end of something, you're at the beginning of something else.

—*Fred Rogers*

Scaling is about replicating the adoption of the solution in different environments to achieve enterprise-wide impact. The classic situations where replication is needed include scaling across a network of production facilities, different geographic markets, different customer segments, or different organizational groups. We will refer to these replication targets simply as "units" in this chapter.

Scaling requires designing the most effective replication approach to roll out across every unit and creating an efficient method to reuse and adapt the digital solution to the specifics of different units.

Designing an effective replication approach

Start by defining which solutions to scale and where. This typically requires different unit leaders to agree on the value in their particular unit, understand what is expected of them, free up the right financial and human resources, and agree on their accountability for the expected benefits. Next, you need to determine the sequencing of units where the solution will be deployed. There are typically three important considerations in the design of the sequencing: time to value, ease of implementation, and unit readiness. Exhibit 29.1 is an example of how one mining company used these considerations in sequencing its scaling effort.

Next, it's time to select a scaling archetype. Choosing the right archetype depends on the overall complexity of the solution, organizational readiness to absorb the change, and urgency to scale the transformation across the enterprise. Different solutions can use different archetypes (see Exhibit 29.2). The three main options are:

1. **Linear waves.** This approach is about scaling sequentially from one unit to the next, with a central team building out capabilities at each new unit. This approach is slower, but it enables steady progress, ensuring value capture at each unit before moving on to the next. This approach makes the most sense with fewer, high-value units such as mines or refineries.

2. **Exponential waves.** This approach is about launching in successively larger waves. The first wave might have two units, the second wave four, the third one eight, and so on. It often requires using a train-the-trainer model. For example, leaders from the units on the rollout plan might be included in the implementation of the first two units so they can learn and be ready for their own upcoming implementation effort. Exponential waves create

impact more quickly, but the quality of the implementation can be more difficult to maintain. This approach works best with a large number of (lower-value) units.

Define the scaling sequence

Mining example

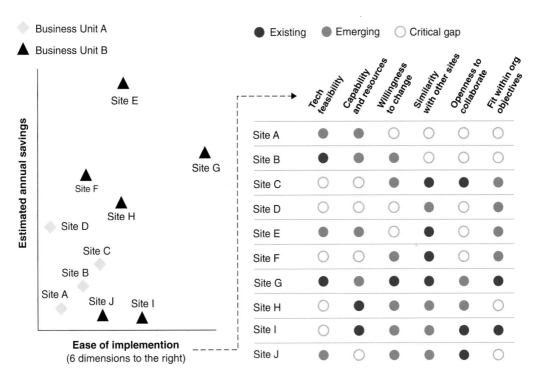

EXHIBIT 29.1

3. **Big bang.** This approach is about deploying a solution across the entire organization at the same time. For example, a scheduling solution for airline routes would make sense to deploy everywhere at once. This archetype requires building capabilities for all critical roles at the same time, often using coordinated implementation teams deployed across the organization. This approach works best in network businesses.

Different ways to follow the scaling pathway

Example type	Define which solutions to scale and where	Determine the sequencing of units	Select a scaling archetype	Approach
Mining Mining company developed a set point optimizer solution for its ore concentrators	Set point optimizer Scale across all 12 concentrators	Sequence concentrators by potential impact, IT maturity, and sensor data availability	Linear waves	Implement site by site Start at every site with data assessment, customization, training, then launch Build custom solution for site 1 and communize data model in sites 2 & 3 to enable more rapid implementation on site 3+
Automotive Automotive company developed family of quality control solutions for different products (i.e., systems and components)	Scale bundle of solutions Scale across vehicle platforms	Sequence plants by potential impact and similarity of platforms	Exponential waves	Roll out across plants producing same product with a lead plant, follow by waves of 2,4,8+ plants Build custom solution for one product platform, standardize approach for product platforms 2 and 3 to prepare for scaling
Airline Airline company developed a revenue management solution to help its 250 cargo sales reps globally to maximize cargo revenues on its commercial airline network	Revenue management solution Scale across all 1,200 network routes	All routes prioritized equally	Big bang	Roll out training to all cargo sales reps Develop production version of solution for all routes "Flip the switch" with solution integrated into backend cargo planning system

EXHIBIT 29.2

Creating a solution reuse method – the concept of assetization

What if a company built each component of its product from scratch with every order, without any standardized or consistent parts, processes, and quality-assurance protocols? Chances are good that any executive would view such an approach as a major red flag preventing economies of scale and introducing unacceptable levels of risk – and would seek to address it immediately.

Unfortunately, when it comes to scaling digital and AI solutions, companies often find themselves redoing a lot of work. This is a scale killer. Scaling effectively relies on being able to reuse as much of the solution as possible when deploying it across the enterprise.

To capture the reusability benefit, the digital and AI solution must be packaged as a set of modules or assets (thus the term *assetization*). This makes it easier to adapt it to the inevitable differences in unit conditions. For example, a mining company might have copper concentrators that were built with different ore processing technologies. While the digital solution to optimize yield might have a common machine learning engine, the data pipelines to ingest data from the ore processing equipment will likely be specific to each plant.

The first thing to do in developing a solution reuse approach is to recognize that digital solutions have different levels of reusability (see Exhibit 29.3). Some solutions are highly specific and customized and can hardly be reused. Others are completely standardized and can be packaged into software applications. Somewhere in between lies a broad class of solutions where 60–90% of the solution can be reused. Most proprietary digital and analytics solutions that companies develop fall into this category.

The core principle of effective assetization is reusability to achieve efficient and speedy rollout. Effective assetization requires managing three elements (see Exhibit 29.4):

1. **Implementation process steps.** These are the step-by-step delivery and operational guidelines that are needed so teams can use the digital solution. Essentially, this is a standardized way to train people in how to use and manage the solution, including using specific modules for unit-specific needs.

Types of digital and AI solution based on degree of standardization

	CUSTOM SOLUTION	ASSET	STANDARDIZED SOFTWARE PRODUCT
DESCRIPTION	Solution to solve a specific problem. Custom solutions sometimes reuse code snippets, but are generally built from scratch	Solution to solve a problem that is common across multiple units (e.g., plants, markets or BUs), but requires unit-specific customization. A core code-base, UI, and delivery recipe is leveraged and maintained at the enterprise level	Standalone enterprise software application that serves multiple end users with little to no customization
EXAMPLE	Specific analysis to investigate a root cause for deteriorating equipment	An AI-based advisory system to optimize production yield in plants	Statistical analysis tool suite
DEGREE OF STANDARDIZATION	10%	60–90%	>90%
COMPONENTS	Data (typically offline)	Data (frequently online)	Data (frequently online)
	Model (often developed in a notebook and rarely put into production)	Core codebase, modeling framework, UI	Standard software package
		Delivery recipe and deep SME support	Enterprise rollout and user training
		User training & adoption support	"Helpdesk" support
		Enterprise product management	Enterprise product management (internal or 3P)
		MLOps and ongoing performance mgmt	

EXHIBIT 29.3

Recipe for effective assetization

PROCESS	TECHNOLOGY	PEOPLE
Diagnostic guide Step-by-step guide to identify, size and prioritize deployment opportunities. Includes a standard approach to impact assessment	**Code building blocks** Modular and reusable components (may apply to many use cases)	**Experts for delivery/scaling** Subject matter experts, data scientists, business translators
Operations and support guide Step-by-step instructions on how to run and maintain asset, roles & responsibilities, escalation protocols	**Analytics pipeline** Prebuilt, easy-to-configure, end-to-end code for a specific use case	**Capability-building program** Definitions of what the roles and responsibilities are, training program to build or reinforce capabilities
Delivery guide Step-by-step methodology to deploy the asset – including standard and customized components	**Standards for code building and collaboration** Document defining cross-program standards and collaboration guidelines for developing analytics applications	**People to maintain/innovate** Product owner, ML engineers, enterprise product owner
	Documentation of domain knowledge Description of the use case, where the value is, and learnings about modeling the process (e.g., process description, operational KPIs, issue trees)	**Organization structures** Governance, how teams are formed and the roles interact, and relationship to other organizational units
	MLOps infrastructure Technology stack for application deployment, monitoring, performance management	

Not exhaustive

EXHIBIT 29.4

2. **Modular technology components.** This is about using blocks of code that can be consumed through APIs and easily swapped out without affecting the rest of the solution. This speeds up tailoring to a specific situation when scaling. In the example featured in Exhibit 29.5, a mining company used a modular architecture broken into multiple layers to maximize code reuse at other mining sites even though the sites' technology and data environment were different.

Example of a modular architecture for a setpoint optimization solution

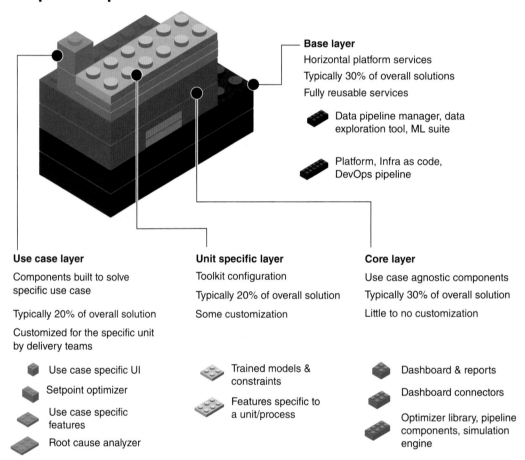

Base layer
Horizontal platform services
Typically 30% of overall solutions
Fully reusable services

Data pipeline manager, data exploration tool, ML suite

Platform, Infra as code, DevOps pipeline

Use case layer
Components built to solve specific use case

Typically 20% of overall solution

Customized for the specific unit by delivery teams

Use case specific UI

Setpoint optimizer

Use case specific features

Root cause analyzer

Unit specific layer
Toolkit configuration

Typically 20% of overall solution

Some customization

Trained models & constraints

Features specific to a unit/process

Core layer
Use case agnostic components

Typically 30% of overall solution

Little to no customization

Dashboard & reports

Dashboard connectors

Optimizer library, pipeline components, simulation engine

EXHIBIT 29.5

3. **Solution support people.** You will need a team of subject-matter experts (e.g., ML engineers, enterprise product owners) who understand how to deploy the solution and adapt it to different environments. These people should know how to train users and implement organizational change.

A thoughtful assetization approach can lead to substantial deployment speed and efficiency gains. Exhibit 29.6 shows the deployment of set-point optimizers in two different industrial settings, and the gains in deployment speed through effective assetization. The more standardized the units, the greater the benefits, a point reflected in Exhibit 29.6, where a power generation fleet achieves even more benefits from assetization because most of the solution is common across plants (as opposed to mineral processing operations, which tend to be more site and ore specific).

Deployment times reduction through assetization

Mineral processing and power generation examples
Number of weeks to deploy solution

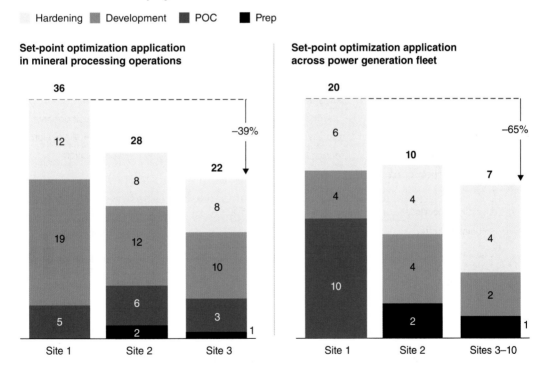

EXHIBIT 29.6

To ensure that solution reuse becomes part of the overall enterprise approach to scaling, consider creating a funding model and an incentive structure that encourages reuse. This usually means (a) budgeting explicit investments to assetize the solution after it has passed the MVP stage, (b) establishing central funding and resources to support deployment, and (c) measuring unit adoption and incentivizing unit leaders accordingly.

Case example: Driving adoption and scaling of 400 AI models

Vistra, a leading energy company, invested in an approach to rapidly scale AI solutions developed for the optimization of its power plant fleet. These solutions were composed of 400 AI models tuned to optimize different parts of power plant operations.

From the beginning of the solution development process, designers worked with operators to understand what their day-to-day activities looked like. The AI tools had to make operators' lives easier, so the screen that displayed the AI solutions and recommendations, for example, was integrated into an interface that operators already used so they didn't need to monitor an additional screen. The displays themselves were designed to be easy to read. A solution displays a green signal if the plant is running optimally, and a red one when it isn't, with a corresponding recommended action that includes the value attached to implementing that recommendation.

When a solution demonstrated its value at a pilot site and was approved for scaling, a team of software and ML engineers immediately took over to refactor, modularize, and containerize the code. That way, there was a single software "core" package for each deployment that could be updated and improved. Some customization was always needed because each plant has its own unique characteristics.

Dedicated customization teams made up of data scientists, engineers, operators, and power generation experts worked with each plant to tailor the solution to that plant's unique conditions. The team built an MLOps infrastructure to bring live data from each of Vistra's power units into a single database (read more on MLOps in Chapter 23). It used GitLab software to manage version control for code and containerize the code so it could easily be deployed to any environment. The team also created dashboards to monitor model performance and usage, and manage the continuous improvement of each model.

Finally, the effort involved three levels of training: for the front lines (to learn how to use the models), the tech team (to learn how to develop and maintain AI models), and the leadership team (to understand how to use AI models and transform how the business operates).

Chapter 30

Ensuring impact by tracking what matters

Don't mistake activity for achievement.

—John Wooden

A surprisingly high number of CEOs don't have a clear view of how their digital and AI transformation is doing.[1] Are we making progress toward a more digital business model? Are we building digital capabilities like we said we needed to? Is this paying off in terms of customer experience and bottom-line impact?

No one will debate the need for measuring transformation progress. But the question is what to measure and how. Performance tracking can quickly crumble under its own weight when poorly designed and without the right supporting tools.

A quality performance infrastructure includes (1) designing the right performance management KPIs, (2) tracking with a stage-gate process and supporting workflow tools, and (3) standing-up an effective transformation office.

Performance management architecture and KPIs

Being clear on what performance metrics to measure is half the battle. In digital and AI transformations, key performance indicators (KPIs) tend to fall into three families: value creation metrics, pod health metrics, and change management metrics (see Exhibit 30.1).

Digital and AI transformation performance management architecture

	VALUE CREATION	POD HEALTH	CHANGE MANAGEMENT
GOAL	Measure impact of digital solutions on core business/operational KPIs	Measure health and maturity of pods	Measure progress in building new capabilities and mobilizing the organization
METRICS	Operational KPIs	Pod maturity KPIs	Capability building and change management KPI
EXAMPLES	Customer adoption (%) Online sales (% of sales) Process yield (%) Cross-sell rate (%)	Pod staffing adequacy OKR achievements Agile/DevOps maturity Release frequency	# of pods mobilized Employee engagement Talent hiring/upskilling Milestone achievements
UNIT OF ANALYSIS	Solutions and domains	Pods	Specific capabilities, leadership, employee engagement
RELEVANT FOR	C-suite, domain leaders	Domain leaders and pod owners	C-suite and transformation leader

EXHIBIT 30.1

Value creation tracking through business/operational KPIs

Digital solutions typically target one or a few business/operational KPIs that can usually be translated in financial or customer benefits.

These metrics matter to domain leaders and C-suite executives. They also offer convincing proof points to investors on the progress of the digital transformation.

Exhibit 30.2 shows an example from an international bank that reports to investors every quarter on its key digital transformation metrics, namely mobile app adoption by customers, digital sales, transaction migration out of the branch network, and headcount reduction in branches.

A value driver tree is a helpful tool for identifying where digital and AI solutions are expected to improve core operational KPIs. The tree is also used to link the OKRs of the pods working on that solution, thus creating a unified representation of how the improvements will be achieved.

Exhibit 30.3 shows an example for a retirement insurance provider. The revenue for such a business is driven by the number of companies that have contracted for a retirement plan, the average number of participating employees per plan, and the average revenue per participant.

As the tree gets decomposed, it gets into operational KPIs such as the number of proposals made to potential customers and the win rate. It is typically at this level that digital solutions will impact the performance of the business. In this example, the leader of the commercial domain has decided to develop three digital solutions, as shown in Exhibit 30.3. Solution 2 in this example is focused on making it easier for participants to enroll. Two pods will be working on this solution. The first pod will work on streamlining the application, while the second will develop an API to prepopulate the employee information.

The commercial domain leader should track progress at the operational KPI level. For solution 2, this would be the percentage of completed applications and the user satisfaction level (not shown in the value driver tree). The pod owners, on the other hand, should be tracking key results that are directly controllable by the pods and where progress can be realized in weeks or a few months at most. A good example in this case is the reduction in the number of steps to complete the application, which typically can be achieved in a few months.

Classic business operations KPIs tracked in banking digital transformations

Example from investor reporting by a top international bank, *2016–2020*

Are my apps being used by customers?
% of digitally engaged customers

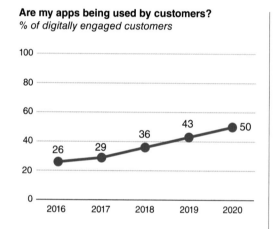

Is it easy to buy my banking products online?
% of total sales

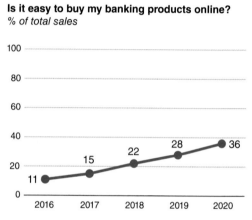

Are transactions coming out of branch network?
% of total transactions in branches

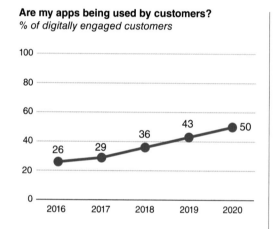

Are processes being automated?
Headcount in branch network
100 = 2016

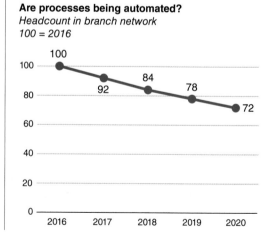

EXHIBIT 30.2

A value driver tree to identify where digital solutions impact KPI

Retirement insurance example

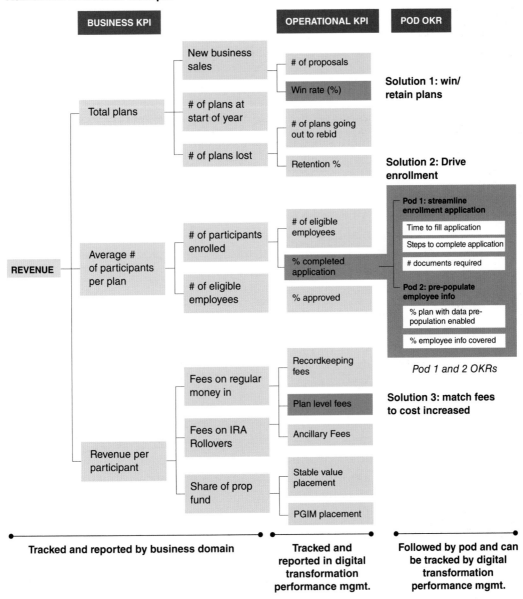

EXHIBIT 30.3

Exhibit 30.4 shows how the OKRs are organized for each pod, along with the phasing of expected key results and the end-state improvement targets. It also shows the underlying assumption for how the solution will reduce application abandonment rates and drive more enrollment.

The formulation of these assumptions can be difficult. It's hard to know a priori how much reduction in the abandonment rate will be achieved with a streamlined application and prepopulated employee data. This requires judgment. Therefore, it is very important to phase the key results and observe how version 1 of the solution impacts abandonment rates, thus building conviction to continue the efforts for V2 and eventually V3, or pivot the pods' approach to more promising avenues.

Designing this driver tree and tracking the corresponding KPIs is fundamental to the overall success of the digital transformation. It provides a clear North Star, ensures strong focus on value creation, and creates clear accountability.

Assessing pod health

The pod is the "fighting unit" in a digital and AI transformation. You cannot successfully deliver a digital transformation without healthy, mature pods.

Many digital transformations progress more slowly than initially planned because their pods are poorly configured (e.g., part-time pod members, inadequate skills), did not adopt modern ways of working (e.g., agile, DevOps), or lack critical capabilities (e.g., product management, user experience design). In our experience, the difference in productivity between a low- and high-performing pod can be 5× or more. Measuring and managing pod health really matters.

The pods' health assessment is done using three lenses:

1. **Pod configuration metrics.** This gets at a simple question: Is the pod properly staffed? Seems obvious enough, but every company

has resource constraints, and pods can run for a long time without the proper resourcing. You really want to get to two core questions: Are the pod's resources dedicated? And is each role filled with an individual who has the right skills to contribute? This assessment is best done by the pod owner and the domain leader. The QBR is an excellent opportunity to assess this as part of QBR reporting.

Business/operational KPIs linked to pod OKRs

Case example: OKR mapping – Driving retirement insurance enrollment

Solution business case

400,000 abandoned applications last year and enrollment NPS of 10	Solution will reduce application abandonment rate from 20% to 5% resulting in 300,000 additional applications and industry leading NPS of 50	2/3 of completed applications typically become enrolled resulting in 200,000 additional enrollees	Average margin per participant of $500	$100 million EBITDA NPS = 50

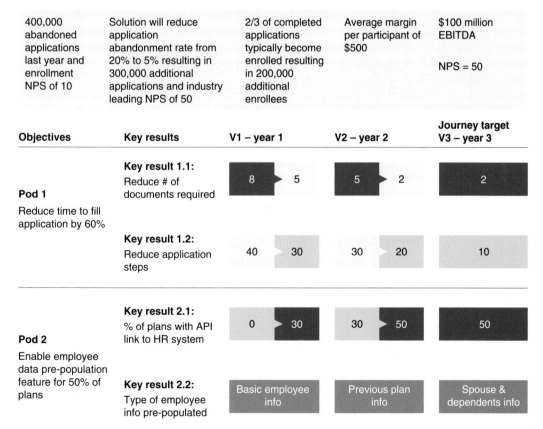

Objectives	Key results	V1 – year 1	V2 – year 2	Journey target V3 – year 3
Pod 1 Reduce time to fill application by 60%	**Key result 1.1:** Reduce # of documents required	8 ▶ 5	5 ▶ 2	2
	Key result 1.2: Reduce application steps	40 ▶ 30	30 ▶ 20	10
Pod 2 Enable employee data pre-population feature for 50% of plans	**Key result 2.1:** % of plans with API link to HR system	0 ▶ 30	30 ▶ 50	50
	Key result 2.2: Type of employee info pre-populated	Basic employee info	Previous plan info	Spouse & dependents info

EXHIBIT 30.4

2. **Pod performance metrics.** This gets to the functioning of a pod. These metrics are usually extracted from backlog management tools, e.g., Jira, Azure DevOps, Digital.ai (thus the importance of training pods in a consistent way to use these tools). While there are debates in the industry on the best metrics to track, we recommend tracking the metrics below. The first four are known as the standard DORA (DevOps Research and Assessment) metrics. (Exhibit 30.5):

- *Deployment frequency,* to measure the average time between successful code releases to production per application. If releases are constrained by business reasons, then the deployment frequency to user acceptance testing (UAT) can be measured as a proxy.

- *Lead time to changes,* to measure time from the end of the development cycle to deployment in production. This metric informs how efficient (and automated) the process is from the time a pod checks in code to the time a new solution is integrated, tested, and deployed.

- *Mean time to recover (MTTR),* measures the average time it takes to recover from a product or system failure. It indicates whether the system has been architected for resiliency, and how quickly you solve downtime incidents to get your systems back up and running.

- *Change failure rate,* to measure the percentage of deployments that result in a failure in production. Change failure rate takes all your workflows over a period and calculates the percentage that ended in failure or required remediation (e.g., required a hotfix, rollback, fix forward, patch).

- *Velocity,* to calculate how long user stories within a particular sprint have taken to complete against their estimate. Velocity can be used to measure how much work can be completed in each iteration and helps to predict how long future sprints, or an overall project, will take to complete.

- *Code churn,* also called rework, indicates how often a given piece of code – e.g., a file, a class, a function – gets edited. For example, you can measure what percentage of code gets rewritten up until three weeks from when it was first merged.

Pod performance measurement

Example from a global wealth management company   ■ Elite   ■ High   Medium   ■ Low

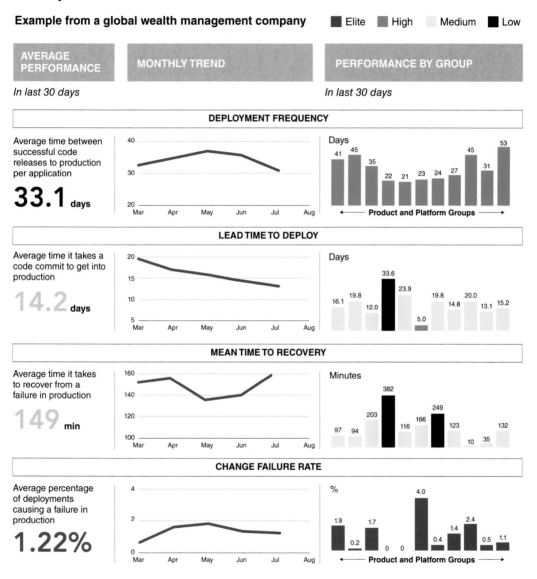

EXHIBIT 30.5

3. **Pod maturity metrics.** This gets to the underlying practices that drive pod performance and overall effectiveness. Different survey instruments exist to measure pod maturity. The survey is filled by

pod members and/or the pod's agile coach, the latter typically providing a more independent viewpoint and better calibration. Exhibit 30.6 shows an example of output for a family of pods.

Ideally these different metrics are automated in the pod's workflow, but this takes some time to implement, and it only makes sense to do so once a certain scale is reached (i.e., more than 20 pods).

Change management progress

These metrics measure the progress in building new capabilities and the health of the transformation itself. Are we mobilizing pods as planned? Are people engaged? Are we progressing in building enabling capabilities and talent? In our experience, perfection is the enemy of good (and completion) when building change management measurement. Implement the basics and build from there:

1. **Leadership mobilization.** Conduct periodic surveys with the top 200–300 executives in the company to understand the importance of digital to their management agenda, their sense of progress, and their assessment of their own effectiveness in leading the change. Complement this with interviews.

2. **Capability-building progress.** We have found a few core metrics to be quite representative of the progress made in building the four delivery capabilities discussed in Sections Two through Five. On talent, are you making progress in building your digital bench (i.e., recruiting or upskilling) and are you retaining your best technologists? On operating model, are you mobilizing pods at the rate you had planned and how good are the product owners on these pods? On technology, how many pods are capable of releasing code to production and what is their release cycle time? And on data, how many solution pods are data constrained and unable to progress, and how many pods are consuming data from any given data product?

Pod maturity measurement

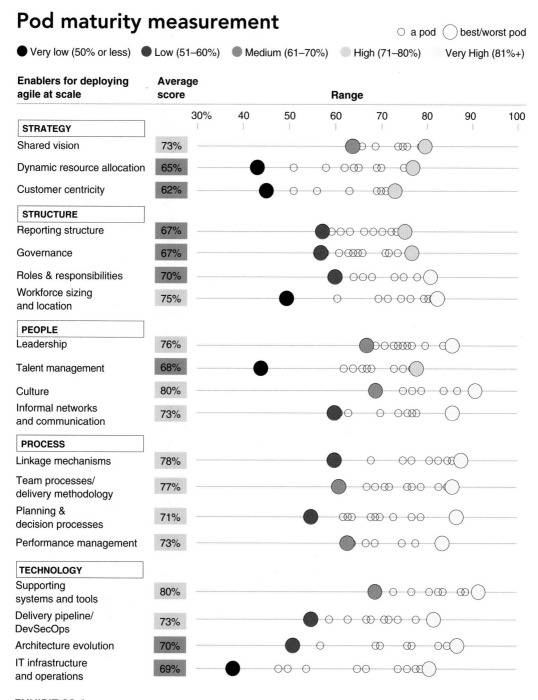

EXHIBIT 30.6

3. **Employee engagement.** The annual employee engagement survey is a good opportunity to measure overall excitement, skill development, and personal growth. It may also be a good idea to segment the survey for those more directly impacted by the transformation – for example, those working on pods or the users benefiting from the new solutions being developed.

Tracking with a stage-gate process

Robust transformation programs ensure that solutions are stage-gated. We have found it helpful to run each solution identified through a five-gate process. These are the same five gates that our firm has been successfully using in general transformations. The gates are described in Exhibit 30.7.

Gates L1 to L3 are essentially solution incubation gates that are part of the domain reimagination effort. As the solution progresses through formal gate reviews, the business case and delivery requirements become more precise. Gate L3 is a go/no-go gate that leads to a full mobilization of the delivery pod.

The L4 gate is often matched up with the delivery of a solution MVP. L5 corresponds to an adoption and/or scaling gate where version 1 (V1) is adopted by customers/users and meaningful value has been delivered. Through yearly planning (or QBR planning), the specifications for V2 are defined and another cycle starts. The solution continues to evolve, improve, and deliver more value. At some point, the solution may reach maturity. Then the development team is reduced and only a core support team stays behind.

The discipline of this gating process should not be underestimated. As the digital and AI transformation scales to more domains, this gating process brings a consistent language and investment discipline that can be managed through yearly planning and/or QBR. As companies learn what works (and what doesn't), build capabilities, and find new sources of value, they dynamically refresh their digital roadmap, business cases, and resourcing needs.

Transformation tracking through stage gates

Domain reimagination phase

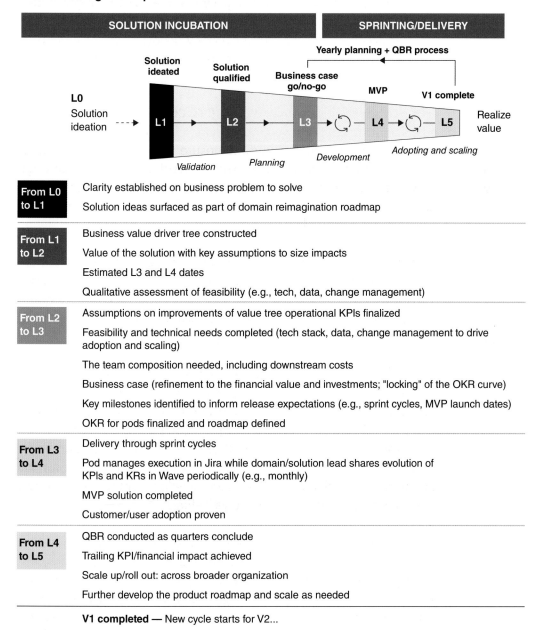

From L0 to L1	Clarity established on business problem to solve
	Solution ideas surfaced as part of domain reimagination roadmap

From L1 to L2	Business value driver tree constructed
	Value of the solution with key assumptions to size impacts
	Estimated L3 and L4 dates
	Qualitative assessment of feasibility (e.g., tech, data, change management)

From L2 to L3	Assumptions on improvements of value tree operational KPIs finalized
	Feasibility and technical needs completed (tech stack, data, change management to drive adoption and scaling)
	The team composition needed, including downstream costs
	Business case (refinement to the financial value and investments; "locking" of the OKR curve)
	Key milestones identified to inform release expectations (e.g., sprint cycles, MVP launch dates)
	OKR for pods finalized and roadmap defined

From L3 to L4	Delivery through sprint cycles
	Pod manages execution in Jira while domain/solution lead shares evolution of KPIs and KRs in Wave periodically (e.g., monthly)
	MVP solution completed
	Customer/user adoption proven

From L4 to L5	QBR conducted as quarters conclude
	Trailing KPI/financial impact achieved
	Scale up/roll out: across broader organization
	Further develop the product roadmap and scale as needed

V1 completed — New cycle starts for V2...

EXHIBIT 30.7

Large-scale digital transformations mobilize hundreds of pods and deliver as many digital solutions. While the tracking and reporting can initially be done in spreadsheets and slides, this quickly becomes untenable.

In our own work, we often use two software packages for transformation tracking and reporting. Our first tool is an all-purpose general transformation tracking tool that tracks the stage-gating of solutions and the underlying use cases, and the core performance KPIs. In essence, it tracks the investments and value created by the digital solutions. We like to use WAVE,[2] but other tools are also available in the market. Our second (LINK) is designed to track the health of pods and support the agile ceremonies, including managing cross-team dependencies.

Transformation office

To help manage all the digital initiatives on an ongoing basis, a transformation office (TO) is always necessary. The TO is the umbrella team that oversees all elements of the broader digital and AI transformation across the business – from ensuring quality domain roadmaps to reporting on the performance and health of the transformation.

Depending on the scale of the transformation, the TO is often composed of professionals from finance, HR, communications, IT, and subject matter experts (e.g., legal, procurement). Its primary responsibilities include: launching the transformation; supporting the development of the digital roadmap; tracking that the targeted value is actually being captured; detecting early signs of potential value leakage; removing roadblocks; reviewing and refreshing the roadmap based on progress; ensuring advancement in building capabilities; and managing change throughout.

The TO is empowered to make important decisions (e.g., stage-gate approvals, team and budget allocations) and push the organization by asking tough questions and holding people accountable.

The TO is much more forward-looking than a traditional program management office (PMO). It anticipates bottlenecks and proactively addresses them. Its focus is on problem-solving, accountability, and maintaining pace.

Exhibit 30.8 shows a classic transformation governance structure including the TO setup.

Transformation office setup

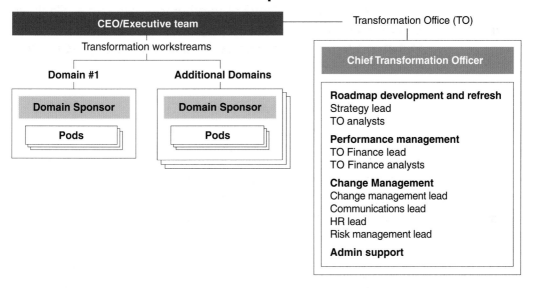

EXHIBIT 30.8

The transformation officer (TO) needs to understand the business, be well respected, and be willing to push people and "spend" their relationship capital to drive the transformation. For this reason, the TO is often an in-house executive.

As the digital and AI transformation matures and becomes business as usual, there will be less need for the TO and it will eventually be disbanded. Digital efforts at this point are integrated as part of the new operating model (see Section Three).

Notes

1. Matt Fitzpatrick and Kurt Strovink, "How do you measure success in digital? Five metrics for CEOs," McKinsey.com, January 29, 2021, https://www.mckinsey.com/capabilities/mckinsey-digital/our-insights/how-do-you-measure-success-in-digital-five-metrics-for-ceos.
2. For more about WAVE, please visit mckinsey.com/capabilities/transformation/how-we-help-clients/wave/overview

Chapter 31

Managing risk and building digital trust

Risk comes from not knowing what you're doing.

—*Warren Buffett*

Risks happen. And digital and AI transformations surface a whole new and complex set of interconnected risks. Rapid digital and AI innovations are taking place in an environment of increased regulatory scrutiny, where consumers, regulators, and business leaders are increasingly concerned about vulnerabilities across cybersecurity, data privacy, and AI systems.

From unintentional outcomes such as implicit bias in AI algorithms, to tragic accidents involving self-driving vehicles, and personal information leaks, no business, industry, or government is safe from digital and AI risks.

These issues are the reason consumers and regulators alike expect companies to establish and enforce strong digital trust practices. Digital trust means confidence that an organization protects consumer data, enacts effective cybersecurity, offers trustworthy AI-powered products and services, and provides transparency around AI and data usage.

Leaders who have established strong digital trust are less likely to experience downside risk through negative data and AI incidents, and are statistically more likely to outperform.[1] Many consumers – particularly those who are digitally savvy – consider trustworthiness and data protections to be nearly as important as pricing and delivery times.

For the purposes of this book, we will focus on the four digital trust capabilities that most directly support a digital transformation, as discussed next.

Triaging the risks

This is similar to a classic risk triaging effort that you would do as part of an enterprise risk management effort, but this time is focused on the digital solutions, models, and data assets that are on the digital and AI transformation roadmap. As you assess these risks, you will identify the risks, classify them in a risk taxonomy, and "score" them based on what the impact would be if it did happen. Regulators have already required organizations to conduct impact assessments for data processing impact assessments (APIAs), and, increasingly, algorithmic impact assessments (AIAs).

The output of this effort is an easy-to-understand heat map of risks. The score triggers additional questions, and signals where risk and legal experts are most needed. It will help you prioritize where the policies need to be reviewed.

Reviewing policies

Comprehensive digital trust policies address the use of data, analytics, and technology, and provide a North Star for the organization. These policies must be broader than a traditional data privacy policy, and address topics such as use and handling of personal data, guardrails for use of technology, the fairness of code-based models, as well as protocols around software, IoT systems, cloud solutions, and design prototypes.

Expect to be reviewing your policies in the following areas:

- **Data:** Succinct, plain-language policies for the collection of sensitive data, clearly defined data retention policies, due diligence on third-party personnel and/or vendors, and ongoing audits
- **Tech and cloud:** Strategy for prioritizing IT risks, continuous cyber training for all personnel, and an incident response program
- **AI/ML and analytics:** Clear standards and thresholds for AI risk, including transparency and explainability, automated AI model monitoring systems, and bias and fairness checks for AI models

For example, if a solution includes the ability to target various demographics or engage in varied pricing, the business will need to implement specific protocols – mandatory across the enterprise – to prevent bias. That should be specified in your AI policy.

Reviewing the full set of policies to address these new risks takes time. Ask your risk management or legal team to develop a structured approach to do this over 12–24 months.

Operationalizing your risk policies

The best policies in the world will fail if teams do not have the capabilities to quickly and consistently check for and implement digital trust practices. There are simply too many data sources and digital and AI systems to test and validate.

Companies should focus on building three operational capabilities:

1. **Embedded control functions.** We have seen numerous cases where development teams have spent considerable time and money creating and deploying new solutions, only to have to go back to the drawing board, or worse, shelve their work permanently, when they encounter risk issues (e.g., not having customer consent to use their data). Such issues often result from traditional operating models where legal, governance, quality assurance, and other risk experts work in silos, providing their input only at specified "gates" in the development process, many of which come after substantial work on the solution has been completed.

   To redress this issue, you need to develop a risk triage checklist that pods go through under guidance from a risk professional to surface risks requiring additional expertise from legal, cybersecurity, data, privacy, compliance, or other control functions that the company might have. Once the assessment and mitigation measures have been agreed on, the pod includes them in its backlog of work. For example, it may be concluded that customer data needs to be blinded for certain demographic data fields before the ML model is built.

   This process of risk triaging, expert assessment, and execution of mitigation measures is usually built in a digital workflow that eases traceability and scaling (Chapter 14 offers more details on this).

2. **Specialized talent.** This is a highly specialized field at the intersection of regulation, ethics, and technology. You should consider assigning an overarching enterprise lead for digital trust, accountable for building and managing the business's digital trust capability. Some companies even name a chief trust officer.

   There is usually a need to deepen expertise in "privacy engineering" – people who are skilled at managing and maintaining data privacy applications, developing automated tests for security and compliance, and refactoring applications to bring them into compliance.

3. **Automation of risk controls.** Automating trust is the process of turning trust policies into code ("policy as code"), such as compliance requirements ("compliance as code") and risk standards ("security as code"). These automated risk controls are activated whenever anyone submits new code. This approach radically speeds up development and deployment, and cuts back on risk. For AI systems, this might include MLOps tools that automate compliance with new regulations.

Raise awareness and pattern recognition

Everyone in the enterprise is responsible for digital trust. That has become an article of faith in leading companies. To build up a culture of responsibility, the trust message must come from the top. Leaders must sponsor, enable, and role-model digital trust practices across the organization. Those practices can include implementing training programs focused on digital trust; publishing core values around the use of data, digital, and AI technologies; and including digital trust metrics in performance reviews.

For customers to have confidence in an organization's efforts to protect their data, they must be aware of these efforts and policies. Sometimes such communications are required by regulators. For example, New York State includes a provision that requires companies to publish on their website their audit process for confirming fairness in AI-driven employment and recruitment systems, including what tools their data scientists use for identifying bias in AI. Leaders in digital will also regularly and proactively communicate their work to the marketplace to build a competitive advantage and shift the landscape of consumer expectations.

Finally, it's important to share digital risk management efforts with relevant regulators to help them understand the new ways of working and associated benefits. In this way, companies can reassure regulators of active steps taken to ensure compliance and collect feedback to inform further measures.

In their words: Balancing user value and digital trust

AI is in almost everything now, and it does a lot of things that most of us find delightful. For example, I love it when YouTube or Spotify recommends something that I would never have thought of or when my phone guesses what I want to do and provides a prompt. But in the rush to produce user value and get these products to market, some companies haven't given sufficient attention to the side effects these tools can create.

It's analogous to when the auto industry was beginning to consider safety features for automobiles. Then the mindset was, "Well, the seatbelts work 20% of the time. We'll figure it out eventually." And the response from customers and others was, "No. Figure out how to make the seatbelts work now." It's the same with tech. Companies know how to innovate in the ways needed, but they have to invest in those areas and work harder at it.

—Mark Surman, president and executive director of the Mozilla Foundation

Note

1. Jim Boehm, Liz Grennan, Alex Singla, and Kate Smaje, "Why digital trust truly matters," McKinsey.com, September 12, 2022, https://www .mckinsey.com/capabilities/quantumblack/our-insights/why-digital-trust-truly-matters.

Chapter 32

So, what about culture?

Capabilities are clearly manifested only when they have been realized.

—*Simone de Beauvoir*

We get asked this question all the time: What about culture?

Business leaders recognize the importance of culture but are often stymied about what it takes to build a digital culture – the mindsets and behaviors that support and accelerate their digital and AI transformation. In our experience, this is often because people consider culture in vague terms, as a set of mindsets and behaviors to develop without a clear sense for how or even why.

In fact, culture is the result of a set of actions, incentives, new skills, and leadership attributes.

The entirety of this book adds up to the actions needed to build a digital culture: building pattern recognition of executives on the possibilities offered by digital and AI, hiring new tech talent, bringing IT closer to the business, learning new ways of working, making technology and data easily consumable to foster innovation across the company, developing product owners, etc.

While digital culture is an outcome of all of these efforts, being intentional about developing a digital culture starts with being clear about the leadership attributes you expect from your leaders – and tracking progress against them (see Exhibit 32.1).[1]

Leadership attributes in digital enterprises

Customer-centricity
Has the customer at the center of all activities, sparing no effort to provide an outstanding experience

Test, learn, and grow
Is able to assume risks to test new innovations and views mistakes as a source of learnings

Collaboration
Collaborates well across functions and business units for the benefit of customers and the enterprise

Data-oriented
Embeds data in real-time decision making

Sense of urgency
Acts/reacts quickly, and is sensitive to the needs of each situation

Empowerment
Empowers employees to make decisions and creates the environment for it

External orientation
Constantly learns from other companies, partners, and customers

Constant delivery of value
Prioritizes quick delivery of value to the customer and improves products and solutions continuously

EXHIBIT 32.1

Addressing a company's organizational culture head-on during a digital and AI transformation reinforces a focus on the required shifts in mindsets and behaviors that will be needed for the transformation to be successful over time. Establishing a baseline and periodically measuring through cultural surveys is a good way to understand progress against the prioritized cultural attributes.

A digital and AI transformation requires more skill building change than any other type of transformation. That's because the scope and speed of the change put significant pressures on the entire institution. Without well-structured and sustained investments in training and grooming of new talent, the gravitational pull of the legacy organization can create real change resistance.

Invariably, successful companies end up focusing on three fundamental skill-building efforts: leadership upskilling, broad-based change management programs, and heavy reskilling efforts for pivotal roles.

Invest initially in the leadership team

A digital company runs differently, and it requires leaders to lead differently. Business leaders at digital enterprises are customer fanatics, they understand digital technologies (at least the basics) and the process for developing digital solutions, they are familiar with agile and know how to play their roles in an agile process, they embody collaborative leadership, and they exemplify a "can-do" attitude.

In their words: Evaluating leaders for new skills

We recently revamped our management evaluation criteria, adding a set of attributes. We used to select our management team based on three characteristics: the ability to think, execute, and lead teams. These are hard skills, if you will. Last year, we added six other attributes that are much softer skills. This is very important, particularly in an environment like Ping An's, which is very aggressive.

We're now looking at things like a person's adversity quotient, and their ability to be open and receptive. This is something we started with our top 150 people in senior management that will eventually trickle down to the rest of the organization. It's a shift that has to happen, especially because so much technology innovation is cross-discipline and requires the collaboration of different teams. It's more and more important for people to be able to work with other people.

That sounds very simple, but it's a huge change because these softer factors are hard to measure.

—Jessica Tan, co-CEO of Ping An

Many leaders at large established companies don't have these attributes. But leaders can build them up through an intentional and disciplined program. In our experience, three specific practices are most helpful:

1. **Go & see visits.** One of the most powerful early investments that can be made is to take the leadership team (and even the board) on a two- or three-day visit to relevant companies. A typical visit includes a couple of Big Tech digital natives, a few traditional companies that are far along on their digital and AI journey, and perhaps a few start-ups in the industry. The goal is to learn how digital-first companies operate.

2. **Digital 101.** Executive teams need to understand at least the basics of digital technologies and new ways of working to be effective leaders in the digital era. Most executive teams undertake at least 10 hours of training on the basics of digital, either in the classic "classroom" model or in a self-serve online training format so they can tailor the learning journey to their needs. The contents of this book is indicative of what executives should know. Over time, a program to continue building the leadership's tech acumen should be considered.

3. **Leadership in a digital age.** Once the digital transformation is underway, many companies invest in a program that takes their top executives through an exploration of their leadership style and how it needs to evolve in a rewired enterprise. The emphasis is usually placed on embracing a learn-it-all (versus "know-it-all") culture, a more collaborative culture (versus "my resources and my P&L"), and a true customer-centric culture (versus saying you are customer focused but not really embracing it). This is typically delivered over four to six half-day sessions organized for groups of 10 to 15, followed by individual coaching.

Typically, a leadership training program would focus on the top two or three levels in the organization.

Case example: Investing in digital leaders at Roche

To build an agile culture as part of its digital transformation program, Roche, the pharmaceutical company, launched an intensive change process among senior leaders. More than 1,000 of these leaders were invited to learn a new, more agile approach to leadership through a four-day immersive program that introduced them to the mindsets and capabilities needed to lead an agile organization.

Within six months of the senior leader program, many participants had launched agile experiments with their own leadership teams and organizational units, engaging thousands of people in co-creating innovative ways to embed agility within the organization. Compared with the initial expectations of 5–10% of participants running a follow-up session with their teams, 95% chose to do so.[2]

Even with all these investments in upskilling the leadership team, the hard reality is that many executives are not ready for the journey. Looking back at mature digital transformations in banking and retail, for example, it is common that about 30% of the top 300 will require a leadership change favoring executives with a more suited leadership profile.

Finally, if you don't make explicit changes to management incentives and promotion criteria for these top 300 leaders, you will be continuously fighting an uphill battle with your upskilling programs. We have seen companies only promote executives who had demonstrated deep understanding of customer needs and pain points, and a constant focus on measuring and improving customer satisfaction. Others emphasize the importance of cross-functional collaboration assessed through 360-degree peer feedback.

Build broad learning programs that can scale

To bring large parts of the organization along on the journey, many organizations develop dedicated training programs that can scale. They often invest in developing a corporate "academy" as the engine to develop and deliver learning curricula and journeys to build the required awareness, skills, and behaviors across the organization.

For example, the Singaporean multinational bank DBS set the goal of building a strong experimentation culture and becoming a 30,000-employee start-up. It invested heavily to develop a learning infrastructure to produce a data-first mindset across the organization, establishing multiple programs such as a curriculum that equipped employees with the skills of a data translator (someone from the business who knows enough about data and analytics to conceptualize and implement new high-value digital solutions); an innovation hub that organized 300+ hackathons and workshops; a "hack-to-hire" program that resulted in hiring more than 200 employees; and a back-to-school program fostering a culture of peer-to-peer learning (you can read more about this case in Chapter 34).

With these programs, the bank managed to train over 5,000 employees in various digital and analytics capabilities. Of these, 1,000+ employees were upskilled and moved into more pivotal roles for the digital transformation. Employee engagement increased by six percentage points, and there was a 40% improvement in employee retention.

Case example: Building a "school" for 40,000 employees

Majid al Futtaim (MAF), a real estate and retail conglomerate based in the Middle East, developed a "school" of analytics and technology (SOAT) to build the capabilities of its 40,000 employees to support the company's analytics transformation.[3] MAF detailed the priority learning objectives for five segments: senior executives, tech experts and business practitioners, mid-level managers, front-line staff, and entry-level practitioners. It then architected learning curricula and journeys to achieve these objectives (see Exhibit 32.2).

School of Analytics and Technology

Majid al Futtaim example

Introduction to analytics & technology	**Understanding and applying analytics use cases**	**Power of technology**
Understand the importance of analytics and technology and the benefit it can bring	Lead into a more thorough use of analytics & technology	Understand how technology can improve the way we do things and get exposed to the latest technological trends and threats

The "school" encourages employees to . . .

Embrace flexible and new ways of working	Demand data-driven support of assumptions	Challenge analytics approach and analyses	Promote the use of analytics and technology	Push the envelope when it comes to applying the latest trends in analytics and technology

EXHIBIT 32.2

MAF prioritized the senior executives, technologists, and mid-level managers who were working on analytics and AI solutions, to ensure that the SOAT curriculum targeted the most critical business needs. SOAT leaders were staffed in cross-functional pods to rapidly design, build, test, deploy, and iterate learning curricula. The school also pulled in technologists from within the organization to bring relevant experiences to supplement the content. Programs included a healthy mix of simulations and games to bring skills to life in real-world scenarios and make the content accessible to everyone.

Metrics have shown positive outcomes across multiple vectors, including learner experiences, individual knowledge development, and application one month from program completion. Positive changes were also found in observed and sustained skills and behavior changes (based on 360-degree feedback) six months after program completion, and enablement of business outcomes (e.g., successful delivery of use cases).

Our most important lesson from broad-based learning programs is to make them relevant and easy to scale. We too often see companies start with ambitious plans only to abandon them later because of execution complexity.

Reskill pivotal business roles

Focus heavy reskilling programs on the pivotal business roles that will need to be radically transformed to capture the value of the digital and AI transformation. Role-specific reskilling programs require significant time – anywhere between three and nine months – and they tend to be industry-specific: merchants in retail, underwriters in insurance, product marketers in banking, agronomists in agriculture, network planners in transportation and logistics, etc. These roles are undergoing massive change with the embedding of data and use of AI.

As an example, a large US food grocer had to reskill 400 merchants who had 20+ years of merchandising experience – giving them phenomenal pattern recognition for assortment, pricing, and promotion decisions. But they needed new skills to do their job in a data- and AI-intensive world. Over a six-month period, the company trained them to use the new integrated workflow tool for advertising planning, vendor on-boarding, vendor funding, and promotion execution. They also learned to use and trust the new promotion recommendation engine for optimizing promotional events. Finally, they were trained to do national category planning with a real-time vendor portal to serve as a starting point for local planning, thus maximizing network collaboration.

The upskilling transition was not without challenges. Not every merchant could make this upskilling transition, leading to 20–30% turnover over two years. Having said that, the company also found it was easier to ramp up new merchants with the new tools and training. In fact, automation, new tools, and process redesign (including new data) brought the bottom-performing merchants up to the top quartile in performance. In other words, the new technology could raise the performance of any merchant to the level of the best ones with 20+ years of experience.

Notes

1. George Westerman, Deborah L. Soule, and Anand Eswaran, "Building digital-ready culture in traditional organizations," *MIT Sloan Management Review*, May 21, 2019, https://sloanreview.mit.edu/article/building-digital-ready-culture-in-traditional-organizations/; Rose Hollister, Kathryn Tecosky, Michael Watkins, and Cindy Wolpert, "Why every executive should be focusing on culture change now," *MIT Sloan Management Review*, August 10, 2021, https://sloanreview.mit.edu/article/why-every-executive-should-be-focusing-on-culture-change-now/; Julie Goran, Laura LaBerge, and Ramesh Srinivasan, "Culture for a digital age," *McKinsey Quarterly*, July 20, 2017, https://www.mckinsey.com/capabilities/mckinsey-digital/our-insights/culture-for-a-digital-age.

2. Larry Emond, "How Roche helps leaders achieve the power of an agile mindset," Gallup, April 29, 2019, https://www.gallup.com/workplace/248714/roche-helps-leaders-achieve-power-agile-mindset.aspx.

3. Gemma D'Auria, Natasha Walia, Hamza Khan, "Majid Al Futtaim's new growth formula: Innovate fast, stay ahead, work the ecosystem," McKinsey.com, April 20, 2021 https://www.mckinsey.com/capabilities/growth-marketing-and-sales/our-insights/majid-al-futtaims-new-growth-formula-innovate-fast-stay-ahead-work-the-ecosystem.

Getting Ready
Section Six

The following is a set of questions to help you home in on the right actions to take:

Is your digital and AI transformation creating the value you expected, and if not, do you know where the issues lie?

Are you spending (at least) as much time/resources/investment on adoption and scaling as you are on solution development?

Who is responsible for adoption? Are the business leaders accountable?

What proportion of the digital solutions developed are being continually used in the enterprise? What proportion of them failed to scale?

Do you have a set of metrics and goals for your digital transformation that are just as clear as they would be for a traditional cost, or sales, transformation?

Do your investor or board presentations reflect a sufficiently deep understanding for where digital and AI is moving the needle for your customers and your operations?

Can your top team clearly articulate the progress made with your top 10 digital solutions, and how much value was created?

What are the new risks and digital trust issues surfaced by digital and AI, and are you managing them to increase customer trust?

What kind of "digital" culture would you like to have in three years? How will you know when you get there?

Transformation Journey Stories

An exploration of how three companies have driven successful digital and AI transformations

This book has tried to go deep below the surface to expose and curate the most important details of what it takes to plan and execute a successful digital and AI transformation. In detailing what it takes to develop the relevant six core capabilities – roadmap development, talent, operating model, technology, data, and adoption and scaling – the reader, however, is in danger of missing the bigger picture of how each of these aspects needs to work as a whole.

In considering the bigger picture, it's important to focus on two key aspects. First is the necessary integration between the elements of the transformation – you can't expect top digital talent to perform effectively unless they can work within an operating model that pro-vides them sufficient autonomy and agility; similarly, you can't expect a great digital solution to deliver value if the business doesn't adopt and scale it. And, second, there is the element of baseline capabilities that you need to hit. Being strong in a few of them, for example, and weak in the others will doom a business's digital efforts.

This story of integration and capability excellence can best be told by showing how companies have done it. So, this final section will show how three different organizations navigated their own digital and AI transformations. These are leading companies in their respec-tive industries and they are also digital leaders. Each have been on a digital journey for years, even a decade for some – and none of them would say they've arrived. On the contrary, the more they progress, the more opportunities that progress allows them to uncover.

Chapter 33: Freeport-McMoRan turns data into value

Chapter 34: DBS – A multinational bank becomes a digital bank

Chapter 35: The future of play takes shape at the LEGO Group

Freeport-McMoRan turns data into value

A copper mining business's AI transformation journey

Freeport-McMoRan has a reputation as a savvy operator in the mining industry. The company operates a fleet of relatively mature, large-scale copper mines in the Americas, which means that the company's performance is highly leveraged to global copper prices: in a high price environment they generate significant cash, but at the bottom of the price cycle, some of the mines struggle to break even.

The company's expectations for growth required significant capital and lengthy permitting and construction efforts. Seeking another path, Freeport turned to artificial intelligence (AI) to see if it was possible to get more out of the assets they already had.

Over a five-year journey, the company successfully designed and executed its "Americas Concentrator" program to unlock the equivalent of an entire processing facility's worth of incremental annual copper production through the use of big data, AI, and agile. No new capital deployment was required.

About Freeport-McMoRan

- Company description: Freeport-McMoRan Inc. (FCX) is a metals and mining company that carries out the production of copper, gold, and molybdenum. It was incorporated in 1987.
- Number of employees and contractors: More than 60,000
- Market cap: $60 billion
- Revenues: $22 billion in 2022
- Geographic spread: The company's portfolio of assets includes the Grasberg minerals district in Indonesia, and mining operations in North America and South America, including the large-scale Morenci minerals district in Arizona and the Cerro Verde operation in Peru.

Freeport's leaders enabled the success of its AI program. Key to the journey were:

1. A visionary leader of North American operations, who was convinced that Freeport would need to evolve to survive and thrive, and wanted to learn from cutting-edge practices used in other industries.

2. A courageous continuous improvement leader, whose curiosity, drive, and deep subject matter expertise drove the combined team to continuously ask "What's possible?" and then get after it at pace.

3. A savvy information and innovation officer who had the foresight to establish a common data infrastructure and architecture to support all processing operations, and to enable swift deploy-

ment of AI tools across sites with modest tailoring. This allowed much of the site-level focus to be on agile practices, training, capability building, and change management.

4. An open-minded general manager at the pilot transformation site who had the creativity and self-confidence to try new things and learn from what worked.

5. A chief executive officer and chief financial officer who championed the program to external audiences, which energized and buoyed the multidisciplinary team driving the effort.

As an initial test case, Freeport selected a mature mine with an enthusiastic GM keen to try the AI transformation program. By demonstrating the value of AI in Bagdad, Arizona, the company sought to learn how machine learning (ML)/AI could enhance their existing algorithmic analytics and advanced process control (APC) systems already deployed. The resultant improvement gave Freeport's leadership pause on the capital required for a planned series of improvements, and resulted in cutting over half of the planned capital spend.

Over the course of six months, a small team of metallurgists, site operators, and engineers worked to develop and train an AI model to recommend changes in settings to safely increase the mill's processing rate. During the next several months, copper production increased 5%. In one quarter, the Bagdad site's throughput exceeded 85,000 tons of ore per day – 10% more than the previous quarter – while its copper-recovery rate rose by one percentage point and its operations became more stable. Improving throughput *and* recovery is an elusive goal in metallurgical processing, and Freeport achieved this in an asset that had been in operation for more than 50 years.

The company's leadership recognized that scaling the potential of the ML/AI across their Americas mines would unlock a system-wide production increase of 125,000 tons per day, which would yield 200 million pounds of copper per year representing $350–$500 million in EBIDTA.[1] This would be comparable to bringing a new concentrator on line, but without spending the $2 billion or waiting the 8–10 years that such major capital projects typically require.

With **leadership aligned** around the opportunity, Freeport launched the "Americas Concentrator" program to roll out this AI capability to its mines. The key challenge in this effort was to industrialize the capabilities developed at the Bagdad site so they could scale.

Freeport had a strong foundation of knowledge of where to focus based on a recently completed operating performance benchmark. The company also had a head start on data because it had previously standardized mine performance measurement and reporting data, and enriched it by installing additional network equipment and performance sensors on the company's trucks, shovels, and stationary machines. They also built a central **data warehouse** to store this data, allowing the company to capture and correlate second-by-second performance readings in real time.

With the operating performance benchmarks and a solid data foundation in place, the company turned its attention to building its analytics and engineering skills. They made significant progress with a first class of 16 upskilled data scientists who came from process engineering or metallurgy backgrounds across the company, and supplementing them with external data engineering experts from a partner. Attracting top agile coaches, product owners, and data and analytics engineers was challenging, so they turned to a "buy (hire), build (upskill), borrow (contract)" talent strategy. This approach allowed them to build up **a talent bench** that could help them move quickly while also developing core skills internally that would provide them with a long-term competitive advantage.

One approach to attract and keep talent that Freeport adopted was to ensure that data scientists and engineers were working on management's top priorities, something that top talent is often not able to do at Big Tech companies. One apprenticing data scientist, for example, joined Freeport just a year earlier as a junior metallurgist working at a mine in Arizona. She had some experience with computer programming in college and was excited by the opportunity to learn new skills. Less than three months later she was presenting her work modeling and optimizing concentrators to the president of the business.

This new way of thinking about talent extended to the operating model as well. Developing AI models at pace required a change to how the company worked. A culture of planning and development built around a set of safeguards had served the company well, but it had its drawbacks, chiefly on pace. For the Bagdad AI pilot, the mine shifted to an **operating model** that emphasized agility, continuous improvement, and quick, low-risk tests without compromising safety. The key success element to this change was assembling a cross-functional mix of experts from the mine and a central data-science group who could evaluate and execute on change initiatives.

To quickly ramp up teams and build skills, Freeport brought in coaches to train people in agile working methods, from the basics of building a backlog to building "minimum viable products," that were good enough to start with rather than laboring to perfect products before launching them. Teams quickly learned how to work in two-week sprints, developing data-modeling functions or operational changes, testing them, learning, and adding updates to a backlog.

Company leaders made the crucial decision to add metallurgists and plant operators as part of the development team at every site. When each new set of recommendations came out during the testing phase, the AI developers, operators, and metallurgists on the team would assess the recommendations: Why were they made? Did they make sense? Would they work? In this way, the teams uncovered flaws that the AI developers then quickly fixed, which in turn helped the agile team learn more quickly. Through this process, the team trained the AI tool, while the metallurgists' and operators' trust in it grew so they were more willing to adopt it when the tool was ready.

The new AI model and interactions facilitated a dialogue and deeper understanding of the process between operators and metallurgists. The AI model was a barometer for what is possible in three-hour increments as opposed to running the plant at one setting throughout the day for the average material received.

The initial team had developed a ML model, which they called TROI, for Throughput-Recovery-Optimization-Intelligence. This product helped predict how the processing plant would behave and how much copper could be recovered under any set of conditions. The optimization algorithm, known as a genetic algorithm, used the principles of natural selection to evolve settings that would produce the most copper given a particular type of ore, and issue recommendations every one to three hours depending on the operation.

To make TROI work at other sites, however, Freeport had to "**assetize**" the models. That essentially meant refactoring and repackaging them so that they could be more easily adapted to other plants. The modular way the tool was built allowed 60% of core code to be reused easily, while the remaining 40% would have to be customized for the new site, such as training the models on the site-specific data. To further simplify these localization efforts, the company invested in developing a centralized code base that site-specific modules could call on rather than having to recreate the necessary code for each specific module.

Running and scaling these models efficiently was possible because Freeport had migrated its **data architecture** to the **cloud**. They used **DevOps**, **MLOps**, and **CI/CD** tools and practices based on clear standards to rapidly develop and deploy in a controlled manner. Freeport was able to further take advantage of the cloud by automating many processes, such as developing the data pipeline, which had been a laborious process of pulling data from dozens of manually updated spreadsheets.

As the company's agile teams proliferated, the management of the overall process had to evolve. With multiple agile teams running in parallel, for example, obtaining resources was difficult. Freeport solved this issue by putting a senior **product owner** in charge to help coordinate teams and improve allocations. A finance director was assigned to manage impact tracking and reporting for the overall domain, as well as helping sites manage their funding requests and measure progress. And finally, they instituted a quarterly master planning system (similar to **quarterly business reviews**) where top leaders from the company come together to set **objectives and key results** and focus resources on the high-priority areas.

With a road-tested transformation recipe in hand and most of their "Americas Concentrator" vision achieved, Freeport then turned to other areas of their business where they could apply their AI capabilities. They identified multiple prospective domains, including capital project execution, maintenance, and leaching operations where they are applying an evolution of the playbook that made their "Americas Concentrator" program a success.

Note

1.   Based on $4/lb copper price and unit costs of below $2/lb.

Chapter 34

DBS – A multinational bank becomes a digital bank

A multinational bank's digital and AI transformation journey

In a fast-evolving digital world, DBS leadership could see that meeting the needs of a new generation of tech-savvy customers required becoming a truly digital bank. DBS's CEO laid out the challenge for the bank in surprisingly simple terms: Think like a start-up, not like a bank.

To start the process of thinking like a start-up, DBS top management looked not to other banks or financial institutions, but to tech giants for inspiration. The CEO and his top leaders **visited and learned** from the top tech companies around the globe and brought what they learned back to shape the "future DBS." That learning crystallized into a clear **vision** to "Make banking joyful." This vision reflected the goal to make customers happy by making banking effortless and making DBS "invisible." DBS was clear that it would no longer benchmark itself against other banks, but rather against the top global technology companies.

About DBS

- Company description: DBS Group Holdings Ltd is the largest banking group in Southeast Asia by assets. It provides retail, small and medium-sized enterprise, corporate, and investment banking services, principally in Asia. The company was founded in 1968 and is headquartered in Singapore.
- Number of employees: 36,000
- Market cap: SGD 91 billion (69 billion USD)
- Revenues: SGD16.5 billion (12.5 billion USD) in 2022
- Geographic spread: Operates in 19 markets, including Singapore, China, Hong Kong, India, Indonesia, Malaysia, Taiwan, UAE, and Japan

---

The team took these learnings to heart in building a **commitment** to apply the lessons it learned visiting the world's top tech companies and have DBS become a tech leader itself. That aspiration was reflected in the mnemonic GANDALF, which stood for: G – Google; A – Amazon, N – Netflix; A – Apple; L – LinkedIn; F – Facebook. The D in the middle stood for DBS with a bold aspiration to join the league of iconic technology companies. Borrowed from the movie *The Lord of the Rings*, GANDALF became the rallying cry for DBS's ambitious digital transformation.

In developing their **digital transformation roadmap** to deliver on this commitment, DBS leadership focused initially on the most important customer journeys that deep analysis had identified would have the biggest impact or address the biggest pain points. One, for example, was account opening for current accounts and another was waiting time at ATMs. These "Iconic Journeys," as they were called, laid the foundation in terms of learning and capabilities to help them move quickly into phase two, where DBS launched 100 journeys in various domains in the business, including finance, employee experience, and additional customer journeys. Each one was led by one of the most senior leaders in the organization.

To ensure they stayed focused on the customer, DBS created a steering committee called the Customer Experience Council (made up of the CEO and key leaders such as business unit heads and service heads) to track progress and **manage performance**. The group met once a quarter to review the progress of all the journeys, focusing specifically on customer experience metrics and EATE metrics (early engagement, acquisition, transacting, and deepening engagement).

As DBS looked to scale their capabilities, they turned to an **operating model** built around **platforms**, a flavor of the products and platforms operating model that DBS adapted to its own circumstance. DBS created 33 platforms aligned to business segments and products, where each of the 100 customer or user journeys were "housed." Each platform had a "2-in-a-box" leadership model, which meant each was jointly led by a leader from the business and one from IT. This platform approach allowed DBS to scale more effectively because it eliminated the historical silos between the business and technology function, which had made it impossible to support truly cross-functional agile teams.

Many of the platform leads were internal hires who had expertise in the corresponding field. Together, the platform and tech lead were responsible for delivering on the goals of that platform in terms of growth, revenue, or customer experience. Each journey team had a journey manager (like a **product owner**) who ran the **agile** team of usually 8–10 people. They would create a journey statement that included an objective, the value they were targeting, and a time frame for achieving that target. The focus on **customer experience design** was foundational to the teams' work. Leadership, for example, pushed for process improvements that benefited the customer. As a result, the credit card origination process, which had taken 21 days, was reduced to just four days.

To enable these teams to function effectively for the long term, top management realized they needed to develop a deeper **talent bench**. DBS made the crucial strategic decision to bring 70% of its tech talent in-house (versus 20% historically). They turned to non-traditional ways of finding the talent they needed, including hack-athons, which were an integral part of DBS's early transformation years. DBS also used these hackathons as opportunities to train senior DBS executives to become familiar with cutting-edge tech-nologies and methodologies like human-centered design. To help attract talent in more locations, DBS also established three tech-nology hubs. Through this and other efforts, DBS could boast of having over 10,000 technologists – about a third of its workforce and double the number of bankers.

As DBS ramped up its tech hiring and instituted a platform operating model, it resolved to build an **engineering culture** of doers who had the freedom to practice their craft on cutting-edge technology. A core component of delivering on this goal was to move to the **cloud**, invest in automation, and develop microservices to support platforms. By 2021, 90% of its technology services were insourced (up from just 15% in 2015). Some 99% of applications are now cloud based and aggressive automation has optimized operations significantly, with one system administrator being able to run 1,200 virtual machines.

Building on this technology foundation was a commitment to become a **data-driven organization**. So DBS launched a comprehensive set of data initiatives, including modernizing data governance, intro-ducing a new data platform (SWLWTE), and driving culture change across the organization. DBS turned away from slide decks and used dashboards instead to drive data-driven decision-making, track performance, and assess impact. The deep changes in how DBS managed its data allowed them to radically change the way they served their customers. For example, the consumer bank adopted AI to deliver "intelligent banking" that provided more than 50,000 personalized daily nudges to its consumers. In human resources,

AI/ML solutions helped better predict when an employee might be considering leaving so HR could intervene (resulting in DBS having the lowest turnover rate in the industry in Singapore – 10% compared to the industry average of 15–20%).[1]

The shift to cloud gave DBS the scale and speed to use AI and ML with its **data** across multiple domains, such as: in marketing, to provide personalized solutions in context; and in human resources, to better predict when an employee might be considering leaving. For example, in compliance and fraud teams, DBS used AI and analytics to develop a comprehensive end-to-end surveillance process for anti–money laundering and to better combat the financing of terrorism. The initiative combined multiple models using rules, network link analysis, and machine learning, with a range of internal and external data sources to generate faster and better insights on money-laundering threats.

Through its AI initiatives, DBS is estimated to have generated S$150 million in additional revenue and another S$25 million from loss prevention and increased productivity in the past year alone. DBS has more than 1,000 data experts to continue to innovate.

DBS was able to **scale** the value it generated with its digital and AI solutions by investing in an institutional **learning program** to build an array of needed skills. A 60–70 person transformation team developed, among other things, "DigiFy," a module-based learning pathway that allowed employees to understand and apply concepts like agile ways of working, big data, journey thinking as well as digital technologies. As a "live" curriculum that is continuously updated, "DigiFy" equipped the entire organization with baseline digital skills and kept them up to speed with the rapidly evolving digital landscape.

The transformation team managed the supporting tools so that individuals and teams could do the agile work. To meet the technical training needs of the more than 10,000 technologists in the bank, DBS set up the DBS Tech Academy. This provided technologists with a technology curriculum that was developed in house and focused on domains such as site reliability engineering, cybersecurity, and machine learning. While DigiFy provided baseline digital acumen for all DBS employees, the DBS Tech Academy built deep engineering expertise, which enabled the bank to go broad and deep in developing its digital capabilities.

This commitment to scaling led DBS to commit to standardizing and packaging as many assets as possible – from a learning module to a training program to a journey-mapping methodology to an analytics product. That focus was central to its ability to "industrialize AI" by, for example, digitizing workflows (including end-to-end AI project management with standard templates and best practice guides), developing a set of best practices to guide analytics delivery, creating an analytics repository where teams could easily access reusable code, and developing a data/feature mart that stored common features that could be used for other analytics development. DBS complemented this formal training and scaling initiatives with more informal efforts to build a digital **culture**, such as redesigning workspaces to encourage collaboration and innovation, frequent peer reviews and storytelling around successes and failure (i.e., learnings).

The impact to date has been impressive. Some 65% of DBS customers are using digital tools and services. For the bank's consumer and SME businesses in Singapore and Hong Kong, the proportion of digital customers rose by 27 percentage points over the past seven years to 60% in 2022. With more diverse product holdings and more transactions, digital customers consistently generate more than twice the income on average of traditional ones. As a result, the cost–income ratio of digital customers is half of traditional ones. The ROE of digital customers is 39%, 15 percentage points higher than traditional customers. Furthermore, DBS has been the recipient of several top global awards over five consecutive years (2018–2022).[2]

The journey isn't over. DBS continues to look at new business opportunities by building on its technology capabilities, including innovating in cross-border financial movements as well as establishing a number of blockchain-enabled businesses. These initiatives are all in the service of unlocking new sources of value and delivering on its promises of making banking joyful for customers.

Notes

1. "DBS: Purpose-driven transformation," Harvard Business School, July 29, 2022, https://www.hbs.edu/faculty/Pages/item.aspx?num=62948.
2. "DBS named World's Best Bank for fifth year running," DBS.com, August 25, 2022, https://www.dbs.com/newsroom/DBS_named_Worlds_Best_Bank_for_fifth_year_running#:~:text=Piyush%20Gupta%2C%20DBS%20CEO%2C%20said,customers%2C%20employees%20and%20the%20community.

Chapter 35

The future of play takes shape at the LEGO Group

A global toy brand's digital transformation

The LEGO Group's digital transformation journey started with a fundamental question: How can we secure the legacy of one of the world's most-loved brands in an increasingly digital era?

With children increasingly turning to screens, shopping behavior becoming digital, and logistics dependent on technology, the LEGO Group developed a vision to own the future of play. That required becoming digital to the core and a tech leader.

The first stage of the journey was focused on technology. The IT function upgraded their systems to allow technologies to work better together, implemented agile programs for their tech teams, and started migrating workloads to the cloud. But the CEO and top team knew they needed a more radical and fundamental change – technology was crucial but alone wouldn't deliver on their vision. They needed to use technology to reshape everything from customer experience to global supply chain management. This more extensive goal required the LEGO Group to change their architecture, operating model, talent profile, and tech and analytics competencies to become a tech leader.

About the LEGO Group

- Company description: The LEGO Group is a Danish toy production company based in Billund, Denmark. It manufactures LEGO-brand toys, consisting mostly of interlocking plastic bricks. The LEGO Group has also built several amusement parks around the world, each known as LEGOLAND, and operates numerous retail stores.
- Number of employees: 25,000+
- Market cap: N/A (privately held company)
- Revenues: 64.6 billion DKK ($9.3 billion USD) in 2022
- Geographic spread: Europe, North America, South America, Asia–Pacific, Middle East, and Africa

---

An important early realization was that a vision this fundamental couldn't be outsourced or handed to an executive as a project. The LEGO Group's **leadership** decided they needed to collectively own their digital transformation from the start. In an intense period, almost 100 business leaders and the entire management group formulated a five-year aspiration to become a truly digitally enabled consumer goods company.

To begin to translate that aspiration into a roadmap, the leadership group identified the business capabilities that are fundamentally dependent on technology, data, and analytics and that could be improved by investing in over 90 identified initiatives. For each, they sized the potential impact, how to measure that impact, and what investment was needed to get that impact.

To help get their arms around these opportunities, LEGO leadership grouped these business capabilities into a set of 10 domains based on relevancy (e.g., capabilities related to consumer experience were grouped in the consumer domain). With this in hand, leadership mapped out the underlying solutions and the corresponding technology, data, and talent needs for each.

This process had a number of benefits. One is that it helped **align** leadership by providing them with a shared understanding of the opportunities and the requirements to deliver them. Another is that it generated real excitement and **conviction** among leadership to see how much was possible.

The team determined the priority domains where they first wanted to create great digital experiences: consumers (those who played with LEGO products, mostly children); shoppers (those who bought LEGO products directly from LEGO); customers (those who sold products for LEGO, i.e., retail partners); and colleagues (those who worked at the LEGO Group). They worked those priorities into a comprehensive **roadmap** that prioritized and sequenced the key digital solutions for each user group or domain. This included the identification of technology, data, and team resource needs for each solution, as well as the estimated investments and required returns for each. The company's Board agreed to make a significant investment over a five-year period to build out the necessary digital solutions and supporting technology and analytics capabilities.

To execute this plan, leadership knew they needed a **leader** with real experience with the complexities of a digital transformation.

So they hired a chief digital and technology officer (CDTO), Atul Bhardwaj, who had led digital transformations at Tesco and Media-MarktSaturn. One of the most important decisions he made was to adopt an **operating model** where teams were assigned to, and had responsibility for, each product needed to deliver a specific solution (a variation of the **product and platform** model). Some product teams focused on delivering user-facing solutions and the underlying applications and workflows, such as optimizing the website experience. Others focused on data and technology systems to support these development teams, such as migrating applications to the cloud to help speed up application development. Another set of product teams focused on developing data products that were shared across multiple domains, such as customer and identity data, and product master data.

A critical component of this operating model was having clear ownership. Each domain had a sponsor from the executive team and a leader from both the business and IT who jointly had responsibility for delivering the outcomes in their domain. Working in partnership with these leaders, the sponsor created roadmaps, and aligned on both solution sequencing and solution design. At the product team, or pod, level, a business lead assumed the product owner role, and, working closely with an engineer, had responsibility for managing and prioritizing the backlog to deliver on their specific KPIs. This focus on integrating the business into the **product management** structure was critical for ensuring that the business adopted the solutions that product teams would develop.

Product owners from the business worked in cross-functional teams with a lead engineer and a team that had about 8–10 people, including engineers, agile coaches, technical program managers, data scientists, designers, and analytics experts. The ultimate goal of this team structure was to erase the distinction between "business" and "tech." All members of the product teams shared KPIs and incentives, but technical roles reported to the CDTO ultimately, who managed their career development, training, and growth.

To manage this product-oriented operating model, the CEO, the CDTO, and the domain "sponsors" allocated budgets and resources annually. Domain leads, however, reviewed progress of the product teams monthly, and later on a quarterly basis (or **quarterly business reviews**). The reviews were focused on tracking outcomes and well-articulated KPIs that drove those outcomes, such as changes in the implementation of technology enablers (e.g., the share of modern APIs implemented per subdomain/product team) and the share of applications migrated to the cloud.

These product teams also held the key to what the CTDO calls the essence of digital transformation: data. That's because it's the data that is the key to delivering advanced user experiences, improving operations, and lowering unit costs. Each domain owned its data, and was accountable for both maintaining it and making it easily consumable by other domains. In this way, the business eliminated data confusion and ensured that each **data product** was the single source of truth. This approach to data ownership also allowed the LEGO Group to build out their data platform, which both housed these objects and made them available to other teams through a self-serve model, including to data scientists who could run advanced analytics and AI against them.

Delivering the digital solutions against the aggressive timeline defined in the roadmap required the LEGO Group to bring in **engineering talent**. This was particularly urgent because they had fewer than 30% of engineers on staff, and about 70% of their code was developed by external resources. A lack of senior engineers at the director/senior director level added to the challenge. To attract talent, the LEGO Group attended developer conferences and launched a social media campaign to highlight the latest technologies developers used and the deep technical problems they were solving. They also opened a digital studio in Shanghai, which grew from seven to 75 digital and analytics experts, and one in Copenhagen, where 200 new digital and analytics experts work. In short order, they increased the number of systems and software engineer roles by 2.5×, most of them with cloud skills.

This infusion of engineering talent helped the LEGO Group meet two specific needs. One was an aggressive application and system modernization effort to create much more flexible, fast, and self-service capabilities. This included paying down their technical debt, automating infrastructure operations such as pipelines, migrating up to 80% of key workloads to the cloud, and developing platform-as-a-service and SaaS capabilities to radically reduce the use of monolithic applications. The second was the incorporation of **advanced engineering practices**, such as DevSecOps to integrate security into the development process from the beginning (with a continuously measured National Institute of Standards and Technology score), CI/CD practices to both accelerate and improve coding quality, and MLOps to develop and manage AI models.

A core focus was to ensure that users would **adopt** the solutions the teams developed, and that those products could **scale**. So the LEGO Group instituted a policy that all technology solutions should be designed and **architected for global use** from the start. That meant using prescribed API standards and a specific, company-wide data taxonomy that included clear definitions of data domains and objects, clear relationship mapping and documentation, and clear accountability for these data domains. The CDTO had the authority, and often invoked it, to veto "local" efforts that did not meet these principles. This approach allowed teams to work in parallel without getting stuck or slowed down in regression testing and team-to-team communication.

A few years into this phase of their digital transformation the LEGO Group is seeing improvements and knows it's on the right path. The LEGO Group cited strong e-commerce and omnichannel retailer partnerships as important contributing factors for their performance. Revenue grew 17% while operating profits grew 5% compared with the same period the previous year, according to the LEGO Group's earnings report. It also noted that accelerated investments in its digital transformation have delivered wide-ranging benefits, including improved online experiences for shoppers and partners and expanded building experiences for consumers.[1] The website has been rebuilt to scale, while downloads of its LEGO Builder app increased 42% compared to 2021.

These new enterprise-wide digital capabilities that the LEGO Group has developed are opening new growth avenues for the company. The LEGO Group is expanding into new domains, including partnering with Epic Games to explore the future of play in the digital arena and the metaverse. This gaming ambition is paired with a willingness to create a virtuous ecosystem of touchpoints around the consumer, stretching from physical in-store experiences to active engagement on several social platforms where children are increasingly present. The LEGO group is investing in building an array of new capabilities, including game engineering and game design.

Note

1. "The LEGO Group delivers strong growth in 2022 and invests in the future," LEGO.com, March 7, 2023.

Acknowledgments

From the three of us

Rewired reflects the innovation, hard work, and pragmatism of our clients. They have embraced the idea of building new enterprise capabilities to outcompete in the age of digital and AI. We have had the privilege to accompany them on this incredible journey. This book is really a mirror of their experiences.

We are particularly thankful to the three companies – DBS, Freeport-McMoRan, and the LEGO Group – which offered their journeys as guidance and inspiration for this book. These stories reminded us that this journey continues to evolve.

This book would not have been possible without the support, guidance, and insights from our colleagues and more than 200 client service teams. We have relied on their hard work galvanizing lessons over thousands of hours for more than six years. We have also benefited from their sharp insights captured in hundreds of articles published on different aspects of the digital and AI transformation journey that helped shape the thinking in this book. We owe them a debt of gratitude and we thank them for their partnership.

The three of us are part of McKinsey Digital, an amazing group of more than 5,000 cutting-edge engineers, technologists, and designers; world-class experts in software development, AI, cloud, agile, product management, user experience design, and other specialties; and capable business transformation leaders. We thank them for continuing to push us on this amazing journey exploring the power of digital to transform companies and industries.

Special thanks to our colleague Barr Seitz, who has been instrumental in editing this book, sharpening our thinking, and bringing the perspective of the reader throughout this effort. This book would not have been possible without him.

And thank you to Bill Falloon and Wiley, who saw enough merit in our thoughts on digital and AI transformation to turn our musings into a book.

From Eric

To my wife, Marie-Lyse, who has been curious about this book and sparked many interesting conversations. And to my daughters, Anne Marie and Claire, who inspire me in their own ways with their amazing talents; thank you for the support and freedom to complete this project.

From Kate

To the three amazing boys in my life, Ben, Harry, and Zac, who make me laugh every day and keep my head in the clouds and my feet on the ground. They won't read this, but I love you tons.

From Rodney

To my wife, Laura, and to my children, Zachary, Asher, and Dahlia, who have overheard me discuss this topic on enough Zooms and calls that they could write a book, too. And to my parents, Esther and Barrie, so they can read it and better understand what I do!

Contributing Leaders

We want to acknowledge the leaders and practitioners who lent their expertise and invested their time (and sweat and tears, no doubt) to help complete this book.

Overall guidance

Rob Levin, Johannes-Tobias Lorenz, Alex Singla, Alexander Sukharevsky

Section One: Creating the Transformation Roadmap

Tanguy Catlin, Alejandro Diaz, Bryce Hall, Vinayak HV

Section Two: Building Your Talent Bench

Vincent Bérubé, Sven Blumberg, Maria Ocampo, Suman Thareja

Section Three: Adopting a New Operating Model

Santiago Comella-Dorda, Julie Goran, Kent Gryskiewicz, David Pralong, Shail Thaker, Belkis Vasquez-McCall

Section Four: Technology for Speed and Distributed Innovation

Aamer Baig, Klemens Hjartar, Nayur Khan, Oscar Villareal

Section Five: Embedding Data Everywhere

Antonio Castro, Holger Harreis, Bryan Petzold, Kayvaun Rowshankish

Section Six: The Keys to Unlock Adoption and Scaling

Ryan Davies, Liz Grennan, David Hamilton, Mark Huntington

Section Seven: Transformation Journey Stories

Chapter 33: Sean Buckley, Harry Robinson, Richard Sellschop

Chapter 34: Shefali Gupta, Vinayak HV, Joydeep Sengupta

Chapter 35: Karel Doerner

In addition, we would also like to thank the following contributors to this effort:

Mohamed Abusaid, Chhavi Adtani, Aziz Almajid, Juan Aristi Baquero, Sebastian Batalla, Kimberly Beals, Jonathon Berlin, Salesh Bhat, Dilip Bhattacharjee, Etienne Billette, Jim Boehm, Jan Vanden Boer, Victoria Bough, Sam Bourton, Jan Shelly Brown, Matt Brown, Yahya Cheema, Devon Chen, Josephine Chen, Melissa Dalrymple, Jay Dave, Mathieu Dumoulin, Jeremy Eaton, Ben Ellencweig, McGregor Faulkner, Scott Fulton, Or Georgy, Martin Harrysson, Jeff Hart, Dave Harvey, Yaron Haviv, RJ Jafarkhani, Steve Jansen, Noshir Kaka, James Kaplan, Marami Kar, Prateek Khera, Gina Kim, Minki Kim, Kathryn Kuhn, Steve Van Kuiken, Klaas Ole Kürtz, Laura LaBerge, Clarice Lee, Larry Lerner, Amadeo Di Lodovico, Jorge Machado, Ani Majumder, David Malfara, Brian McCarthy, Lauren McCoy, Tom Meakin, Sidd Muchhal, TJ Mueller, James Mulligan, Björn Münstermann, Raju Narisetti, Kaitlin Noe, Sona Patadia-Rao, Naveed Rashid, Ranja Reda-Kouba, Marti Riba, Gérard Richter, Myra D. Rivera, Katharina Rombach, Aldo Rosales, Tamim Saleh, Katie Schnitzlein, Stuart Sim, Pamela Simon, Rikki Singh, Henning Soller, Arun Sunderraj, Anand Swaminathan, Shravan Thampi, Gregor Theisen, Caitlin Veator, Anna Wiesinger, and Linda Zhang.

Thank you!

Index